Divined Intervention

Divined Intervention provides an innovative institutionalist account for why religion enables political activism in some settings, but not others. The author argues that *decentralized* religious institutions enable grassroots collective action, and he uses a multimethod approach to test this explanation against several theoretical alternatives, all in Mexico. Utilizing nationally representative Mexican survey data, the book's statistical analyses demonstrate decentralization by the Catholic Church is positively associated with greater individual political activism across the country. Using case studies centered in Chiapas, Yucatán, and Morelos, the author shows that religious decentralization encourages reciprocal cooperative interactions at a local level. This then increases the ability of the religion to provide goods and services to its local adherents, and these processes prompt the growth of organizational capacities at the grassroots, facilitating secular political activism.

Because this theoretical framework is grounded in rational choice conceptions of human behavior, it shows how local institutions, religious or otherwise, politically organize at the grassroots level. The book also offers an improved understanding of religion's relationship with political activism, a topic of ever-increasing significance as religion fuels political engagement across the globe. It further synthesizes seemingly disparate approaches to the study of collective action into a cohesive framework. Finally, there is some debate as to the impact of ethnic diversity on the provision of public goods, and this study helps us understand how local institutional configurations can enable collective action across ethnic boundaries.

Christopher W. Hale is Assistant Professor of Political Science at the University of Alabama.

DIVINED INTERVENTION

Religious Institutions and Collective Action

Christopher W. Hale

University of Michigan Press
Ann Arbor

First paperback edition 2023
Copyright © 2020 by Christopher W. Hale
All rights reserved

For questions or permissions, please contact um.press.perms@umich.edu

Published in the United States of America by the
University of Michigan Press
Manufactured in the United States of America
Printed on acid-free paper

A CIP catalog record for this book is available from the British Library.

Library of Congress Cataloging-in-Publication data has been applied for.

First published in paperback January 2023

ISBN: 978-0-472-13181-5 (hardcover : alk. paper)
ISBN: 978-0-472-12654-5 (ebook)
ISBN: 978-0-472-03928-9 (paper : alk paper)

For Sofi

Contents

Digital materials related to this title can be found on
the Fulcrum platform via the following citable URL:
https://doi.org/10.3998/mpub.11413696

Contents

Acknowledgments

When I began working on this project back in January of 2010, I could not have imagined the extent to which it would consume the next ten years of my life. I also could not have imagined the extraordinary array of individuals and institutions whose support was essential to its completion. I will be forever grateful for their assistance. Most obviously, I wish to thank Carolyn Warner, Michael Hechter, David Siroky, and Magda Hinojosa for serving as the faculty advisers to my dissertation. David and Magda both provided a great deal of encouragement and substantive knowledge that helped guide my efforts, and David has become a valued coauthor with our work on irredentism. I would like to thank Michael for taking me under his wing in the fall of 2007 to work on my first published article. I have always found him to give valuable and honest assessments of my work.

My profound gratitude goes to Carolyn for chairing my dissertation and for what must have been countless hours of reading through draft grant proposals, dissertation prospectuses, dissertation chapters, journal articles, and a draft version of this book manuscript. Without that commitment and interest, this project would not be what it is today, and I cannot repay the debt incurred for what she has contributed to my career. I would also like to thank her and our coauthors (Ramazan Kılınç and Adam Cohen) for inviting me to contribute to our book project *Generating Generosity in Catholicism and Islam: Beliefs, Institutions, and Public Goods Provision*. That experience helpfully prepared me to undertake my own scholarly manuscript.

The Institute for the Study of Religion, Economics, and Society (IRES) at Chapman University funded my continued work on this project through a postdoctoral fellowship during the 2014–2015 academic school year, and I have also had the good fortune to participate in several graduate student workshops and conferences sponsored by IRES over the years. I wish to thank Jared Rubin, Christopher Bader, and Andrea Molle for their support and advice. I would particularly like to thank Laurence Iannaccone, the director of IRES, for his counsel, support, and general good humor. I'll never forget Larry working through a backward induction game tree with me to work out stresses associated with the job market.

I appreciate that my colleagues at the University of Alabama's Department of Political Science have created a supportive atmosphere for junior faculty. I would like to thank several individuals who participated in our department's external colloquium series and provided helpful comments on this project including Karrie Koesel, Anthony Gill, Ani Sarkissian, John McCauley, and Carew Boulding. My appreciation also goes to George Thompson for his advice on the book through the University of Alabama's Publisher in Residence program.

I have been fortunate to find Paul Djupe as an advocate for my work, and he provided me with helpful feedback at an early stage of this project during the 2012 Midwest Political Science Association's Annual Meeting. I appreciate Guillermo Trejo's willingness to share his dataset with me before it was publicly available back in 2010. My thanks also go to several additional people who provided comments or advice on the project including Eli Berman, Marcus Janssen, Christopher Butler, Chris Herbst, Ramazan Kılınç, Daniel J. Levine, Stanley Brodsky, Gama Perruci, Holger Albrecht, Dina Bishara, and Nicholas Kerr. This project has gained remarkably from advice given by several anonymous reviewers at various stages of its development, and I further appreciate the helpful comments provided by the anonymous reviewers of this book manuscript. My thanks also go to the entire production team at the University of Michigan Press. I would particularly like to thank Elizabeth Demers for her interest in this project and for her editorial support.

Additionally, I would like to thank all faculty, staff, and graduate students at the School of Politics and Global Studies at Arizona State University during my tenure there as a graduate student for their support, guidance, and for creating a generally positive atmosphere where I could pursue my studies. A special thanks goes to Maureen Olmsted at the Center for the Study of Religion and Conflict for support in pulling grant applications together. Thank you to my many friends at the law firm of Odin, Feldman, and Pittleman for their warm friendship and for making graduate school possible by employing me over several summers. Furthermore, thank you to the faculty and staff at the Universidad Autónoma de Yucatán, including Dr. Luis Várguez Pasos, Dr. Francisco J. Fernández Repetto, and Lic. Gabrieloa Quintal Avilés. I also wish to thank my research assistants, Laura Carrillo, Amra Morquecho, Alma Medina, and Jasset Puc. I particularly want to express my gratitude to all of my interview respondents.

Bringing this book to completion was greatly facilitated by a year-long Book-Writing Leave Fellowship (2017–2018) sponsored by the Global Religion Research Initiative of the Center for the Study of Religion and Society at the University of Notre Dame. The book is also based on work supported by the National Science Foundation under Grant Number 1159485,[1] the Society for the Scientific Study of Religion, and from both the School of Politics and Global Studies and the Graduate College at Arizona State University. This manuscript includes material drawn, with revisions, from "Religious Institutions and Civic Engagement: A Test of Religion's Impact on Political Activism in Mexico," *Comparative Politics* 47 (2) (January 2015): 211–30 and from "Religious Institutions and Collective Action: The Catholic Church and Political Activism in Indigenous Chiapas and Yucatán," *Politics and Religion* 11 (1) (March 2018): 27–54. The revised material is reprinted with permission from City University of New York (*Comparative Politics*) and Cambridge University Press (*Politics and Religion*).[2]

Finally, I would like to thank my friends and family whose support has made all of this possible. In particular, I would like to thank my parents, Gary and Shelia Hale, and my sister, Gina, for their unwavering encouragement. They inculcated a sense of curiosity and appreciation for reading from an early age that has served me well. Above all, I would like to thank my wife, Erica. She has been an extraordinary companion and I couldn't think of a better person to create a loving home with. Our first trip to Guatemala many years ago sparked an interest that would become the foundations for this project. She has supplied a great deal of patience and guidance as I have pulled this endeavor together, and she knows better than anyone that I could not have completed it without her. I would also like to thank Erica for the sacrifice and unbelievable effort associated with bringing our daughter, Leandra Sofía, into our lives. Our *Sofiita* has provided us both with a new appreciation for the word joy.

ONE

Of God and Coffee

Something arose from the production of coffee.
Catholic priest in Chiapas, Mexico (Interview 45, 2012)

A Catholic priest named Miguel Hidalgo famously rang his church bell during the early morning hours of September 16, 1810. After delivering a stirring speech known as the *Grito de Dolores* that became a rallying cry against Spanish colonial rule, he organized an army of indigenous peasants tens of thousands strong to initiate what would become the Mexican War of Independence.[1] At the same time, Church leadership strongly disapproved of his actions and supported the Spanish Empire. Following his capture and before his execution in 1811, Hidalgo was excommunicated by his Catholic superiors. His head was hung in Guanajuato by political authorities supported by the Catholic Church as a chilling warning against insurrection, and it would be several years before the independence movement regained momentum (Eakin 2007, 190–91). This famous episode from Mexican history demonstrates the complicated relationship between religion and collective action, and religious institutions across many different cultural and geographic settings have both supported and inhibited political activism. How do we reconcile this seemingly contradictory impact? *Why is it that religious institutions support secular political activism in some settings, but not in others?* In providing an answer, this study also contributes to our understanding of a more general question: *How do local communities develop capacities to organize at the grassroots?*

To further illustrate, let us travel to twentieth-century Chiapas, the southernmost state in Mexico. With some dramatic flair, it could be said that coffee and God ignited the political liberation of its indigenous peoples, with "God" serving as a metaphor for theology, resources, and personnel within the Catholic Church. For decades, the peasants of this Mexican state toiled under the abuse of their landlords and a neglectful government. Politically voiceless, they suffered their injustices without organized complaint for the better part of the twentieth century. These impoverished farmers certainly faced considerable obstacles to making their voices heard. They lacked access to the most basic public services, and few received a state-sponsored education to give them the skills to organize. In 1960, it was seemingly unimaginable that they could mount an organized challenge against the Mexican government.

By the end of the 1990s, however, the peasants of Chiapas had helped prompt multiparty democratization in Mexico. The state flowered with all manner of indigenous organizations that actively agitated for political, social, and economic change. Most dramatically, the Zapatista Army of National Liberation staged an armed insurrection against the Mexican government in 1994, and indigenous guerillas captured several cities throughout Chiapas. While the Mexican army quickly secured control of these cities and drove the Zapatistas into the mountains, the episode stunned the nation and contributed to a series of events that would see the end of authoritarian single-party rule by the year 2000. Though dramatic, the Zapatista uprising was only one example of indigenous collective action. It was the culmination of thirty years of active political organization and protest. How had Chiapas undergone such a dramatic transformation? How had it gone from decades of acquiescence to militant political resistance?

"God" played an indispensable role in these developments. Beginning in the 1960s, the Roman Catholic Church instituted a series of theological and organizational reforms that revolutionized Chiapan politics. In unprecedented ways, Catholic bishop Samuel Ruiz García entrusted his adherents with new responsibilities. The Church allowed indigenous individuals to reinterpret key scriptural passages and to develop their own themes for reflection and discussion. At the same time, it advanced a new progressive framework known as liberation theology that emphasized political liberation through active engagement with secular political affairs. The book of Exodus, in particular, stirred hope through its depictions of a powerful God performing miracles for his aggrieved people (Kovic 2005, 53, 110; Womack 1999, 30, 132; Harvey 1998, 62–63). Indigenous communities interpreted these passages against their own marginalized status and used biblical stories to help inspire change. Church reforms moved through the region like wildfire, emboldening indigenous peasants with new ideological frameworks for action.

Meanwhile, "coffee" provided the pathway for the grassroots development of organizational resources that enabled political activism. The Catholic Church engineered a strategy for its adherents to run communally owned and operated economic enterprises called cooperatives. These cooperatives produced coffee, textiles, transportation services, and many other products. Their decentralized management encouraged individuals within villages and across the state to interact, increasing the solidarity of indigenous communities. As they became increasingly capable of producing valuable goods and services for their members, they slowly and organically developed an organizational infrastructure at the grassroots. This new organizational framework, rooted in a decentralized design consciously created by the Catholic Church, directly mobilized political engagement and contestation. Unlike the stories detailed in the book of Exodus, the indigenous populations of Chiapas did not depend on miracles from on high for their emancipation. They developed their own power to organize and to make political demands through the production of coffee and other products. They were the authors of their own political liberation. It was a divined intervention.

In contrast to Chiapas, the Mexican state of Yucatán has seen little indigenous political activism. Like Chiapas, Yucatán's large indigenous population lives in poverty, is poorly educated, and sees little room for socioeconomic advancement. Furthermore, many indigenous peasants lost their jobs and livelihoods with the collapse of the Mexican government's support of Yucatán's economy in the 1980s. However, the Catholic Church has not promoted opportunities for political engagement. Why, despite their similarities, did the Catholic Church encourage the grassroots development of political activism in Chiapas but not Yucatán?

Fundamentally, this study is about how local communities develop capacities for political activism at the grassroots, and it draws heavily from literature across the social sciences examining collective action. I am particularly concerned with how local community groups structure the interactions of individuals and provide incentives to organize. I focus my inquiry on religious institutions, one of the most common types of local community groups, and I argue the governance structure of religious institutions powerfully impacts their ability to develop political activism.[2] Specifically, I argue that where religious institutions are decentralized, they overcome local collective action problems and create an organizational infrastructure enabling political activism.[3]

Because my theoretical framework is grounded in "rational choice" conceptions of human behavior,[4] this study offers further insight into how local institutions, religious or otherwise, develop grassroots potential for collective action. It also offers an improved understanding of religion's relationship with political activism, a topic of ever-increasing significance as religion fuels all manner of political engagement across the globe. The book further contributes to our scholarly understanding by synthesizing seemingly disparate approaches to understanding collective action into a cohesive framework. Finally, there is some debate as to the impact of ethnic diversity on public goods provision, and this study helps us understand how local institutional configurations enable collective action across ethnic boundaries.

Holy Warriors and Good Servants

Religious institutions have prompted political engagement across a wide variety of geographic settings and religious traditions. For example, religious institutions provided enormous support to the Civil Rights Movement across the Southern and Midwestern United States. The black church facilitated internal, grassroots mobilization for politically and economically disenfranchised African American communities by providing social networks, material resources, and ideological frameworks (Calhoun-Brown 2000; Harris 1994; McAdam 1982; Morris 1981).

The range and scope of Muslim political engagement is sweeping. Islamism has stimulated activism in the Middle East and Northern Africa since at least the nineteenth century (Sarkissian 2012, 610). While militant organizations such as al Qaeda and Hezbollah have orchestrated political violence (Berman and Laitin 2008; Wiktorowicz 2004, 5), nearly half a billion Muslims currently participate in democratic governments (Stepan and Linz 2013, 17). In 2001, Islamic groups were mobilizers of protest movements in Egypt, Pakistan, and Indonesia following American military intervention in Afghanistan (Wiktorowicz 2004, 1–2), and they also played a key role in setting the table for democratic opposition leading up to the Arab Spring (Stepan and Linz 2013).

Buddhism has been at the very center of prodemocracy movements in Thailand, Myanmar, and Tibet. Buddhist movements in Thailand, for example, created democratic training centers, and Buddhist political parties have helped launch important constitutional changes during the transition to democracy (Cheng and Brown 2006, 18–19). Across Latin America, the progressive Catholic Church enabled movements against authoritarian governance during the 1970s and 1980s. It also empowered indigenous protest movements across Ecuador, Bolivia, Guatemala, and Mexico (Yashar 2005).

In contrast, Karl Marx once famously described religion as the "opiate of the people" (Koesel 2014, 1). Examples abound across regions and religious traditions suggesting religious institutions stifle political activity and enable a conservative status quo. Consider Roman Catholicism. The Catholic Church historically resisted liberal and democratic change throughout the nineteenth and early twentieth centuries in Europe and Latin America (Blackbourn 1991; Lannon 1987; Vanden and Prevost 2015, 141), and it either endorsed or acquiesced to fascism in Vichy France, Italy, and Germany (Warner 2000; Heilbronner 1998). Robert Putnam noted that the Italian Church has traditionally encouraged disengagement from political concerns (Putnam 1994, 107–9) while in Latin America, Catholicism buttressed several dictatorships from the 1960s through the 1980s (Gill 1998; Klaiber 1998).

Furthermore, the Muslim populations of Western Europe have not made common political demands despite clear incentives to do so. In Germany, religious organizations gain tax breaks and can establish their own schools when they register with the state. However, Germany's Muslim population has not been able to organize to obtain these benefits (Warner and Wenner 2006, 464). Similarly, the French government has passed a variety of measures specifically discriminating against its Muslim population. The negative effects of these laws are palpable and have forced many Muslim girls out of the public-school system (Warner and Wenner 2006, 467; Soper and Fetzer 2007, 935). Despite these seemingly powerful incentives and grievances, "there has been no Muslim civil rights movement, and no principal interest organization has arisen to speak for Muslims in the political realm" (Pfaff and Gill 2006, 805).

The dictatorships of the 1960s and 1970s in South Korea were careful to fold institutional Buddhism effectively into state structures, eliciting declarations of allegiance from Buddhist believers. While the Roman Catholic Church has been a thorn in the side of the Communist Party of China for its outspoken support for democratization in Hong Kong, Chinese authorities continue to rely on the support of large Buddhist organizations and the Anglican Church (Cheng and Brown 2006, 18–27). In Russia, the Orthodox Church receives several protections from the state while providing the Russian government with an important source of legitimacy. Meanwhile, a variety of Russian religious groups "actively battle for access to state resources, influence, and followers" (Koesel 2014, 166–67).

This brief survey suggests that many of the very same religious traditions that support militant political engagement in some settings encourage acquiescent obedience in others (Koesel 2014, 2017), and any attempt to peg overarching religious traditions to specific collective action outcomes is likely to be fruitless. A more productive endeavor might be to understand why any given religious institution might facilitate secular political activism in one setting, but not in another, and this work uncovers why a particular religious institution varies in its ability to create political activism.

Understanding Religion and Collective Action

Previous Work

For further insight on the relationship between religion and political activism, we might reasonably consult the broader multidisciplinary literature on collective action. This previous work is often preoccupied with explaining the emergence of political activism. I briefly summarize the literature here but interested readers will find greater detail in chapter 2. The scholarship on collective action has broadly coalesced into "political process" and "rational choice" approaches to understanding collective action that often talk past each other. The **political process** approach argues collective action emerges when activist groups possess three critical features: framing, opportunity, and resource mobilization (McAdam 1982, 37; McAdam, McCarthy, and Zald 1996, 3–7; Snow et al. 1986, 464–81). The literature on religion and collective action has tapped each of these three dimensions separately, but there has been little self-conscious work devoted to drawing recent innovations together under a coherent framework.

Scholarship in the political process tradition emphasizing *framing* has argued that collective action depends on ideological frames that inspire popular engagement. These strategically developed shared ideas and concepts help coordinate the efforts and expectations of activists. To use contemporary examples, the National Rifle Association's emphasis on the Second Amendment coordinates the activities and goals of individuals interested in limiting gun regulation in the United States. The very phrase Black Lives Matter, on the other hand, serves as a call that coordinates the activities and goals of activists seeking to limit law enforcement abuses.

As the concept of framing has been applied to the study of religion, new religious beliefs are thought to potentially influence political engagement when they constitute politicized theologies that form a new "insurgent consciousness" among their adherents and inspire them to advocate for social change (C. Smith 1991; Philpott 2007, 511; Hurd 2008; Philpott 2000; Fox and Sandler 2006; Thomas 2005; Mitchell 2007).

Second, scholarship suggests *opportunities* for activism emerge when previously restrictive political environments suddenly open. A commonly used case demonstrates how incremental liberalization in the 1980s by Eastern European communist political leaders created a new opportunity for activist groups, eventually facilitating the end of communism in the region (McAdam 1996a, 26–27; Brockett 1991; Kriesi et al. 1992; Kitschelt 1986; Oberschall 1996). Though these explanations often focus on the incentives of *political* elites to create such openings, we can also apply this perspective to understanding the behavior of *religious* elites in religious institutions. When a religion is the dominant and unchallenged religious supplier, its leadership can ignore the social concerns of its adherents and instead curry favor with the rich and powerful. However, new religious competitors pose serious threats because they steal adherents, and religious leadership can no longer take the concerns of most of its members for granted. Accordingly, when formerly monopolistic religious institutions face competition from new competing religions, religious leadership is more likely to support secular political activism (Gill 1998; Trejo 2012). Thus, religious competition creates an opportunity for activism within the religious institution.

Finally, the literature emphasizing *resource mobilization* suggests activists are greatly assisted when they can link into preexisting institutional resources rather than having to build such infrastructure themselves. Religious organizations often provide places to meet, bases of recruitment, communications networks, administrative services, and leadership that activists can draw upon (Becker and Dhingra 2001; Putnam 2000; Loveland et al. 2005; Caputo 2009; Verba, Schlozman, and Brady 1995; Morris 1981; McAdam 1982; Calhoun-Brown 2000; Harris 1994; Wickham 2004; Wiktorowicz 2004). Though the political process model is quite useful, the resource mobilization perspective presumes religions automatically provide these types of resources and subsequently treats them as "vending machines" dispensing activism (Djupe and Gilbert 2006; Hsiung and Djupe forthcoming). Less consideration has been given to how and whether religions develop capabilities for resource mobilization in the first place, and we lack a clear understanding of when it is that mainstream religions possess organizational capacities for collective action.

Where the political process approach explains collective action as a result of framing, opportunity, and resources, the **rational choice** approach focuses on the incentives of individuals to contribute to mutually beneficial causes. From this perspective, collective action is difficult to achieve because individuals have incentives to free ride. Political activism is not a costless endeavor. It entails sacrifices of time, resources, and potentially even one's safety, and it is difficult to exclude the benefits of political activism from those who did not participate. For this reason, each person possesses an incentive to free ride off the efforts of others. To the extent that most individuals share these incentives, we can imagine little potential collective action is realized.

The approach is characterized by its emphasis on examining individual incentives to explain larger outcomes, and it has been applied to the study of religion and extreme forms of political activism. Strict sectarian religious groups are often most adept at overcoming free-rider problems because they weed out opportunists through strict prohibitions against popular activities. "Radical religious communities—Amish, Mennonites, Hutterites, and ultra-Orthodox Jews . . . require that members demonstrate their commitment to the group through some costly or painful sacrifice, often giving time early in life to some religious cause" (Berman 2011, 16). Only the most highly committed members will be willing to pay costs associated with extreme sacrifice and stigma, and these same individuals are well-positioned to engage in high-cost activities such as terrorist violence that are sensitive to defection (Iannaccone 1994; Berman 2011).

Both the political process and rational choice approaches have greatly informed our knowledge of the relationship between religion and political activism, and yet mysteries remain. Though the political process approach tells us activist groups need resource mobilization, it is less helpful in explaining how those resources develop in the first place. While the rational choice approach focuses on how individuals overcome free-rider problems, it does not explain how they coordinate activities around common goals, nor does it address the broader political environment that may inhibit opportunities for engagement. Neither approach, to this point, provides a compelling account for how mainstream religious institutions create capacities for collective action at the grassroots. In response, I introduce a new rational choice institutionalist explanation that elaborates how religious institutions develop the organizational capacities necessary for resource mobilization. However, my theory is nestled within a broader political process framework that also takes framing and opportunity seriously.

Religious Decentralization and Collective Action

The central theoretical argument guiding this book is that where religious institutions are characterized by decentralized governance, communities develop heightened capabilities to engage in political activism. While some previous research has also suggested decentralization within religious institutions affects collective action (Warner 2000; Warner and Wenner 2006, 457; Trejo 2012; Levine 1988, 254; Verba, Schlozman, and Brady 1995, 380–84; Djupe and Gilbert 2006; Kalyvas 1996), I make three advances on this prior research. First, I develop a new theory of religious decentralization explicitly rooted in an institutionalist understanding of how institutions structure and affect individual behavior. Second, religious decentralization has been ambiguously defined in the past, and I develop a more precise understanding grounded in this institutionalist perspective. Finally, while previous research has been suggestive of a relationship, I test the impact of religious decentralization on political activism systematically and rigorously with empirical data utilizing a multimethod approach.

By religious decentralization, I refer to settings where a religious institution is governed at a local and nonclerical level. My emphasis then is on who governs within the institution. When we think of governance, we might think about who makes decisions within a particular group. However, governance involves more than decision-making. It also entails responsibility for observing the behavior of fellow members (monitoring) and punishing members when that behavior fails to live up to membership obligations (sanctioning). In decentralized religious settings, it is the adherents of the religion, rather than clergy, who are given monitoring, sanctioning, and decision-making responsibilities within the religious institution. Decentralized monitoring by religious communities occurs when local, nonclerical actors shoulder responsibility for ensuring other religious members engage in cooperative behavior in highly visible and relatively costless ways. Individual laity subsequently possess greater access to information regarding the cooperative (or uncooperative) behavior of other members within the religious institution and also possess more confidence their own contributions to the religious group will be reciprocated by others (Ostrom 2009, 200–201; Putnam 1993, 172).

Decentralized sanctioning in religious institutions entails the responsibility nonclerical religious actors have for punishing monitored transgressions. To the extent sanctioning decisions are decentralized, they are made by members of the religious institution and are not likely to be overridden or commuted by members of the clergy. Religious institutions produce a variety of spiritual and material goods and services for their members that we might refer to, in the terminology of economics, as religious club goods, and religious members sanction noncontributors by excluding them from these goods and services (Iannaccone 1994; Berman 2011; McBride 2007, 405–6).

With decentralized monitoring and sanctioning, individual adherents at a local level increasingly know their own contributions to the religious group are likely to be reciprocated by others, and they feel confident cooperating. As more adherents contribute, the value of the goods and services the religious group can provide to its members grows. I used coffee as an example of club goods production in Chiapas, but there are many goods and services that religious groups provide to their members. For example, religious groups often provide housing or rudimentary healthcare and welfare services for their adherents (Berman 2011, 16–19, 75) With effective club goods provision, the group fosters dependence and entices new members. As a result, reciprocal interactions grow, the religious institution provides ever-increasing value to its members, and it develops the organizational infrastructure that can then be used to facilitate collective action (Ostrom 1990; Rydin and Pennington 2000; Hechter 1987, 123; Ostrom 2009). In this way, a religious organization internally develops institutional capacities for political activism at the grassroots.

However, I recognize decentralization creates only organizational potential for collective action. To develop a comprehensive accounting of the relationship between religion and collective action, we must also understand why that potential gets applied to political activism. We must understand why a community of individuals, now collectively organized with an organizational infrastructure, would apply its nascent resource capacity to political activism rather than allow such potential to lie dormant.

The political process model informs us that for a religious institution to prompt political activism, institutional capacities for resource mobilization must be accompanied by a framing "political theology" (Philpott 2007) that advocates for active political engagement. Furthermore, religious elites must have incentives, typically in the form of religious competition, to lend the weight of their institutions to secular political causes (Gill 1998; Trejo 2009). By combining the insights of the political process and rational choice approaches to collective action, I provide a framework for understanding variation in frames, opportunity structures, and capacities for resource mobilization that allow religious institutions to engage in political activism. As a result, I expect that *where religious institutions are characterized by religious decentralization (enabling resource mobilization), politi-*

*cal theologies that frame and encourage dissent, and religious competition that
provides opportunity, they are most likely to facilitate secular political activism.*

As I elaborate in the concluding chapter to this book, my theory is applicable to many types of local institutions and should prove useful to understanding the mobilizing potential of religious traditions beyond Roman Catholicism. It should also prove applicable to the study of grassroots mobilization potential of nonstate institutions and voluntary associations more broadly. I would expect institutional decentralization accompanied by appropriate frames and opportunities would prompt grassroots activism across many different types of local groups. Furthermore, much literature has demonstrated a negative association between ethnic diversity and the ability of communities to produce public goods for themselves. This study provides some tentative guidance for how ethnically diverse communities can overcome these difficulties, effectively coordinate and overcome collective action problems, and create a vibrant, multiethnic movement for social reform. Specifically, local institutions may enable multiethnic collective action when they are decentralized and encourage the joint production of excludable goods and services across ethnic boundaries.

Religion and Political Activism in Mexico

The Catholic Church and the Mexican State

For reasons elaborated in the next section, I locate my study of the relationship between religion and political activism in Mexico, and this manuscript makes allusions to several historical episodes involving the Catholic Church and the PRI political party (*Partido Revolucionario Institucional*). Some readers may not be familiar with the relationship between the Catholic Church and the Mexican state, however, and a brief discussion of historical context is necessary before continuing.

From the late fifteenth century through the beginning of the nineteenth century, the Catholic Church legitimated Spanish colonial rule across Latin America, amassed considerable secular fortunes, and was deeply entwined in political affairs. Though subservient to political authority, the Church provided what were essentially the only organized religious services,[5] educated the people, and became the single largest landholder in the region (Gill 2008, 115–19, 146; Camp 1997, 24; Klaiber 1998, 3–4; Vanden and Prevost 2015, 37–38, 136; Blake 2008, 22). Things changed considerably following the collapse of the Spanish Empire in the early nineteenth cen-

tury, however, as many newly independent liberal governments expropriated the Church's resources and sought to remove it from the public sphere
(Gill 2008, 127–30; Blake 2008, 25–26; Camp 1997, 25).

Within Mexico specifically, the 1917 Constitution and the passage of
the 1926 Calles law propagated anticlerical measures. Religious orders
were closed, primary education was secularized, and religious clergy were
required to register with the government (Wilkie 1966, 222; Camp 2014,
151). In response, the hierarchy suspended religious services. Rural peasants, already aggrieved by agrarian crises resulting from the Mexican Revolution (1910–1920), rebelled in support of the Church throughout the
countryside across central and western Mexico. This insurrection, which
became known as the *Cristero War*, lasted three years and mobilized more
than twenty-five thousand combatants before an informal truce finally
emerged between the Church and the Mexican government. To end the
conflict, the Mexican state tacitly agreed not to interfere in internal matters of the Church so long as the Church refrained from speaking out on
political matters (Jrade 1985; Blancarte 2006, 426; Chand 2001, 153; Camp
2014, 151).

This resultant modus vivendi had important implications for the trajectory of politicized Catholicism in Mexico. The Church lacked "moral
authority" in that it was not seen as having played "a favorable role in
[Mexican] national history and its myths" (Grzymala-Busse 2015, 330).
Subsequently, from the 1930s through the 1970s, the Church was inwardly
oriented, conservative, and characterized by an extreme reluctance to get
involved in political matters (Camp 1997, 12, 30, 91, 273; Gill 2008, 116,
154; Chand 2001, 153, 177).

This situation persisted for some time, but the collapse of the PRI
political party's seventy-year authoritarian rule of Mexico (1929–2000) had
important implications for the Mexican Catholic Church. The PRI had
ruled Mexico through extensive (and corrupt) clientelistic patronage networks, and the system worked so long as the PRI could dole out economic
rewards to its core supporters. However, once economic crisis hit Mexico
and the rest of Latin America during the 1980s, the government was forced
to reorient Mexico's economy toward a neoliberal model. The PRI could
no longer buttress its supporters as it once had, and new political opportunities opened for independent political actors to emerge and challenge the
system (Blake 2008, 324–34). It was in this context during the 1980s that
some within the Mexican Catholic Church chafed at illegitimate electoral
measures utilized by the PRI to maintain its position of power. Several
bishops issued public pronouncements in favor of democratization and

fair elections (Gill 2008, 160; Chand 2001, 195; Camp 1997, 51). As PRI control eroded, Mexican president Carlos Salinas (1988–1994) reached out to the Church and traded constitutional changes to its status in exchange for support (Gill 2008, 162–63). The Church was subsequently recognized as a legal entity in 1992 for the first time since the Mexican Revolution. Clergy were allowed to vote in elections, although they were prohibited from explicitly supporting particular candidates or parties (Gill 2008, 163–64; Blancarte 2006, 426).

Finally, and beginning in the 1960s, the Mexican Church faced further challenges from the sudden popularity of evangelical Protestantism (Stoll 1990; D. Martin 1990; Gill 1998; Chesnut 2003; Trejo 2012; A. Smith 2016). Mexico has not seen the massive defections from Catholicism that other countries in the region have seen at a national level, but there are areas of Mexico, particularly its indigenous south, where Protestantism has made significant inroads. Competition from Protestants is something the Mexican Catholic Church takes seriously, and it devises a variety of strategies to keep its flock from converting to alternative religious denominations (J. Dow 2005; Trejo 2012; Camp 1997, 94–97).

Mexico as a Case

Though religion has affected collective action across many different religious traditions, my study focuses on Mexican Catholicism. The Church provides a common core religious tradition across Mexico, and it is subsequently helpful in controlling for several characteristics that might confuse the analysis if I were examining multiple religious traditions. As in Latin America more generally, the Catholic Church provides a "unique historical laboratory from which to pursue rigorous social-scientific research" (Gill 1998, 3).

While the Church often is rightfully considered centralized (Kollman 2013), there is a misperception that it is uniformly governed by the Vatican from Rome. In any given country, the Church typically consists of a national bishops' conference. These national bodies can often hold very different views from each other on a variety of social and political matters. For example, some bishops' conferences in Latin America challenged the military dictatorships of the 1960s and 1970s while others supported them (Gill 1998; Klaiber 1998). The Catholic Church is further divided into administrative territories called dioceses and archdioceses (Camp 1997, 276; Kalyvas 1996, 29–30). Each country is typically divided into many of these administrative divisions,[6] and each diocese is presided over by a bishop who enjoys nearly autonomous authority to run it as he sees fit. At the same time, bishops govern with different styles of leadership, and though many Mexican bishops display a strong proclivity for authoritarianism, several show a strong commitment to bottom-up and democratic decision-making (Camp 1997, 262–63). As a result, there is a great deal of observable variation in how Mexican Roman Catholicism governs itself. Mexico is particularly intriguing in this respect because it is divided into nearly ninety administrative dioceses and archdioceses, the most of any Spanish-speaking country in Latin America.

Not only does the governance of the Catholic Church differ across Mexico, several additional variables of interest vary meaningfully as well. While political activism is vibrant in Mexican regions such as Chiapas, Jalisco, and Mexico City, there is much less activism in settings such as Tamaulipas and Yucatán (Sabet 2008; Mattiace 2009). Furthermore, while some Mexican bishops espouse politicized theologies that exhort their adherents to action, the majority avoid these types of messages (Chand 2001, 199; Camp 1997, 272–73). There is also a great degree of variation across Mexico as to the degree the Catholic Church is challenged by Protestants (Trejo 2009; J. Dow 2005). Helpfully, the Mexican government has taken detailed statistical demographic records of its citizens, and researchers have access to an abundance of individual-level and demographic data. In sum, Mexico provides marked observable geographic variation in several variables that are important to this study including political activism, diocesan organization, the presence of a politicized religious theology, and Protestant competition.

For these reasons, I test my theoretical framework in Mexico, and I do so with a two-pronged and multimethod research strategy incorporating the rigorous use of both statistical analyses and case studies. First, I evaluate whether religious decentralization, the presence of a political theology, and Protestant competition are generally associated with increased propensities for Mexican citizens to engage in political activism, and here statistical analyses are advantageous. In addition to testing whether these general associations exist, however, I am also interested in assessing whether religious decentralization prompts political activism through my theorized causal pathway, and qualitative case study analyses are extremely useful for this purpose.

My statistical analyses allow me to test the impact of my principal variables of interest on political activism. Because statistical analyses typically utilize many observations, they possess a great degree of generalizability, and they help assess whether two variables share general associations with each other. Accordingly, I constructed an original dataset detailing religion's impact on political activism across Mexico from a variety of sources. I measure political activism with data collected from the Mexican National Survey of Political Culture and Citizen Practices (*Encuesta Nacional Sobre Cultura Política y Prácticas Ciudadanas*), a nationally representative dataset that assesses the political behavior of Mexican citizens. I added data to the survey from supplementary sources detailing the organizational structure of the Catholic Church, ideological tendencies of individual bishops, regional demographic information describing the religious makeup of individual communities, and several other measures of theoretical interest as more explicitly specified in chapter 3. The resultant dataset includes over thirteen thousand individual observations, and within this book I employ a variety of statistical models to test my theoretical framework along with several alternative explanations.

Chiapas, Yucatán, and Morelos

My statistical analyses provide evidence of a general association between religious decentralization and political activism across Mexico. However, qualitative methods are advantageous when researchers want to understand, in depth, the mechanisms of how causes produce effects, and I examine the relationship between religion and political activism in the Mexican states of Chiapas (the Catholic Diocese of San Cristóbal de las Casas), Yucatán (the Catholic Archdiocese of Yucatán), and Morelos (the Catholic Diocese of Cuernavaca).

My qualitative research strategy comprises two stages. First, I identify whether religious decentralization took place within each of my cases. I find that the Catholic Church in both Chiapas and Morelos is characterized by religious decentralization, while the Catholic Church in Yucatán is centralized. Second, I assess whether decentralization is linked to political activism through my hypothesized causal pathway. This is to say that where religious decentralization is present, we should see that it leads to greater reciprocity among religious adherents, greater club goods provision by the religious institution, and subsequently to the emergence of organizational infrastructure that can be utilized for political activism (George and Bennett 2005, 176–77; Bennett 2010, 208–9; Mahoney 2010, 131; Brady, Collier, and Seawright 2010, 29; Lijphart 1971, 683–84; D. Collier, Seawright, and Munck 2010, 37–38; King, Keohane, and Verba 1994; Tarrow 2010, 108–10; D. Collier, Brady, and Seawright 2010). Within Chiapas and Morelos, I show that decentralization induced reciprocity, club goods provision, and the development of organizational infrastructure. Because the Church is not decentralized in Yucatán, however, this process did not develop.

I examine indigenous communities specifically because they often lack resources to organize politically, and they provide a compelling arena for the study of collective action. Borrowing from the Mexican census, I define Mexico's indigenous population as the individuals in the country who speak an indigenous language. While there are several countries in Latin America whose indigenous population is larger than Mexico's as a proportion of the population,[7] Mexico has the largest indigenous population in Latin America when considering the total number of people (Mattiace 2003, 1–3; United Nations 2014). Estimates vary depending on the source, but according to the 2005 Mexican census just over six million people in the country over the age of five speak an indigenous language, constituting nearly 7 percent of the population. This population is clearly disadvantaged relative to its mestizo counterparts. Indigenous individuals are less likely to have access to clean water and basic sanitation, less likely to have finished high school, and far more likely to have homes with dirt floors (INEGI [Instituto Nacional de Estadística y Geografía] 2009). Furthermore, the ruling PRI political party organized rural indigenous populations into peasant and indigenous confederations. The purpose of these organizations was to de-emphasize indigenous identities and also to make organizing political activism more difficult (Mattiace 2003, 3, 30–31; G. Collier and Quaratiello 1999, 69; Eisenstadt 2011, 8).

Chiapas and Yucatán, for their part, respectively demonstrate the highest and lowest levels of indigenous political activism across Mexico.[8] Chiapas contains a vibrant civil society with an array of political groups and community organizations that consistently mobilize political activism (Mattiace 2003; Harvey 1998; Washbrook 2007; Trejo 2009; Eisenstadt 2011). It experienced 2,382 separate indigenous protest events[9] from 1976 to 2000, the highest count of all Mexican states (Mattiace 2009, 161; Trejo 2004, 70, 73; 2010). Furthermore, the Catholic Church is widely considered to have driven political engagement in the region (Kovic 2005, 7–8; Trejo 2009, 323–42; Yashar 2005, 74; Womack 1999; Mattiace 2003; G. Collier and Quaratiello 2005). Bishop Samuel Ruiz famously mediated negotiations between the government and the rebel Zapatistas after their insurrection (Barmeyer 2009, 42–43), and his progressive Catholic leanings have been credited with helping to produce political activism across the state. "The key role of Roman Catholicism . . . features in nearly all accounts of social processes and events in Chiapas" (Domínguez 2004, 397).

The unit of analysis in my qualitative investigation is the Catholic diocese, the central governing administrative unit of the Catholic Church. Chiapas is divided into three dioceses, but my study focuses explicitly on the Diocese of San Cristóbal de las Casas[10] in the mountainous and indigenous northeastern part of the state. Eighty percent of the indigenous population inhabiting the State of Chiapas resides within the Diocese of San Cristóbal de las Casas. While I refer to "Chiapas" and the Diocese of San Cristóbal interchangeably, the reader should keep in mind my study is focused on the Diocese of San Cristóbal. It is also the diocese where the vast majority of Chiapan indigenous political activism has taken place.[11]

In stark contrast, Yucatán experienced only sixty protest events from 1976 to 2000 (Trejo 2010),[12] and it is characterized by the lowest levels of indigenous protest (Mattiace 2009, 161; Trejo 2004, 70, 73; 2010). Associational activity centered on indigenous activity is highly limited as there are practically no indigenous political organizations (Cocom 2005, 146). In short, "ethnic identity has not been politicized in Yucatán, and ethnic mobilization and organization have been sporadic and short-lived" (Mattiace 2009, 148). Beyond indigenous organization, there is little political activism generally. While a few independent organizations and groups formally embedded within Mexico's corporatist peasant leagues have organized movements for wage reform, these have typically not lasted (Diggles 2008, 154–55; Mattiace 2009, 145–46). Generally, peasants in Yucatán have not demonstrated much militant political engagement (Baños Ramírez 1988, 334). Furthermore, the Catholic Church has not served as a vehicle for political activism in Yucatán. The Church inhibited the work of progressive priests who attempted to initiate activism (Mattiace 2009), and it emphasized spiritual rather than secular concerns among its parishioners (Trejo 2009).[13] In contrast to Chiapas, the borders of the Catholic Archdiocese of Yucatán and the Mexican State of Yucatán are the same.

Finally, Chiapas and Yucatán share many similarities.[14] Both possess large indigenous populations and high rates of poverty (CDI [Comisión Nacional para el Desarrollo de los Pueblos Indígenas] 2000; Székely Pardo et al. 2007, 249, 260). The authoritarian PRI political party encountered robust political party competition during the 1980s and 1990s in both states (Mattiace 2009, 147–48; Diggles 2008, 153; Harvey 1998, 156–60), and each is also characterized by high levels of Protestant competition (J. Dow 2005).[15]

While my analysis of Chiapas and Yucatán is useful for a variety of reasons, some readers may fear something unique to indigenous modes of political activism may influence my results. Examination of the Diocese of

Cuernavaca in Morelos helps alleviate these concerns by inspecting religious decentralization in a nonindigenous context, and the investigation serves as a shadow case intended to provide "brief points of comparison for the case(s) of primary interest" (Gerring and Cojocaru 2016, 407). Only 4.7 percent of the population of Morelos is indigenous (compared to an average of 7.1 percent among Mexican states), and only 2.3 percent of the population of the state speaks an indigenous language (CDI 2000).[16] At the same time, Morelos is characterized by an extensive history of political activism, particularly under the stewardship of Bishop Sergio Méndez Arceo from 1952 to 1982. Though Morelos was not marked by widespread levels of political activism between the Mexican Revolution and the 1960s, a vibrant movement advocating for teachers', workers', and peasants' rights exploded suddenly in the 1970s and 1980s. As in Chiapas, the Catholic Church is credited for prompting collective action throughout the state (Mackin 2003), and I provide evidence it did so because it was decentralized.

Qualitative Data

I drew data for my qualitative analyses from secondary historical sources[17] and more than seventy semistructured interviews I personally conducted throughout Chiapas, Yucatán, and Morelos during fieldwork dating from the spring of 2011 through the fall of 2012.[18] My access to indigenous communities was greatly helped by Church clergy, local government officials, and community leaders. I selected my interviewees on the basis of their associations with a variety of organizations including the Catholic Church, Protestant denominations, government, civil society, and I further interviewed regular churchgoers and citizens. With semistructured interviews, the researcher prepares specific questions, but the ebb and flow of the interview determines the order and approach used in asking them. These interviews have the advantage of generating reliably comparable data while allowing for the possibility of unanticipated responses (Bailey 2007, 95–112; Leech 2002, 665). The interviews lasted about forty minutes on average, although some particularly informative interviews lasted well over an hour. The vast majority of interviews were conducted in the interviewee's home, place of work, or place of worship.[19]

I also relied on referrals from other interviewees in a procedure called "snowball sampling." This type of purposeful sampling is useful when targeting both elite and marginalized populations in a qualitative study that uses a relatively small number of respondents. In my case, I was interested in interviewing both types of individuals: clerical elites within the Catholic Church as well as ordinary indigenous adherents who themselves are often politically marginalized. Random samples like those used in statistical analyses may not be a dependable strategy to get a researcher in touch with the types of individuals who will provide the most helpful information (Cohen and Arieli 2011, 423–35; Tansey 2007, 765–72). "Choosing someone at random to answer a qualitative question would be analogous to randomly asking a passer-by how to repair a broken down car, rather than asking a garage mechanic—the former might have a good stab, but asking the latter is likely to be more productive" (Marshall 1996, 523). Because I was sensitive to the risk of producing biased replies protecting particular interests, I specifically recruited respondents who reflected a spectrum of socioeconomic statuses, religious positions, and relationships with the government whose responses could be triangulated against each other.

Finally, I conducted my interviews in cities that were representative of the level of activism in both Chiapas and Yucatán. To identify such representative cities, I computed standardized residuals following a regression on indigenous protests using Guillermo Trejo's *Mexican Indigenous Insurgency Dataset* (Trejo 2010). A detailed description of that analysis along with a brief description of each city is available in Appendix Table A.11, and most of my interviews were conducted in San Cristóbal de las Casas in Chiapas (along with several smaller communities), and Tizimín and Valladolid in Yucatán.

Alternative Explanations

Finally, several other theoretical accounts might alternatively describe the development of collective action across Mexico, and I assess the potential impact of these alternative explanations in both my statistical and case study analyses. As I detail in the following section, economic deprivation, the decline of PRI authoritarian rule, legacies of Church and state conflict, and ethnic heterogeneity all may have influenced Mexican political activism, and I develop hypotheses to test these accounts against my own theoretical framework.

Economic Deprivation (Grievances)

Economic deprivation has long been conjectured to explain collective action. Widespread poverty, socioeconomic discrimination, or frustrated economic expectations are thought to prompt protest movements because

individuals became dissatisfied with their economic status and seek to
change it (Gurr 1970; Snow et al. 1986, 465; Zald 1996, 265). The substantial literature on collective action, both in the political process and rational
choice traditions, has rebuffed the idea that economic deprivation automatically produces collective action. Both perspectives consider economic
deprivation to be widespread. Because political activism is relatively rare,
pervasive economic deprivation does not seem to explain the relatively
small number of protest movements we see (Oberschall 1996, 94–95).

However, more recent work has demonstrated an empirical relationship between economic deprivation and insurgency and has revived interest in studying deprivation (Cederman, Weidmann, and Gleditsch 2011;
Besançon 2005; Siroky and Hale 2017; Hechter, Pfaff, and Underwood
2016). While economic grievance may be insufficient to prompt collective action on its own, it may increase the demand for social change. As
Mexico adopted neoliberal economic reform beginning in the 1980s and
instituted painful austerity programs, there was certainly cause for grievance. Accordingly, a hypothesis formulated to test the influence of economic deprivation might expect that Mexican regions experiencing higher
socioeconomic deprivation are associated with higher individual propensities to engage in political activism.

Political Opportunity: Political Party Competition

My theoretical explanation considers religious opportunities that create
possibilities for political activism through religious competition. However,
what of openings within the political establishment? Where political parties effectively compete against each other, there is greater representation
of views within the political sphere. Political party competition can further
be a sign of political liberalization within a previously closed authoritarian regime. The larger the number of parties, "the more difficult it is to
confine electoral interest articulation to the 'cartel' of entrenched interests
that is represented by the established, bureaucratized parties" (Kitschelt
1986, 63; McAdam 1982).

Within Mexico, increased party competition during the 1980s and
1990s may have opened political opportunities for action. The PRI party
governed Mexico under a single-party system for fifty years, but the situation changed in the 1980s as its political authority eroded. Emergent
party competition may have heightened interest in political participation
as Mexican voters increasingly perceived they had a legitimate choice

(Birch 2010; Franklin 2004; McCann and Domínguez 1998). Though Mexico has generally been characterized as a three-party system since its democratization, there is a great degree of variation in the number of competitive parties across the country. Some municipalities are dominated by a single party while others might have as many as five parties actively competing against each other (IFE 2010). Alternatively, political competition might further the bargaining power of religious institutions vis-à-vis the state. Within Mexico, the Church might have been emboldened to advocate on behalf of its interests where the PRI sought support to fend off challenges from political rivals (Gill 2008, 159). Political party competition might have increased Mexican political participation as Church leadership, to heighten its negotiating position with the state, actively encouraged the political participation of its laity.[20] A common hypothesis derived from each of these perspectives, however, would be that municipalities with more political party competition should be associated with heightened individual propensities to engage in political activism.

Political Opportunity: Church/State Interactions

Similarly, the historically contentious relationship between the Church and the Mexican state may have had differential impacts on the Catholic Church's relationship with political activism across Mexico. Conflictual Church/state legacies affect religious groups' opportunities to represent their interests to the state (Fetzer and Soper 2005; Grzymala-Busse 2015). As detailed earlier in this chapter, liberals enacted a variety of anticlerical measures to curtail the power of the Church. The eventual result of this was the Cristero War and its informal truce known as the modus vivendi. The Mexican state did not enforce anticlerical policies so long as the Church refrained from taking public political stances. Bishops in dioceses located in central Mexico, a region disproportionately affected by the conflict, may have been wary of disrupting the uneasy truce with the state. On the other hand, dioceses in peripheral regions, such as the northern and southern regions of Mexico, were far less affected. Bishops in the periphery of the country are accordingly argued to have had more space to act politically and encourage political activism by their laity (Chand 2001, 160–62). From this perspective, we might hypothesize the Church would be more likely to facilitate individual political activism in locations that were not touched by the Cristero War.

Ethnic Heterogeneity

A vibrant body of literature provides mixed but generally supportive evidence suggesting ethnic fractionalization has a negative effect on the production of public goods (Putnam 2007; Alesina, Baqir, and Easterly 1999; Habyarimana et al. 2007; Baldwin and Huber 2010). In other words, the literature suggests that the more ethnically diverse a community is, the more difficulty its members will encounter in their attempts to produce mutually beneficial goods and services, including political activism. Coethnics may be more likely to produce public goods because they share common tastes and other-regarding preferences for each other. Ethnically diverse communities, on the other hand, have different preferences for how they would like to see public goods administered. For example, two distinct ethnic groups might prefer that school lectures be administered in two different languages, and these differing preferences increase costs associated with providing education. Furthermore, cooperation may be heightened when individuals share the same language and cultural heritage as they can more easily monitor and punish individuals when they share similar ethnic attributes (Habyarimana et al. 2007).

According to each of the perspectives elaborated above, we could hypothesize that ethnically diverse communities should be associated with lower individual propensities to engage in political activism. Mexico, for its part, is characterized by measurable variation in levels of ethnic diversity. While most of the country identifies as mestizo (a combination of Spanish and indigenous heritages), approximately 10 percent of the population belongs to any one of more than sixty distinct indigenous groups (Suárez Blanch 2005, 3). Many communities across Mexico are ethnically similar, but several also possess large indigenous populations that themselves are characterized by a variety of different languages and local customs. Chiapas and Yucatán provide a particularly interesting setting to examine this relationship. The indigenous population in Chiapas is characterized by a great deal of ethnic diversity. At least five languages are spoken, and customs can vary drastically across indigenous communities. Yucatán's indigenous population, on the other hand, is characterized by its linguistic and cultural similarity. While we might expect the indigenous populations of Yucatán would have had an easier time organizing for collective action, it was Chiapas that experienced a broad, interethnic movement demanding political reform.

Book Organization

The introductory chapter of this book has sought to familiarize the reader with the purpose of the study, briefly introduce my theoretical orientation, and elaborate my research strategy. Chapter 2 fully elaborates my theoretical framework. I provide definitions for political activism and religious institutions, examine the political process and rational choice approaches to understanding collective action in greater detail than I have sketched here, and I develop an institutionalist theory of religious decentralization that is embedded within a broader political process approach emphasizing the importance of framing, opportunity, and resource mobilization.

Chapter 3 tests the various explanations I have detailed here statistically. I find that religious decentralization, politicized theology, and Protestant competition are each positively associated with individual propensities for engaging in protest activity across Mexico. Not only that, I find that religious decentralization shares mutually reinforcing relationships with both politicized theology and Protestant competition in prompting political activism. In short, determinants of framing, opportunity, and resource mobilization each have significant and mutually reinforcing positive impacts on the propensities of individuals to engage in collective action. Little support, on the other hand, is given to ethnic fractionalization or political competition, and only weak support is given to economic deprivation and Church/state legacies.

Chapters 4 through 6 consist of my qualitative case examinations of Chiapas, Yucatán, and Morelos. Chapter 4 examines Chiapas (the Catholic Diocese of San Cristóbal de las Casas). Local Catholic communities were marked by pronounced decentralized monitoring, sanctioning, and decision-making opportunities. Decision-making was decentralized through the creation of local pastoral councils who advise clergy, the integration of indigenous practices into the traditions of the Church, and the creation of important community leaders named catechists and deacons who were given previously unprecedented power to teach and give sacraments. These catechists and deacons designed their own themes for discussion, and they came to focus on their own local, political, economic, and social problems.

Economic cooperatives created directly by the Catholic Church provided the means for decentralized monitoring and sanctioning. They enabled adherents to produce a variety of goods and services, such as coffee, and were managed completely by laity rather than clergy. Cooperatives provided members with a direct means to monitor the productive contributions of others and sanctioned free riders by excluding them from membership benefits. As cooperatives effectively provided material goods and services, they enticed new membership, provided even greater material rewards, and created new organizational networks that connected previously disparate and isolated communities across Chiapas. These organizational networks subsequently and directly enabled political resistance through a vibrant array of civic associations. Pervasive Protestant competition provided an opportunity for religious elites to allow the religious organization to be used for collective action in Chiapas, while progressive Catholicism provided a mobilizing frame directing communities toward political activism.

Chapter 5 examines the Archdiocese of Yucatán. I found the hierarchy was reluctant to devolve monitoring, sanctioning, or decision-making authority to Catholic adherents. The clergy maintained principal responsibility for decision-making. While adherents participated to some degree in the mass and in their communities, they typically implemented directions given to them by their local priest without the discretion to formulate their own solutions to local problems. Lay apathy, as several priests indicated, was a serious issue. To no extent was Yucatán characterized by the type of cooperatives that were pervasive across Chiapas. As a result, we see few reciprocal networks that go beyond immediate localities, few regional associations, and limited political activism. Despite potential religious opportunities due to Protestant competition and theological orientations encouraging political participation, Yucatán is not characterized by grass-roots infrastructure enabling collective action. The chapter further assesses the potential impacts of economic deprivation, political party competition, legacies of Church and state conflict, and ethnic diversity in explaining the differences in political activism we see between Chiapas and Yucatán.

To assure the reader that nothing particular to indigenous collective action drives the qualitative results of this study, chapter 6 examines the nonindigenous Diocese of Cuernavaca within the Mexican state of Morelos. The diocese decentralized monitoring, sanctioning, and decision-making authority to the laity beginning in the 1950s and 1960s. Decision-making was decentralized through Christian base communities (*communidades eclesiales de base*—CEBs) that, similarly to catechists and deacons in Chiapas, encouraged laity to reflect independently on biblical teachings and to develop their own themes for analysis within small Christian study groups. Just as in Chiapas, local monitoring and sanctioning capacities were provided through economic cooperatives which were a prominent part of CEBs. The organizational framework of the CEBs enabled independent political movements in Cuernavaca beginning in the 1970s along, most notably, issues of workers', teachers', and peasants' rights. They have subsequently supported a host of other political issues. Morelos also provides an opportunity to examine the consequences of religious recentralization following decentralization. Beginning in the 1980s, the Vatican sought to reinstitute centralized control and posted successive bishops to the region who would do so. Despite these efforts, the organizational infrastructure created by decentralization in the Diocese of Cuernavaca, while strained, has endured for nearly forty years.

Finally, chapter 7 summarizes the main findings and implications of the study while suggesting further avenues for future research. Here, I argue my findings can help inform the study of religious traditions beyond Roman Catholicism and to other forms of voluntary local associations. Additionally, I suggest my comparison of events in Chiapas and Yucatán provides suggestive evidence for how multiethnic communities can effectively band together to produce political activism. This is particularly likely when decentralized institutions encourage the production of excludable club goods across ethnic communities.

TWO

Theology, Competition, and Decentralization

Free riders threaten most collective activities, and religious activities are no exception.

(Iannaccone 1994, 1183)

In each community, there is a control. . . . If [members] don't comply, they are left out.

cooperative member, Chiapas (Interview 43, 2012)

If there are rights, there must be obligations.

Church official, Chiapas (Interview 1, 2012)

In the previous chapter, we saw existing attempts to explain the relationship between religion and political activism have broadly coalesced into "political process" and "rational choice" approaches to understanding collective action that often talk past each other. Though both perspectives have provided valuable insights, neither currently explains how large, mainstream religious institutions develop capacities for collective action. In response, *I argue that where religious institutions are characterized by decentralized governance, they enable their adherents to mobilize the resources necessary for political activism.* My framework combines insights from both the rational choice and political process approaches, and I suggest we must combine the analytical scope of both to explain collective action (Siroky, Mueller, and Hechter 2017).

This chapter elaborates my theory of religious decentralization and the theoretical framework guiding my study. It caters to readers interested in theories of collective action and the relationship between religion and politics. Readers specifically interested in Mexican or Latin American politics with less interest in these general theories might skim the chapter and proceed to chapter 3 (the statistical analysis of Mexican survey data) or to chapters 4, 5, and 6 where my arguments are assessed with qualitative case studies in Chiapas, Yucatán, and Morelos.

I begin this chapter by constructing definitions for political activism and religious institutions, my core concepts of interest. I then examine the previous literature investigating the relationship between the two which can be broadly organized as adhering to political process and rational choice approaches to understanding collective action. Following this discussion, I present my own theory of religious decentralization. While decentralization likely produces collective action within many different types of institutions, religious or otherwise, I conclude the chapter by examining the qualities of religious institutions that may make them uniquely situated to prompt political activism.

Political Activism and Religious Institutions

Political Activism

Though social scientists often use the terms political activism, political participation, social movements, and collective action interchangeably, collective action in fact is vast and consists of any instance where multiple individuals interact to produce common and mutually beneficial goods (Olson 1965, 5–7).[1] Many forms of cooperative human activity could be considered collective action, but when political scientists use the term they are often referring to political participation, a specific subset of collective action.

Political participation is any behavior "influencing or attempting to influence the distribution of public goods" (Booth and Seligson 1978, 6; Conge 1988, 244). It is "collective action at the national or local level that supports or opposes state structures, authorities, or decisions regarding [the] allocation of public goods" (Conge 1988, 247). Put succinctly, political participation is any activity, often directed toward political authority, aimed at altering the existing allocation or general character of public goods and services. The reader should note the emphasis on the distribution of public goods, and we will return to that point in just a moment.

In working our way toward an understanding of political activism, we can further divide political participation into conventional (voting) and unconventional (activist) variants. "Conventional" political participation is behavior intended to influence either governmental personnel or policies through established democratic institutions (Verba and Nie 1972; Conge 1988, 242; Pacheco and Owen 2015, 224; Norris 2009, 638). Much of the literature examining the subject has equated participation with voter turnout (Leighley 1995, 181; Whiteley 1995, 212). Voting is typically "low cost" in that participants pay relatively little in terms of time, money, or the risk of injury to engage in it (Pacheco and Owen 2015, 224–25; Aldrich 1993; Lichbach 1998, 6). The costs of establishing democratic institutions, administering elections, and disseminating information about elections and candidates are heavily subsidized by interested actors such as the state, political parties, and the media.

Political activism, on the other hand, refers to unconventional forms of participation that occur outside formal democratic institutions (Conge 1988, 242; Norris 2009, 639; Almond and Verba 1989; Barnes 1979). It is characterized by protest activity including boycotts, petitioning, mass demonstration, occupation, and even political violence (Norris 2009, 639). Activism is a much "higher cost" form of political participation that is active, amateurish, and voluntary (Van Deth 2014, 351–52; Conge 1988, 241–42). It is taken on by individuals unaffiliated with the state or organized parties, and activists do not receive financial compensation for their efforts.

A social movement is a subset of political activism that has received considerable attention in the scholarly literature. Activism becomes a social movement when activist groups develop "organized, sustained, self-conscious" and regular patterns of activity around shared collective identities for the purpose of influencing specific social and political outcomes (Tilly 1984, 304; Tarrow 1989, 17; Diani 1992; Levine 2012, 127). While a social movement is an example of activism, all instances of activism do not necessarily constitute instances of social movements. Studying activism rather than social movements allows me to assess the development of groups in a diverse, vibrant, and engaged civil society advocating for a wide range of political causes (as we will see in Chiapas). My theory is oriented more toward understanding how capacities for activism develop at the grassroots than in understanding how particular collective identities coalesce and orient themselves toward specific social or political issues.

Let us now return to the emphasis noted above on political participation and its relationship with public goods. Public goods include services delivered by the state such as police protection, judicial services, and defense. Once offered, they are extremely difficult to exclude (Cornes and Sandler 1996, 8–9; Hardin 1982). For example, it would be difficult for the United States to deny the security benefits of military superiority from individuals residing within the country who refuse to pay their taxes. Public goods "must be available to everyone if they are available to anyone" (Olson 1965, 14).

Governments, to varying degrees, provide additional public goods such as social security or universal healthcare (Cornes and Sandler 1996, 10). These public goods necessitate income redistribution, are politically contentious, and often require extensive levels of political activism to find fruition. However, the benefits of political activism accrue to activists and nonactivists alike. As Lichbach summarizes, "the benefits of participation, if the group is successful, is a [public good] that can be enjoyed by anyone, regardless of his or her (non)participation" (Lichbach 1998, 6).

Political activism is accordingly prone to the collective action problem. It involves costs of time, resources, skills, and potentially safety (Pacheco and Owen 2015, 224–25; Aldrich 1993; Lichbach 1998, 6). If we assume most individuals are boundedly rational, we assume they minimize known costs while maximizing known benefits. The reason political activism can be a challenge to organize is because individuals have an incentive to free ride off the efforts of others. If they can benefit from others' political activism regardless of their own participation, the rational action is to sit back, let others take on the costs, and benefit from any changes to public policy.[2] Most individuals share incentives to free ride, and accordingly much potential collective action is not realized (Olson 1965, 16; Hardin 1982, 16–17; Ostrom 1990, 5; Lichbach 1998, 6–7; Ostrom 2009, 186).[3]

Religions as Institutions

Religious institutions also constitute an important core concept of this study. Before defining them, however, we should make a few fine-grained distinctions between religion, religious groups, and religious organizations. I start with religion, the broadest of these terms. While it may be impossible to formulate a definition of religion that encompasses all imaginable religious traditions, we can develop a conceptualization that is applicable to most religious adherents worldwide (Gill 2001, 120; Menchik 2017, 576). Generally, religions: 1) emphasize the supernatural, 2) are comprehensive in scope, and 3) are collective efforts subject to the collective action problem.

Religion emphasizes the supernatural (Gill 2001, 120; Grzymala-Busse 2012, 422; Stark and Bainbridge 1985, 3). There are many existential questions that evoke anxiety but that seemingly have no verifiable answer. To use the most obvious example, most individuals have likely at least occasionally preoccupied themselves with the question of what happens to human consciousness after death. Reassuring and demonstrable answers to these types of quandaries are elusive, and individuals often accept imperfect and uncertain substitutes. "When we examine human desires, we see that people often seek rewards of such magnitude and apparent unavailability that only by assuming the existence of an active supernatural can credible [answers] be created" (Stark and Bainbridge 1985, 7; 1996, 36–41). Religion offers individuals reassurances about death, health, material resources, interpersonal relationships, and many other issues of everyday life that often have no immediately apparent solution. It offers at least partially plausible existential assurance by drawing on the supernatural.

In addition to drawing on the supernatural, religion develops comprehensive accountings of human existence. To further explain this, let us briefly consider magic, a potential alternative to religion. Magic might also be considered a substitute for assuaging various existential anxieties. It promises immediate solutions for sickness or for generating wealth. However, magic tends to be specific in its goals and outcomes. Religion, on the other hand, develops systematic theologies meant to structure and define human existence. Unlike secular ideologies or magic, religions are predisposed to deal with "human desires of maximum scope, intensity, and scarcity" (Stark and Bainbridge 1985, 8; 1996, 40). For this reason, religion is often described as "a unified system of beliefs and practices relative to sacred things" (Durkheim 1915, 47), "a system of beliefs and practices oriented toward the sacred or supernatural" (C. Smith 1996, 5; Gill 2001, 120), and a "belief system that structures the relationship of the individual to the divine and the supernatural" (Grzymala-Busse 2012, 422).[4]

Most critically for the purposes of this study, religion is also "an eminently collective thing" (Durkheim 1915, 47), the practice of which is intended to "excite, maintain, or recreate certain mental states" among a group of individuals (Durkheim 1915, 10). It is "a social phenomenon, born and nurtured among groups of people" (Iannaccone 1994, 1183). One's enjoyment of a Sunday morning Christian service, for example, not only depends on one's own contribution to the service, but also on how one is greeted by the other members of the group, how enthusiastically other members sing or pray, and the degree to which others contribute (Iannaccone 1994, 1184). Religion gives "groups of people . . . meaning and direction" (Gill 2001, 120), through a "public and collective belief system" (Grzymala-Busse 2012, 422). These aggregations of individuals espousing collective belief systems constitute *religious groups* that are "communities that define themselves by reference to particular religious beliefs and practices" (Warner et al. 2018, 12).

Much attention is given to religious groups' systematic and supernatural theologies. However, as they are constituted by human beings, they also operate in a world of mundane and secular interests. It is therefore useful to analyze them separately as organizations and institutions. To differentiate religious institutions from religious organizations, we can think of a typical game with rules and players. Institutions function like rules by structuring how players interact with one another, guiding the strategies of the players, and limiting the range of possible actions players can take. Organizations, on the other hand, are like players in a game in that they attempt to maximize their advantage within the framework of the rules to "win" the game through skill, strategy, and by coordinating their efforts (North 1990, 4–5).

Scholarship dating back at least to Adam Smith suggests *religions as organizations* operate according to the same principles of self-interest, scarcity, and supply and demand dynamics that guide the behavior of business firms (Berman 2011, 62). We can think of religious organizations as the players in a game who "win" influence by attracting as many adherents as possible, subsidizing their activities with state funds, and persuading governments to restrict new rival organizations from competing with them (Warner 2000, 28). The rules are the broader social norms and legal rules that influence and constrain the behavior of the religious organization, and a great deal of scholarship has examined religious groups as organizations attempting to maximize their "money, power, and prestige" in society (Koesel 2014, 5; Kalyvas 1996; Gill 1998; Warner 2000; Grzymala-Busse 2015).

I will describe *religions as institutions* more extensively later in this chapter, but for now it will suffice to say we examine religious groups as institutions when we study how their rules and norms structure the interactions of their adherents. Here religions themselves constitute the institutional rules and norms that guide how their members interact within them. This is important because religious adherents interact with each other in a wide variety of ways (Djupe and Gilbert 2006, 118), and in doing so they create mutually beneficial goods and services for each other. To put these activities in the parlance of economics, the cooperative interactions of religious adherents lead to the production of many goods and services for members, both spiritual and material, that we can describe as religious club goods

(McBride 2007, 406; Berman 2011, 16–19, 75). While the tangible material goods religious institutions provide for their adherents are often overlooked, they include services as diverse as housing, education, food, security, and healthcare (Berman 2011, 75).

It is neither cheap nor easy to produce religious club goods, and religious institutions depend on contributions of time, money, and enthusiasm from their members (Iannaccone 1994; Berman 2011). All individuals participating would be better off if they did not have to sacrifice their own time and resources to receive them. However, if all individuals shirk from their individual responsibilities to the group, the ability of the religious institution to provide goods and services to its members suffers. Accordingly, religious institutions, just like other institutions, are keenly susceptible to the "free-rider" problem and must develop solutions to solve it (Iannaccone 1994). One of the primary arguments of this study is that we have not sufficiently examined religions from an institutionalist perspective. The institutional structure of religions influences the interactions of their adherents in ways that can have extraordinary implications for how they produce these club goods and, subsequently, for how they produce political activism.

This understanding of religious institutions may seem narrow to some readers. Why focus on communities and systematized belief systems emphasizing the supernatural when "a non-exhaustive inventory of what constitutes religion includes individual and collective rituals, ethics, canonical texts, doctrine, methods of exegesis, everyday practices . . . [and so on]" (Menchik 2017, 564)? In a thoughtful and provocative article, Jeremy Menchik goes so far as to suggest that definitions characterizing religion as "coherent, unitary, and temporally consistent," are inherently flawed because "a universal definition of what religion is or what religion does is not feasible" (Menchik 2017, 576).

I acknowledge it is not possible for any definition to comprehensively encapsulate what religion is or does. In a similar sense, it may be impossible for any definition to fully capture all of the inherent properties of any concept. However, I concur with Gill that it is possible to develop a general definition of religion that "encompasses the spiritual beliefs and practices of the vast majority of the world's population" (Gill 2001, 120). My focus on the supernatural, systematized belief systems, and collective behavior is consistent with many previous studies and captures the properties of religion that tend to remain constant across religious traditions more so than focusing on doctrine or ethics whose importance may vary substantially across time and space (Menchik 2017, 576).

Previous Approaches

The Political Process Model

To examine the relationship between religious institutions and political activism, I consult an extensive literature on collective action which can be broadly categorized into "political process" and "rational choice" approaches. Largely influenced by Douglas McAdam's political process model (McAdam 1982), the political process approach to examining collective action suggests groups need framing, opportunity, and resource mobilization to prompt political activism. Each of these three factors is considered necessary to prompt collective action, and accordingly none is likely sufficient to prompt it in absence of the others (McAdam 1982, 37; McAdam, McCarthy, and Zald 1996, 3–7; Snow et al. 1986, 464–81).[5]

Framing

Analyses of collective action earlier than the 1970s tended to focus on the importance of grievance in spurring collective dissent. Popular movements demanding social change were thought to be the byproduct of either widespread poverty, social discrimination, or frustrated economic expectations (Snow et al. 1986, 465; Zald 1996, 265; Gurr 1970). The political process approach reacted against this predominant mode of theorizing, however, and suggested socioeconomic grievance alone is rarely a sufficient condition to prompt collective action. Because poverty is everywhere and grievances are widespread, we should see many more examples of collective action than we actually do (Oberschall 1996, 94–95; Javeline 2003).[6]

According to the framing perspective, political activism is not an automatic consequence of political or socioeconomic marginalization. For grievance to lead to collective action, communities must be aware of their marginalization and believe it is possible to change it. If, for example, an impoverished group has been socialized to believe its lower rank in life is an inevitable and immutable consequence of its class or ethnicity, it will not feel compelled to act and change its status. On the other hand, if a marginalized group perceives that its status is a rectifiable injustice, there becomes an increased incentive to engage in political activism (Snow et al. 1986, 466; R. Turner 1969; Piven and Cloward 1977).

If ideology constructs a worldview that either reinforces or challenges the prevailing social order, framing is the purposeful and deliberate creation of stories and symbols to cause individuals to reevaluate their surroundings and stir action. It involves the construction of "specific meta-phors, symbolic representations, and cognitive cues used to render or cast behavior and events in an evaluative mode and to suggest alternative modes of action" (Zald 1996, 262). Frames allow individuals to coordinate solutions to specific problems (Snow et al. 1986, 464; Zald 1996, 265–66), and they constitute "conscious, strategic efforts of movement groups to fashion meaningful actions of themselves and the issues at hand in order to motivate and legitimate their efforts" (McAdam 1996b, 339).

Much of the literature emphasizing the importance of religion in explaining political activism emphasizes framing. Charismatic clergy can "set a tone that suggests addressing political issues is a normal part of church life" (Djupe and Gilbert 2006, 119). Religious institutions are particularly likely to facilitate secular political activism when they foster a political theology that foments an insurgent consciousness. Political theol-ogy refers to how a religious institution thinks about political authority. It is the degree to which religious institutions "support, oppose, modify, or thwart the activities of the state" (Philpott 2007, 507). To say that a politi-cal theology encourages insurgent consciousness is to say that it "perceives, interprets, and explains a social situation in such a way that compels people to collectively organize and act to change that social situation," suggesting that a change of the political socioeconomic order is both "imperative and viable" (C. Smith 1991, 61).

Liberation theology is a particularly relevant political theology that emerged in Latin America during the latter half of the twentieth century. It encouraged the Catholic Church to advocate on behalf of the materi-ally disadvantaged, to promote human rights, and to side politically with the poor rather than the socioeconomic elite (Philpott 2007, 511; Kovic 2005, 49–52; Planas 1986, 6–7; Prokopy and Smith 1999, 3; Betances 2007, 53; Mainwaring 1986; Levine 1981). It was also an explicit attempt by the Church to encourage political participation, reframe adherents' relation-ship to their own poverty, and inspire them to make political demands from their governments.

Liberation theology endeavored to reorient Catholic theology by giv-ing a preferential option to the poor and oppressed (C. Smith 1991, 27). It insisted it was the responsibility of Catholics and the Church to "eradicate all forms of oppression and domination, whether social, cultural, political, economic, or spiritual" (C. Smith 1991, 27). The development of liberation theology created a new frame of insurgent consciousness that facilitated collective action, and the Church is thought to have advocated most vig-orously for democracy where liberation theology was most pronounced

(C. Smith 1991; Philpott 2007, 511). For example, while Daniel Philpott takes institutional configurations seriously, he argues that Catholic support for the Third Wave of Democratization between 1974 and 1990 was most pronounced in Latin America where liberation theology was most deeply entrenched (Philpott 2007, 511). Subsequently, a hypothesis developed from the framing approach would suggest religious institutions will be most likely to facilitate collective action when they produce political theologies.

Opportunity

Political opportunity refers to how changes in political regimes and institutions can either open or close opportunities for activism (Tarrow and Tilly 2009, 441). Previously restrictive political environments can open because of wars, economic changes, demographic changes, and general political instability (McAdam 1982, 41). These external changes allow activist groups to access the political system in ways that had not previously existed, and they often change the calculations of political elites. For example, external structural changes can create new possibilities for political contestation by encouraging elites to forge new alliances, or they can reduce the state's willingness to use repression (McAdam 1996a, 26–27; Brockett 1991; Kriesi et al. 1992; Kitschelt 1986). Such openings increase the opportunities militant actors have to demand change from the political system (C. Smith 1991, 58–59).

The literature emphasizing opportunity has tended to analyze religious groups as organizations, and it has been interested in how external factors compel religious leadership to encourage activism by adherents. By identifying situations that make religious elites likely to form new alliances with insurgent groups, scholars of religion and politics have examined changes in religious institutions that create what we might conceptualize as "religious opportunities" for political activism.

To understand how these openings occur, we must recognize that religious elites in mainstream religious organizations are often unwilling to support secular political movements that defy the dominant political order. Doing so may alienate political authorities or socioeconomic elites who provide valuable political and material support (Gill 1998; Trejo 2012, 32–33; Kalyvas 1996). Consider the Catholic Church in Latin America as an example. If the Church lends meeting spaces, legitimacy, networks of communication, and material resources to disruptive activists intent on challenging the status quo, it risks endangering cozy relationships with political leaders and the material resources it receives from affluent citizens (Gill 1998; Trejo 2012, 32–33; Koesel 2014). For centuries, Catholic adherents in Latin America had few alternatives to the Church to receive religious services. The Catholic Church could take the loyalty of its adherents for granted as it had few serious competitors. Because of this, it could foster positive relations with society's few rich and powerful, and it did not have to be responsive to the social concerns of most of its poor and disenfranchised flock.

When there is religious competition, on the other hand, religious adherents have the option to leave their religion and look for one that is more receptive to their needs. Guillermo Trejo, drawing on insights developed by Anthony Gill, contends that the arrival of Protestant religious competition in Chiapas empowered Catholic parishioners by giving them an exit option. They could receive Christian services from organizations competing with the Catholic Church, and these organizations were often more responsive in administering to poor populations by providing them with material welfare and education services. As a result, they were successful in converting many individuals away from Roman Catholicism. The Catholic Church could no longer take the support of its parishioners for granted, and it was forced to reinterpret its doctrine and scriptures to accommodate them. Religious competition prompted Catholic religious elites to form new alliances with previously marginalized groups to deter conversions to Protestantism. A religious opportunity subsequently emerged allowing the resources of the religious organization to be lent to secular political causes (Gill 1998; Trejo 2009). Simply put, the opportunity perspective as applied to the study of religion and collective action would hypothesize that where there are higher levels of religious competition, religious elites are more likely to support secular political activism.

Resource Mobilization

Finally, resource mobilization is another avenue through which religions contribute to collective action. Individuals are often mobilized for collective action within groups like families, community organizations, religious institutions, and work associations (McCarthy 1996, 141–45). "Drawing from related, existent organizations is a more efficient means of building organizational membership than recruiting random, unorganized individuals" (C. Smith 1991, 60). A great deal of previous scholarship has suggested that religious institutions provide organizational networks and resources that are essential for collective action (Becker and Dhingra 2001; Putnam 2000; Loveland et al. 2005; Caputo 2009; Verba, Schlozman, and Brady 1995; Morris 1981; McAdam 1982; Calhoun-Brown 2000; Harris 1994; Wickham 2004; Wiktorowicz 2004). They can provide activist groups with members, leadership, places to meet, administrative services, and communication networks (C. Smith 1991, 59–60). It is likely at least partially for these reasons that religiosity is consistently found to have a positive association with individual political participation across a variety of empirical settings (Putnam 2000; Putnam and Campbell 2010; Skocpol and Fiorina 1999; Seligson 1999; Klesner 2007).

Applying the perspective to political activism in Latin America, Deborah Yashar argues that transcommunity networks were a necessary condition for the emergence of indigenous political activism across Latin America. Churches, unions, community groups, and other nongovernmental organizations often unintentionally provided organizational structures necessary to support collective action. Yashar finds that churches helped to build rural networks between communities in Guatemala, Ecuador, Bolivia, and Mexico. "Churches often provided the means of communication, the locus of interaction, and literacy skills that linked one community to another" (Yashar 2005, 74). Within Chiapas specifically, she points out that the Catholic Church "organized indigenous fora, brought resources to indigenous communities, and encouraged more active forms of localized organizing" (Yashar 2005, 74). Yashar argues that in Chiapas, liberation theology provided an ideological framework that unified a plan of action within individual dioceses and across the region. Religion also brought institutional resources as Bishop Samuel Ruiz provided training and financial resources to indigenous communities.

The political process approach has compellingly argued that religious organizations often provide critical resources that facilitate collective action. However, it has tended to assume they automatically are capable of providing these resources (Djupe and Gilbert 2006, 117; Hsiung and Djupe forthcoming), and little attempt has been made to assess how or whether they provide such mobilization potential in the first place. Put somewhat bluntly, the approach might hypothesize that where there are religions, there is political activism. Unlike the framing and opportunity versions of the political process approach, the perspective does not offer much insight into variation in resource mobilizing potential across religious institutions. As a result, there is still a need for theories accounting for how mainstream religions develop capacities for resource mobilization.

The Rational Choice Approach

The political process approach helps us understand the importance of frames, opportunity structures, and resource mobilization. However, the rational choice perspective argues that collective action is the result of individual incentives to free ride, and it can help us understand how religious organizations mobilize the necessary resources for collective action.

Like the political process approach, the rational choice approach is skeptical that groups automatically mobilize on behalf of common interests. Rather than focusing on groups' political opportunity, framing, or resource mobilization, however, it considers individuals at a grassroots level. From this perspective, most people have little incentive to cooperate to achieve mutually desirable goals because they share incentives to free ride off the efforts of others (Olson 1965, 21). To relate the problem in the form of a simple example, let's imagine a scenario where five college-aged individuals rent a home. Keeping common areas such as the kitchen clean is desired by all. However, maintaining the cleanliness of the kitchen is costly in terms of time and work involved. Any individual in the home would prefer not to pay these costs and have any of the other members do so instead. We can imagine, however, that if all members of the home share these same attitudes, the result will often be suboptimal with a dirty kitchen.

Mancur Olson's formulation of the collective action problem (1965), along with a seminal contribution from James Buchanan (Buchanan 1965), prompted a vibrant preoccupation with strategies to overcome these types of free-rider problems. It can be difficult to keep kitchens in group homes clean because, like political activism, home cleanliness is a public good. These goods are unique because they are both nonexcludable and nonrivalrous. Nonexcludability means that it is either extremely costly or impossible to exclude individuals from the benefits of those goods. So, for example, if I live in a house with four other individuals and I am the only one who puts in the time and effort necessary to keep the kitchen clean, it is extremely difficult for me to exclude the others from the benefits of cleanliness even though none of them helped. They can all enjoy a clean kitchen, and I cannot prevent that. There is, accordingly, a strong incentive for them to free ride off my efforts. Nonrivalry, on the other hand, means that one individual's ability to consume a good does not diminish the ability of another individual to consume that same good (Cornes and Sandler 1996, 4). In other words, two individuals would be able to enjoy the benefits of cleanliness in the kitchen in much the same way as five individuals would be able to. The benefits of a clean kitchen are not diminished by increasing numbers of individuals.

Political activism, as we have already seen, seeks to influence the development and distribution of public goods. If individuals living in an authoritarian government desire democratization, democratic regime change is a mutually desirable outcome. However, activism to achieve democratization is extremely costly. The results of regime change accrue equally to everyone, regardless of whether they paid the costs in bringing it about, and it is extremely difficult to exclude noncontributors from the benefits of democratization. Because of this nonexcludability and nonrivalry of benefits and the extreme costs involved in protesting for democratization, there is a strong temptation to free ride off the efforts of others, and it can be difficult to create such movements. The key to prompting collective action from the rational choice perspective is to increase the costs associated with free riding, to give individuals incentives to cooperate, and to create general norms of cooperation so that participation becomes an automatic heuristic response rather than a considered strategy.[7]

Religion and Club Goods

Some scholarship within the rational choice tradition has specifically engaged with how religious institutions overcome free-rider problems, and it has been preoccupied with a "club goods" perspective. Unlike public goods, club goods are excludable, meaning it is possible to prevent individuals from enjoying their use. Examples include country clubs that require membership dues, toll roads drivers must pay to utilize, and sporting events in which one needs to purchase a ticket to enter. The key to discouraging free riding is to create an efficient and effective means to exclude noncontributors (Cornes and Sandler 1996, 4, 8). To this end, country clubs exclude nonmembers who do not pay dues with fences and guards, toll roads employ gates to prevent drivers who have not paid from using them, and sporting events use ticket offices and guarded entry points to prevent individuals who have not purchased tickets from entering a stadium. As the reader will see, club goods will importantly inform my own theory because the ability of a religious institution to provide excludable club goods to its members is a key factor explaining their ability to develop organizational capacities for political activism.

The perspective analyzes religions as clubs that provide excludable goods and services to their members. As discussed earlier in this chapter, religious organizations produce club goods that are prone to the free-rider problem (Iannaccone 1994). However, the solution employed by many radical and fringe religious organizations and sects is that they prohibit activities that diminish the resources members are able to provide to the organization (Iannaccone 1994). Individuals who do not adhere to these prohibitions are excluded from many of the goods and services provided by the religion.

Activities that would divert member time and resources, such as smoking, drinking, or socializing in venues outside the religious organization, are prohibited. Some sects also encourage members to take on seemingly bizarre stigmatizing activities including distinctive dress or speech. The intended effect is to ostracize members from the broader community. Only the most committed members are willing to accept these sacrifice and stigma requirements intended to weed out "potential members who might cheat later in life, shirking their responsibilities in mutual aid" (Berman 2011, 16). As a result, strict churches have committed membership that is unlikely to free ride, giving them a distinct advantage in providing goods and services to their members (Iannaccone 1994). They are extremely effective providers of mutual aid within their well-run and internally developed organizations because they have already effectively weeded out low commitment members. This highly committed membership gives them an advantage in perpetrating particularly high cost activities that are sensitive to defection, such as radical terrorist violence (Berman 2011).[8]

The club goods approach to studying religion and collective action has clarified how religious organizations prompt high-level contributions from committed members who self-select into strict groups. My own explanation importantly centers on the capacity of religious institutions to effectively produce club goods. However, while we understand extremist groups develop strong organizational capacities by weeding out free riders, how do we explain why mainstream religious institutions, which often make few serious sacrifice and stigma demands from their adherents, also encourage collective action?[9] Furthermore, as we will discuss in the next section, weeding out free riders is costly. Classic iterations of the club goods approach have implied sacrifice and stigma provide an efficient means for the group to exclude free riders (Iannaccone 1994, 1188), but I explicitly grapple with how decentralized institutional configurations help to overcome these costs. While sacrifice and stigma is an effective screening mechanism for sects, decentralization provides an alternative means to encourage exclusion, and one that is more readily available to mainstream religious institutions who are less likely to deploy sacrifice and stigma requirements.

Religious Decentralization and Political Activism

Obviously, collective action occurs. Even college students occasionally manage to keep their group kitchens clean. The trick is to explain why collective action emerges despite its difficulties, and this section elaborates my theoretical approach to explaining how mainstream religious institutions prompt collective action. First, I introduce my understanding of institutions and the important role they can play in reassuring individuals their cooperative interactions with others will not be exploited. While it is costly for institutions to provide this type of reassurance, I explain how decentralized institutions help mitigate such costs. I then apply the concept of decentralization to religious institutions. Though my explanation is derived from a rational-actor perspective,[10] I further explain how my theoretical account is embedded within a broader political process framework that takes opportunity structures, resource mobilization, and ideological framing seriously. While stressing the theory should be applicable to many types of nonstate and local associations, I conclude with a discussion of the degree to which religious institutions may be uniquely situated among local voluntary associations to prompt collective action.

Institutions and Transaction Costs

The most basic formulations of the free-rider problem assume individuals are located in a "state of nature" whose interactions occur in a vacuum ungoverned by any overarching institutions. In reality, institutions of all kinds regulate human interactions, and they are everywhere. Examples range from national governments to local churches to the informal practices second graders use when trading lunch items. They are the rules and norms that regulate our behavior with each other and that create predictable patterns of interaction. If we imagine human interactions as a transaction where I perform some cooperative behavior in exchange for some reciprocating behavior from you, institutions structure the incentives of that exchange and provide a rough framework for the behavior we can expect from each other. In other words, institutions regulate our behavior and give us expectations about the behavior we can expect from others

(North 1990, 3; Hall and Taylor 1996, 943; Levi et al. 1990, 12; Moe 1984, 739; Kuran 2011; Rubin 2017, 12; March and Olsen 2008, 3–4).

The reason institutions do so is because they help us catch (through monitoring) individuals who shirk their responsibilities and punish (sanction) them accordingly. However, monitoring and sanctioning are not free. We must pay costs, often referred to as transaction costs, to enforce our interaction and provide ourselves with assurance the other party will uphold his or her responsibilities (North 1990, 28, 32; Moe 1984, 750–51; Alchian and Demsetz 1972; Powell and DiMaggio 1991, 3–4).

To help make that point clearer, let's return to our example of keeping a group kitchen clean. While we all might agree to clean up after ourselves, we each have private incentives to use the kitchen without cleaning it because cleaning the kitchen requires time and effort. Unless someone keeps watch twenty-four hours a day, it can be difficult to identify any individual who leaves a mess, and the result unfortunately is often a messy kitchen. One institutionalist approach (albeit extreme) to overcome our kitchen collective action problem might be to buy a video camera. In this way, we could monitor the behavior of everyone using the kitchen. We would also need to impose a sanction for individuals who fail to clean up after themselves, and one common method here might be to employ a fine. However, there are serious obstacles involved with putting such a plan into practice. We would have to buy the necessary video equipment, install it properly, and arrange for someone to review footage and identify non-cleaning perpetrators. Each of these challenges constitutes a transaction cost, and the group would have to grapple with the question of how to compel everyone to contribute and pay for them.

As a result, we housemates might quickly find our scheme to keep the kitchen clean through video surveillance unworkable. This is because monitoring and sanctioning are themselves subject to a "second order" collective action problem (Oliver 1980; Heckathorn 1989). Without a means to compel everyone to contribute to buying video equipment or take turns reviewing footage, everyone has an incentive to free ride. Furthermore, without a way to force housemates to pay fines, our sanctioning mechanism is likely to prove ineffective. As Douglass North explains, "one cannot take enforcement for granted. It is (and always has been) the critical obstacle" to cooperation (North 1990, 33). Accordingly, we cannot simply point to institutional controls of monitoring and sanctioning as an avenue to overcome free riding. We must also explain how an institutional infrastructure providing these controls develops in the first place (Hechter 1990, 245), and it is here where decentralized institutions possess an advantage.

Decentralized Local Institutions

Governments overcome these types of problems through mandatory taxes, and they use the potential threat of force to compel all of us to pay for police, judges, and necessary infrastructure to provide effective monitoring and sanctioning. However, how do nonstate institutions, including religious institutions, overcome costs associated with providing monitoring and sanctioning when they lack similar compulsive force? The key is that monitoring must be highly visible. If individuals can monitor the behavior of others as they go about their everyday activities, such activities become far less costly, and the challenges associated with overcoming transaction costs are substantially mitigated (Hechter 1990, 245–46; Ostrom 1990, 99–100; Popkin 1988, 18). Such monitoring is more likely to occur in decentralized rather than centralized institutions.

In centralized institutions, authority is "concentrated in the hands of only a few members of the group" (Taylor 1990, 225). We can think of these as institutional arrangements where monitoring, sanctioning, and decision-making authority are held within the hands of a small number of people, typically at the top of a hierarchy, overseeing many others who do not share these responsibilities. Effective monitoring and sanctioning can be costly to provide in these scenarios because it is difficult for a small number of individuals in central authority to effectively monitor the behavior of many others without employing (paying) others to do so.

Decentralized institutions, on the other hand, are characterized by arrangements where individuals who consume common, collective resources *monitor*, in highly visible ways, the use of that resource without relying on a central authority. These local consumers also divine their own appropriate *sanctions* when others violate their responsibilities. Furthermore, these individuals typically have *at least some* institutional decision-making authority in their management. Decision-making is important because it facilitates buy-in by the location population for institutional decisions. "The greater the proportion of the group's members involved in solving the collective action problem . . . the more decentralized the solution" (Taylor 1990, 225). Individuals agree to be bound to a set of rules if they believe doing so will enable higher collective benefits than they can achieve on their own and if they believe their own contributions will be reciprocated by others (Ostrom 1990, 99–100).

A decentralized strategy for dealing with our kitchen problem might be to collectively decide upon a single designated time for all housemates to clean the kitchen together, and we would all share monitoring responsibilities. Identifying free riders in this scenario is essentially costless because we know whether everyone showed up to clean simply by looking around (Popkin 1988, 18). Rather than relying on unenforceable fines, we might instead agree to exclude offending individuals from any club goods and services we collectively provide each other. For example, let's assume all of the housemates enjoy going out for happy hour. Perhaps if I do not show up at the designated time to clean the kitchen, the group can sanction me by excluding me from happy hour on Friday evenings. Through these effective and decentralized controls of monitoring and sanctioning, we could identify shirkers and punish them. In this way, we would all have confidence our own cleaning contributions were reciprocated by others in the group.

Decentralized institutions possess some advantages in solving free-rider problems over centralized institutions. Unless centralized institutions make substantial monitoring investments, they do not have access to information about who is shirking to the same degree as individuals consuming institutional resources themselves. This is because the consumers of institutional resources can monitor the behavior of others more cheaply and effectively as they go about their everyday activities, helping to mitigate transaction costs and free-rider problems. Local monitors also bring extensive knowledge and information to bear on local characteristics and the habits of others that may be difficult for a central organization to collect. Sanctioning decisions are more likely to be calibrated to local sensibilities. Accordingly, monitoring and sanctioning capacities are often provided more efficiently by individuals at a local level, and thus developing these formal institutional mechanisms of control are far less costly, and, as a result, less subject to the second order collective action problem (Ostrom 1990, 10–11, 99–100, 185–86; Agrawal and Ostrom 2001; Andersson and Ostrom 2008; Ostrom, Gardner, and Walker 1994, 192–93).[11]

As mentioned, social institutions (like religious institutions) typically do not sanction shirkers with coercive force. Instead, they can sanction their members by excluding them from the goods and services (club goods) they produce for their members (North 1990, 34; Hechter 1990, 246–47; Moe 1984, 751; Hechter 1987). However, for the threat of sanction through exclusion to hold any weight, individuals must need the resources produced by the religious group. If it does not produce desired collective goods and resources particularly well, the threat of exclusion is substantially muted. Accordingly, the more efficaciously a club provides excludable and desired goods and services for members, the more dependent members of the organization are on the group. With effective control through monitoring and sanctioning, the group can incentivize cooperation among its members, and it is now in a position to develop an organizational infrastructure at the grassroots (Hechter 1987). As more and more individuals contribute, the group's resource endowment grows, it can subsequently offer more valuable club goods and services to its members, and it develops a grassroots organizational infrastructure in order to do so. This infrastructure can now be used to mobilize the resources that the political process approach highlights as essential to prompting grassroots collective action.

Religious Decentralization

It is likely not difficult now for the reader to anticipate how I will apply institutional decentralization to religious institutions. Before doing so, I should note others have recognized religious decentralization potentially affects political activism. Some literature suggests decentralized religious institutions make collective action less likely. For example, the decentralized nature of the Catholic Church in France explains why it provided a disjointed response to anticlerical attacks, whereas in Italy the response was much more coordinated due to a centralized governance style (Warner 2000, 71–72). The argument here is that decentralization poses a challenge for coordinating effective responses to political concerns.

On the other hand, other studies have provided largely anecdotal but suggestive evidence that the decentralization of the Catholic Church may have been associated with increased political activism across Latin America and Europe (Levine 1988; Kalyvas 1996). In situations where Church governance was "most genuinely democratic and least directive," the Catholic Church was thought to have the strongest impact on political activism (Levine 1988, 257), and decentralization further appears to have had some positive relationship with the capacity of militant Islamic causes to mobilize terrorist violence (Iannaccone and Berman 2006, 121; Sageman 2004). Religious decentralization plugs individuals into networks that increase communication among adherents, enable recruitment, and that help individuals develop civic skills necessary for democracy to function properly (Levine 1988, 254; Verba, Schlozman, and Brady 1995, 380–84; Djupe and Gilbert 2006).

However, religious decentralization has been vaguely defined, a problem often shared by literature examining decentralization more generally (Treisman 2007, 21). While somewhat difficult to peg down, religious decentralization often appears to be conceptualized across these various works as settings where religious governance, with a focus on doctrinal and institutional decision-making authority, is entrusted to laity in a bottom-up and nearly autonomous manner (Trejo 2009, 327; Levine 1988, 257).

Conversely, when I discuss religious decentralization, I precisely refer to institutional structures that grant decision-making, monitoring, and sanctioning authority over the management of religious club goods to nonclerical members of a religious institution at a local level. Previous conceptualizations of religious decentralization tended to focus on decision-making over doctrine and institutional matters, but they typically ignored important matters of monitoring, sanctioning, and the question of who bears responsibility for governing the production of religious club goods. My conceptualization is differentiated from these in two ways. First, in addition to considering those individuals who create doctrine or manage the institutional hierarchy, it focuses our attention on the individuals responsible for managing material resources. Second, it expands the conceptualization of religious decentralization beyond decision-making to include monitoring and sanctioning responsibilities.

By decentralized *decision-making*, I refer to the ability of nonclerical actors to have at least some role in determining matters of liturgical practice, general doctrine, leadership, and the production of material club goods.[12] Decentralized *monitoring*, on the other hand, occurs when local, nonclerical actors shoulder responsibility for ensuring other religious members engage in cooperative behavior with each other. Decentralized *sanctioning* in religious institutions entails the responsibility nonclerical religious actors have for punishing monitored shirking and transgressions. Sanctioned individuals are generally denied access to select goods and resources created by the religious institution. To the extent these sanctioning decisions are decentralized, they are collectively made by nonclerical members of the religious institution and are not likely to be overridden or commuted by members of the clergy.

Where a religious institution demonstrates decentralized governance, adherents understand that any free riding or cheating behavior is more likely to be noted and punished by their fellow religious group members. As they experience greater levels of cooperation from other members of the religious institution, they become increasingly willing to interact and cooperate themselves. The process creates greater levels of reciprocity (Ostrom 2009, 200–201; Putnam 1994, 172). As more individuals contribute to the good of the group, more resources are poured into the religious institution. It is subsequently able to provide more valuable goods and services to its members. The result is a feedback loop of greater participation and greater benefits provided. As individuals increasingly cooperate over many repeated iterations, cooperation slowly becomes a heuristic norm (Ostrom 1990, 196–97; Koelble 1995, 239; Taylor 1990; Coleman 1990). In other words, and as more fully described further in this chapter, cooperation becomes an automatic response rather than a considered strategy. In the process of providing internal and excludable club goods, an organizational framework and the norms of reciprocal cooperation evolve, perhaps unintentionally, that can be applied to complex and nonexcludable public goods problems such as political activism (Hechter 1987, 123; Rydin and Pennington 2000, 161–62; Djupe and Gilbert 2006, 118; Kalyvas 1996).

Accordingly, I hypothesize that individuals located within decentralized religious institutions should be more likely to engage in political activism than individuals in centralized religious institutions. I further hypothesize that decentralization by a religious institution prompts, in a path-dependent manner, heightened levels of reciprocal interactions in communities, the ability of the institution to offer increasingly valuable club goods to its members, and finally to the development of an organizational capacity that can be applied to political activism.

Rational Choice and Political Process Approaches

My theory of religious decentralization explains how mainstream religious institutions develop organizational resources that can be mobilized for political activism. However, this organizational capacity only creates *potential* for political activism. As I have argued, the rational choice approach and its preoccupation with the free-rider problem is not sufficient on its own to explain how religious institutions mobilize collective action. To understand how that organizational potential is made manifest into political engagement, we must also examine the political process approach to collective action. Within a religious institution, not all adherents may agree on whether political engagement should occur, what types of issues the group should advocate for, or how they should engage in political activity. The inability to coordinate, even given decentralization and potential institutional capacities for collective action, can lead to directionless and weak engagement (Warner 2000; Warner and Wenner 2006). For this reason, framing is extremely important (Hardin 1990, 359–60; Powell and DiMaggio 1991, 5; North 1990; Weingast 1995).

For religious decentralization to prompt political activism, it should be accompanied by a framing "political theology" (Philpott 2007) that advocates for active political engagement. Such a political theology coordinates adherents' effort around common objectives and provides a focused area of engagement for political activism. Charismatic clergy can play a particularly important role here as "political entrepreneurs" who coordinate adherents' expectations around particular goals, disseminate ideas through an institution, and prompt cooperation (Taylor 1990, 234; Popkin 1988, 20; Hall 1986, 276–80; Djupe and Gilbert 2006, 119). We cannot understand why decentralization develops a cohesive social movement, as opposed to a multitude of scattered interests incapable of coordinating activity, without examining the ideological frames that guide action. Similarly, we cannot understand why political activism takes on either progressive or conservative goals without explaining the framing that guides political action. It is only when a political theology of insurgent consciousness exists that organizational potential will seek to apply itself to political activism. Accordingly, areas exposed to politicized theology should be associated with increased individual propensities to engage in political activism.

Second, religions, as specified above, also function as organizations. They seek to advance their interests in society, and they respond to external threats such as the emergence of new religious competitors. Detailing the incentives that inspire religious elites to form partnerships with activists helps us understand why they allow their religious institutions to become politicized in the first place, thus fomenting new opportunities for political activism. Religious competition provides a powerful rationale for political elites to support secular political causes. Accordingly, I expect that increasing levels of religious competition are associated with higher individual engagement in political activism. Within the Mexican empirical context, this should be particularly visible with regard to competition between the Catholic Church and Protestant challengers. In regions where the Catholic Church has faced greater competition from Protestants, we should see greater activism.

By combining the insights of the political process and rational choice approaches to collective action, I provide a framework for understanding variation in the frames, opportunity structures, and capacities for resource mobilization that allow religious institutions to engage in political activism. My theory of religious decentralization provides guidance for whether religious institutions provide organizational infrastructure facilitating resource mobilization, and the presence or absence of religious theologies helps us understand when religious institutions provide frames enabling collective action. Furthermore, the presence of religious competition helps us understand when religious institutions provide opportunities for political activism. I expect religion facilitates political activism when it is institutionally decentralized, characterized by a coordinating political theology encouraging engagement, and when its elites face organizational imperatives to respond to challenges from religious competitors.

Religious Exceptionalism?

Because the theory is grounded in general rationalist assumptions of human behavior, I expect the dynamics of decentralization would work similarly in religious institutions as they would in other types of local voluntary associations. However, there are three characteristics of religious organizations that may make them particularly important to study. The first is their sheer ubiquity and local infiltration. "Religions are probably the largest unit to which individuals claim loyalty," and there are, for example, 1.5 billion adherents of Islam and 2 billion adherents of Christianity (Grzymala-Busse 2012, 423). Much of the world's population is characterized by some form of religious affiliation, and religions often organize a significant proportion of local interactions.

Second, religious elites typically invest in their reputations, and this may give religious organizations a slight advantage relative to other types of institutions in prompting collective action. Religion, as discussed earlier, offers supernatural solutions to many of life's general problems (Stark and Bainbridge 1985, 6; 1996, 39). Because religious adherents cannot substantiate many supernatural promises, religious elites must appear trustworthy. "Religious leaders have a strong incentive to remain trustworthy. The very nature of their job—providing answers to questions that often cannot be verified . . . requires them to invest heavily in their own trustworthiness and credibility" (Gill 1998, 52–53). It is for this reason that religious clergy "typically rank as the most trustworthy profession in opinion surveys" (Gill 1998, 53).

The heavy investments clergy make in their trustworthiness have important implications for collective action. Decentralized institutions help to prompt collective action as individuals learn to reciprocate cooperative activity and have greater assurances that opportunistic behavior will be identified and sanctioned. However, in a newly decentralized institutional environment, the heuristic norms of cooperation take time to develop, and the benefits of cooperation may be uncertain. The religious organization may not yet supply valuable club goods from which individuals fear exclusion, and potential incentives to defect in these early stages may still be strong. In these situations, there is a need for one individual to credibly signal to others an intention to cooperate (Ostrom 1990, 42–44). It is likely that religious leadership, having already invested heavily in trustworthiness and credibility, has an advantage in credibly signaling an intention to cooperate in nascent institutional stages where early assurances of cooperation are critical.

Finally, some critics of my rational choice approach may protest the contention that mainstream religious institutions rely on effective monitoring and sanctioning to develop an organizational infrastructure.[13] Sincere and earnest motivations of faith, they might claim, are lost. I agree the impact of religion on collective action cannot be understood without some reference to transcendent experiences of "humility" and "exaltation" associated with a believer's reflection on the divine (Mitchell 2007). Durkheim and subsequent scholars have extolled the power of collective rituals and shared beliefs in psychologically creating a type of moral community that helps overcome free riding (Durkheim 1915; Graham and Haidt 2010, 143; Atran and Henrich 2010). I certainly concede that some individuals behave altruistically in certain settings, and religious institutions often inspire true believers to action. I do not assume individuals, religious or otherwise, are exclusively motivated by a strictly rational cost-benefit calculus. A great deal of convincing empirical literature demonstrates human behavior entails a mix of rational (self-regarding), altruistic (other-regarding), and reciprocal (tit for tat) actions. Substantial evidence further suggests individuals often behave altruistically and care about fairness and reciprocity in certain settings (Fehr and Gintis 2007; Henrich et al. 2001; Andreoni 1990; Bowles and Gintis 2004; Charness and Rabin 2002; B. Simpson and Willer 2008).

Religious institutions, in particular, appear capable of activating these prosocial tendencies. Some might argue that religious institutions prompt cooperative contributions to the group not through temporal threats of monitoring or sanctioning, but because through theological inspiration, moral persuasion, or the perceived threat of supernatural sanction, religious individuals are predisposed to cooperate (Saroglou et al. 2005; Norenzayan and Shariff 2008; Pessi 2011; Warner et al. 2015; McClendon and Riedl 2015).

However, I assume that while a minority of mainstream religious adherents quite likely are motivated by prosocial or generous religious theology, most are motivated by the same considerations that motivate everyone else. There is a great diversity of commitment among the religious. Mainstream religious institutions, in particular, may be attractive because they often demand little from their adherents (Iannaccone 1992; Iannaccone and Berman 2006, 117), and it stands to reason their members may need additional coaxing to provide cooperative contributions. For example, while Warner and associates' field experiments found that theological primes emphasizing God's grace increased Catholic adherents' propensities to make charitable contributions, the vast majority were not predisposed to make a donation (Warner et al. 2018, 230).

Instead, most individuals, religious or otherwise, are likely motivated by heuristic norms developed through previous and repeated experiences with others. People interact repeatedly over time and learn from those interactions. They come to recognize situations in which they gain and in which they are exploited. They likely do not take the time to gather complete information and make a rational utility calculation for every single interaction they find themselves in, but this is not to say that they do not engage in a rough logic of cost/benefit comparison (they are "boundedly rational"). Drawing on their reservoir of prior experience, individuals tend to cooperate in situations where cooperation has benefited them in the past and defect (or avoid interacting; see Janssen 2008) in situations where they have previously fallen victim to free riding. They develop norms of behavior that are predicated on their prior experiences. Put more simply, if individuals find themselves in social institutions that reward cooperation, most will cooperate over time as a default response without putting much thought into it. Similarly, if they find themselves in social institutions that reward free riding, free riding will become a default response (Ostrom 1990, 196–97; Koelble 1995, 239; Taylor 1990; Coleman 1990; Fehr and Gintis 2007).

However substantial a minority they may be, there are altruistic cooperators, and previous research has demonstrated that religion can further activate the prosocial tendencies of some adherents. In social situations with new and untested decentralized institutions, individuals may only be willing to interact with trustworthy individuals. Religious adherents who have visibly demonstrated consistent prosociality in the past may be safe bets for cooperation during an institution's early going. These true believers are credible cooperators and can provide early cooperative interactions to entice contributions from the remainder of religious adherents under the right (i.e., decentralized) institutional circumstances. It is unlikely, however, that these prosocial cooperators will be sufficient in numbers to prompt large-scale collective action in institutional settings where the majority of members share incentives to free ride.

Now that we have defined the key concepts of political activism and religious institutions, surveyed previous approaches to examining the relationship between the two, and discussed my own theoretical approach, my next undertaking is to test the theory, along with a variety of potential theoretical alternatives. Chapter 3 presents my statistical analysis which seeks to assess whether religious decentralization, the presence of liberation theology, and the presence of Protestant competition are generally and positively associated with political activism across Mexico utilizing Mexican survey data. I assess whether decentralization encourages reciprocity, the development of club goods, and the subsequent development of an organizational infrastructure that can be mobilized for political activism. I further assess the presence or absence of these mechanisms in chapters 4 through 6 with my respective investigations into the Diocese of San Cristóbal de las Casas in Chiapas, the Archdiocese of Yucatán, and the Diocese of Cuernavaca in Morelos.

THREE

Religion and Political Activism across Mexico

Mexico entered unprecedented political territory with the dawn of the twenty-first century. The Institutional Revolutionary Party, more colloquially known as the PRI, was democratically voted out of office in 2000 following seventy years of authoritarian rule. The determinants of Mexican political participation subsequently became a vibrant area of research as scholars sought to determine Mexico's prospects for democratic consolidation. Though Mexicans tend to participate at slightly higher levels than many other Latin American countries, there is great variability. Citizens coming from advantaged socioeconomic conditions tend to participate at much higher levels, and there is also a great degree of geographic variation in levels of political participation across the country (Klesner 2009; Hiskey and Bowler 2005; Olvera 2004, 427).

Given the purpose of this study, it will likely not surprise the reader to learn the Church has played an outsized role stimulating Mexican political activism in recent years. The country is highly religious and predominantly Catholic. Eighty-three percent of the population identifies itself as Roman Catholic, more than 70 percent of the population attends a religious service at least once a month (Camp 2014, 90–91), and churchgoing itself is found to be an important predictor of Mexican political engagement (Klesner 2009). As a result, two-thirds of nongovernmental organizations have some form of religious affiliation. For example, the more than one hundred human rights organizations formed in Mexico during the 1980s had strong affiliations with the Catholic Church. Additionally, more than a quarter of the volunteers for Civic Alliance, a large and influential civic organization that promoted clean and fair elections during the 1990s, came directly from either Catholic Christian base communities, religious orders, or Catholic youth organizations (Blancarte 2006, 429–30, 425; Olvera 2004, 415).[1]

We know the Catholic Church often provides critical resources and helps to mobilize engagement across Mexico, but there are also many examples where it does not. It has not prompted political indigenous activism in Yucatán or Puebla, for example (Trejo 2009; Mattiace 2009), nor has it prompted widespread political activism in some northern Mexican cities such as Nuevo Laredo (Sabet 2008, 81). Under what conditions then can the Catholic Church be expected to influence political activism throughout Mexico?

In the previous chapter, I formulated testable hypotheses explaining why religion facilitates secular political activism in some settings, but not others. The statistical analyses presented in this chapter are meant to test these hypotheses across Mexican individuals on a mass and nationally representative scale. I expect that individuals residing within decentralized dioceses of the Mexican Catholic Church should be more prone to engage in political activism. I also hypothesized that individuals residing within regions characterized by higher levels of religious competition, and individuals residing within areas more likely to have been exposed to a politicized theology, should be characterized by higher levels of political activism. Furthermore, I developed alternative hypotheses in the introductory chapter of this book with contending accounts of how economic deprivation, political party competition, legacies of Church/state conflict, and ethnic heterogeneity might influence collective action.

Within this chapter, I statistically test these hypotheses against each other utilizing an original dataset constructed from a variety of sources. I describe my measures for assessing religious decentralization, religious competition, politicized theology, several alternative hypotheses, and a variety of individual-level controls.

I then run a wide array of statistical models on my data. To be friendly to broad readership, I present the results with figures. Readers interested in greater precision will find full regression tables and robustness checks in the appendix at the end of this book as referenced in the footnotes to this chapter. The results demonstrate religious decentralization, politicized theology, and religious competition are each generally associated with political activism. Furthermore, religious decentralization shares a mutually reinforcing relationship with both politicized theology and religious competition. On the other hand, political party competition and ethnic heterogeneity do not have statistically meaningful relationships. Finally, economic grievance and legacies of Church/state conflict receive only limited support. In short, the results provide support for theories emphasizing the importance and mutually reinforcing impact of religious framing, opportunity, and resource mobilization in producing collective action.

Political Activism

Political activism, my dependent variable, consists of active, amateurish, unconventional, and voluntary political engagement that generally occurs outside formal state institutions. I measure political activism with nationally representative Mexican survey data collected from the National Survey of Political Culture and Citizen Practices (ENCUP 2010), a dataset that analyzes the political behavior of Mexican citizens. My statistical analysis draws on a pooled cross-sectional dataset of more than thirteen thousand individuals surveyed by ENCUP in 2001, 2003, and 2005 in what is "easily the richest dataset available to explore political participation in . . . Mexico's new democracy" (Klesner 2009, 62).

I assess an individual's political activism with two different variables derived from the ENCUP dataset. The first, **"Activism"** is a dichotomous variable (the respondent answered either "yes" or "no") assessing whether an individual self-reported as having participated in any one of the potential forms of political activism assessed by the survey.[2] The measure is useful in helping to differentiate who is politically active from who is not. Because the survey did not ask participants about their frequency of involvement, I have also developed a **"Count Activism"** measure that counts the number of different types of activist behavior an individual has engaged in to further ascertain degrees of political engagement. If, for example, an individual responded that she only attended a march, she is counted as having engaged in one instance of activism. On the other hand, if an individual responded that she had attended a march, petitioned a political party, and complained to authorities, she is counted as having engaged in a count of three activist acts. This allows me, to some extent, to differentiate the degree of active political involvement among respondents.[3]

Independent Variables

I capture religious decentralization (**"Decentralized"**), my primary independent variable of interest, through the number of permanent deacons in each Mexican Catholic diocese. Permanent deacons were introduced into the Catholic Church following the Second Vatican Council of the 1960s. Along with several other major reforms, the permanent deaconate was part of an effort to increase avenues of participation. It directly empowered married laity to perform priestly functions, represent the Catholic Church, and take on leadership positions within the community as ordained ministers. Critically, deacons are not considered priests. Unlike priests, deacons may be married. Also, unlike priests, deacons do not derive their primary livelihood from an institutional affiliation with the Catholic Church. They straddle a position between priests and laity (Catholic Church 1993). The permanent deaconate was an important and radical institutional reform allowing for greater participation in the Church by putting more pastoral agents to work (Chand 2001, 169; Gill 1999, 29–30; Trejo 2004, 222–23; Harvey 1998, 74). It was part of an attempt by the Catholic Church, along with Christian base communities, to "decentralize its operations to reach more parishioners at the grassroots level" (Gill 1999, 30). As we will see in our companion investigation into Chiapas, these individuals were often given important decision-making positions within their communities and responsibility for managing the Church's economic cooperatives.

Catholic dioceses are governed in an autonomous manner by individual bishops, and bishops choose to administer their respective dioceses in very different ways. Importantly, individual bishops may opt whether they want to implement deaconate programs in their dioceses, and nearly half the dioceses in Mexico have no permanent deacons whatsoever. The fear among more hierarchically minded bishops is that such devolution of control may cause the institutional Church to lose influence and control of its message (Gill 1999, 33).

The number of permanent deacons in each diocese, as expressed in the Annuario Pontificio and collected from the Catholic Hierarchy Organization (Cheney 2015), accordingly serves as a statistical means to assess the level of decentralization of that particular diocese. The position provides opportunities for individuals who would otherwise be considered laity to perform liturgical functions and has been noted as an important marker of the willingness of a particular bishop to decentralize control of Church affairs away from the traditional hierarchy (bishops and priests) from as far north in Mexico as Chihuahua to as far south as Chiapas (Chand 2001, 199).[4] I expect higher numbers of permanent deacons in a Catholic diocese are positively associated with increased propensities of Catholics residing within that diocese to engage in political activism.

While religious decentralization creates organizational potential for political activism, the political process approach to collective action suggests there must also be opportunities that encourage active political engagement. With religious competition, religious leaders can no longer pursue cozy relationships with political and socioeconomic elites and may have an incentive to credibly support causes relevant to most religious adherents. They are accordingly more likely to allow the religious institution to support secular political activism. I collected data measuring **"Religious Competition"** at the municipal level from the 2000 Mexican Census (INEGI 2010).[5] These data are used in an effective number of religions index (ENR).[6] Accordingly, my expectation is that increasing levels of the effective number of religions (ENR) in each municipality are positively associated with increased individual propensities of Catholics to engage in activism.

The political process approach further suggests relevant framing must be in place that encourages individuals to become politically engaged. Religious institutions potentially develop an insurgent consciousness wherein individuals become conscious of their socioeconomic status and believe change is possible. Such a politicized theology was most likely to develop in Latin America where liberation theology was predominant. To develop a systematic, testable, and falsifiable measure for **"Political Theology,"** I borrow from Anthony Gill's measure of ideological commitment suggesting the timing of a bishop's appointment influences his receptivity to the influence of liberation theology. Gill argues that bishops appointed under the most progressive popes (John XXIII and Paul VI) were more likely to be influenced by progressive Catholic thinking (Gill 1998, 105–6).

My measure is modified from Gill's to reflect Mexico's unique history. Following John Paul II's selection as pope, the Vatican sent a special envoy to Mexico, Girolamo Prigione, in part to combat progressive trends in the Mexican Catholic Church. Prigione systematically replaced retiring Mexican bishops with bishops adhering to an orthodox, conservative, and generally apolitical social stance (Chand 2001, 183, 198; Camp 1997, 265–66). Accordingly, appointments of bishops made under Prigione's stay in Mexico as Vatican envoy (from 1978 to 1997) are expected to be less amenable to politicized Catholicism than appointments made before or after his tenure. Data detailing the date of appointment of all past and current bishops in each Mexican diocese were collected from the Mexican Episcopal Conference (CEM), and the ideological variable is coded dichotomously with a value of 1 if a bishop was not appointed under Prigione and a value of 0 if he was (CEM 2011). I would expect that Catholic dioceses with bishops who were not assigned by Girolamo Prigione were more likely to have been receptive to expressing a politicized theology, and Catholics residing within those dioceses should be positively associated with increased propensities for activism.

Furthermore, it is possible that resource mobilization possesses a mutually reinforcing relationship with framing and opportunity. I expect the presence of politicized theology increases decentralization's impact on collective action. Decentralized communities, through local abilities to create their own theological interpretations, create even more powerful frames that can then be made manifest through the organizational capacity that decentralization provides. Likewise, political openings made possible by religious competition encourage clergy to proactively advocate on behalf of their parishioners. When combined with increased internal capacities for resource mobilization, this creates even greater propensities for political activism. The interaction term will be created by multiplying "Decentralized" separately with "Religious Competition" and "Political Theology."

Alternative Hypotheses

There are several alternative explanations to be tested that might also explain variation in levels of political activism across Mexico. Political party competition might influence levels of political activism, either because it creates an increased political opportunity for collective action or because it increases the negotiating position of the Church vis-à-vis the state. I develop my measure of **"Party Competition"** using municipal-level data obtained from the Mexican Federal Electoral Institute (IFE). I use a Herfindahl index of the proportion of votes received by each political party at the municipal level (Molinar 1991, 1383–91; IFE 2010; Hiskey and Bowler 2005) for the proportionally represented seats in the Mexican federal lower legislative chamber—the Chamber of Deputies.[7]

Furthermore, histories of Church/state animosities may have a negative impact on political activism. In the Mexican case, Catholic bishops located in geographic regions unaffected by the Cristero War may have had greater space to encourage political activism on the part of their adherents. To test this possibility, I utilized data detailing the number of combatants involved in the Cristero conflict in each Mexican state. Data measuring **"Church/ State Legacies"** was taken from Jean Meyer's historical examination of the Cristero War, *La Cristiada*, vol. 3, *Los Cristeros* (Meyer 1978, 108–9). Meyer presents regional data detailing the number of Cristero combatants involved in the conflict, and I assess the measure as the number of Cristero combatants (per one thousand) in each Mexican state.

Economic deprivation may affect levels of political activism. While much of the literature discounts the impact of economic deprivation on prompting collective action, it likely creates a demand factor for change, and its influence should be accounted for. I derived data for **"Deprivation"** from the United Nations Programs for the Development of Mexico (PNUD 2008) detailing a Human Development Index (HDI) for each municipality in Mexico. HDI considers life expectancy, years of education, and GNI per capita to develop an index of socioeconomic development. Less-developed regions experience more economic hardship than regions ranking higher on the human development index, and we would expect the higher the score on the HDI, the lower the demand for political change. Accordingly, higher scores on the human development index would be expected to be associated with lower levels of political activism.

Additionally, ethnic heterogeneity may have an impact on political activism. Much scholarship has demonstrated a negative association between ethnic heterogeneity and public goods provision. Accordingly, we would also expect that ethnic heterogeneity might also have a negative impact on political activism. There are a great number of indigenous groups in Mexico, each speaking a different language and holding different customs. Theoretically, we might expect that regions marked by higher levels of ethnic heterogeneity would be marked by lower levels of public goods provision, as expressed through heightened levels of political activism. Data on **"Ethnic Heterogeneity"** in Mexico have been collected from the National Commission for the Development of Indigenous Peoples (CDI). The data detail, at the municipal level, the proportion of individuals within a municipality speaking indigenous languages. I use these data to create a Herfindahl measure of separate identities (CDI 2000).

Individual Level Controls

Finally, there are a variety of relevant individual-level variables to control for, all of which were collected from the ENCUP dataset. **"Age"** is a simple numerical number reporting the respondents' age.[8] Respondents were also asked to fill in their economic status into one of several provided categories. I have collapsed these categories into three simple measures of whether an individual self-identified as having **"Good Economic Status,"** **"Regular Economic Status,"** or **"Bad Economic Status."** Here, "Regular Economic Status" is the omitted category, and the remaining economic status variables are interpreted in relation to the omitted "Regular Economic Status" category. "**Gender**" is a dichotomous variable where individuals are coded as 1 if they identify as male and 0 if female.

Religiosity is measured as a categorical variable and based on an individual's attendance of religious services. Individuals who never go to church, or who only go to church for special occasions, are coded in the "**Very Low Religiosity**" category. Individuals who attend church less than once a week are coded in the "**Low Religiosity**" category, individuals who attend church once a week are coded in the "**Moderate Religiosity**" category, and individuals who attend church more than once a week are coded into the "**High Religiosity**" category. I expect that individuals who attend church with greater regularity will be associated with increased propensities to engage in activism. Within the statistical models, the coefficients associated with the religiosity variables are interpreted relative to the omitted "Very Low Religiosity" category.

Modeling Decisions

A variety of statistical models are available to a researcher, and decisions must be made about which models to run based on the nature of the data. This section necessarily details some of those decisions. Less interested readers may prefer to advance to the next section, "Results."

For my primary models, I ran fixed effects logistic regression across Mexican Catholics on the "Activism" variable. Logit analysis is appropriate given the dichotomous (yes/no) nature of the dependent variable. Furthermore, we can imagine any number of additional unobservable or unmeasurable variables that might systematically affect the relationship between religion and political activism. I employ fixed effects to help control for such unobservable observations (Rabe-Hesketh and Skrondal 2012, 530; Allison 2009). The diocese and year are used as the fixed effects, and standard errors are clustered by dioceses. Mexico's nearly ninety dioceses have been drawn specifically to match the demographic and geographic characteristics of the country. The diocese accordingly controls for a wide range of potential geographic, political, religious, cultural, and socioeconomic unobservable effects. The diocese is also chosen as the appropriate spatial fixed effect because it is the central administrative unit of the Catholic Church.

I run many robustness checks with different models, all of which are presented in the appendix at the end of this book. As an alternative to fixed effects, I run random effects (also known as hierarchical models), which have the advantage of being more efficient but do not control for potential omitted variables bias as effectively as fixed effects. Furthermore, though the logit analysis is more appropriate, I also run ordinary least squares (OLS) regression on my "Activism" dependent variable. Though the results presented in the text feature a dichotomous yes/no response of whether individuals engaged in any form of activism, I further counted the number of activism types an individual engaged in for a "Count Activism" variable, and I analyze it with fixed and random effects Poisson, negative binomial, and ordinal logistic regression models.[9] None of these robustness checks substantively alter the conclusions presented here.[10]

Results

Figure 3.1 visually presents the results of my analysis, while interested readers will find the full regression table in Appendix Table A.2. The figure presents variables in the model on the left-hand side along the (vertical) y-axis. The (horizontal) x-axis represents coefficients describing the association of each variable with Activism. Each point to the right of the y-axis within the table represents the coefficient for each variable estimated by the model, and the lines emerging from the right and left of each point represents the 95 percent confidence interval. To the extent that these lines representing the 95 percent confidence interval do not intersect 0, represented by the vertical line emerging from 0 on the x-axis, the variable has a statistically significant association with Activism according to the model.

The statistical results provide supportive evidence for my framework emphasizing the importance of religious decentralization, political theology, and religious competition as each share statistically significant and positive associations with political activism at the 95 percent confidence interval. On the other hand, little supportive evidence is provided for theories of political party competition or ethnic heterogeneity. While my primary model does not provide supportive evidence that relative deprivation shares an association with political activism, its effects are statistically significant in several of the statistical models presented in the appendix. Accordingly, my analyses provide some mixed evidence that as a municipality's human development rises, there is a negative impact on the propensity individuals residing within it engage in political activism. Similarly, my primary models suggest a negative association between legacies of Church and state conflict and political activism at the 90 percent confidence interval, although this finding is not particularly robust

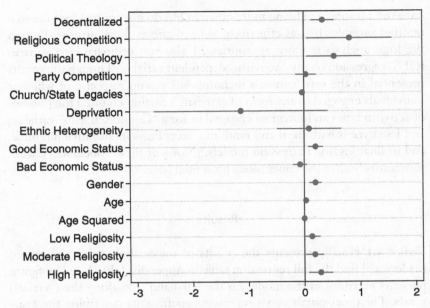

Figure 3.1. Comparative theory test of collective action across Mexico

across the various statistical models presented in the appendix. I would therefore describe my analyses as providing only very weak support for this contention.

We also see that individuals who self-identify as having good economic status are positively associated with political activism. Age demonstrates the expected curvilinear relationship. Religiosity also possesses the expected relationship, with more religious individuals more predisposed to participate. Finally, men are more likely to engage in activist activities than women, consistent with the finding that women are less likely to participate in countries where they hold a low proportion of public office (Klesner 2009, 71; Burns, Schlozman, and Verba 2001).

In the following section, I discuss the implications of these results. In many cases, I provide visual marginal effects plots to further examine the relationship between specific variables and political activism. These models illustrated the probability, predicted by the model, that an individual participates in an activist event given varying levels of our independent variables of interest.[11] The shaded area in each plot represents the 95 percent confidence interval.

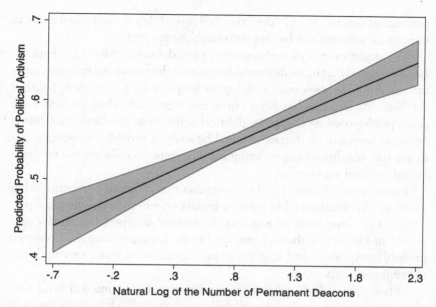

Figure 3.2. Religious decentralization and political activism

Discussion

As we see from Figure 3.1 above, the decentralized variable has a positive and statistically significant relationship with political activism. Catholics residing in dioceses with greater numbers of permanent deacons are positively associated with participating in an activist event. As perusal of the appendix demonstrates, we see that this relationship is robust across a wide array of model specifications.[12] While the model provides positive support for the theory, the coefficients of logistic regression models are difficult to interpret. To make the interpretation of this impact more intelligible, Figure 3.2 demonstrates the marginal impact of decentralization on political activism.

Toward the left end of Figure 3.2, we see that individuals in dioceses with no deacons are characterized by predicted probabilities of just over 40 percent of participating in some form of activism. However, we see that by the time we move to dioceses with relatively high numbers of permanent deacons, the predicted probability of participating in activism increases substantially. For example, by the time the natural log of the number of permanent deacons is 2.3,[13] the predicted probability an individual engages in political activism reaches approximately 65 percent.

The statistical analysis subsequently provides support for a key hypothesis. I expected that individuals residing within decentralized religious institutions should be associated with higher propensities to engage in political activism. We see this has been borne out here. Individual Catholics are more predisposed to engage in political activism as the Catholic Church becomes increasingly decentralized. The analysis provides supportive evidence that conditions engendering resource mobilization encourage individual political activism.

Furthermore, Figure 3.1 above suggests that religious competition has a statistically significant and positive impact on whether an individual participated in some form of activism. To further interpret the results presented in Figure 3.1 above, I present Figure 3.3 examining the predicted probability an individual engages in an activist event given varying levels of religious competition.

When there is little religious competition and only one dominant religion supplier, the predicted probability that an individual participates in activism is about 51 percent. However, in situations where there is religious competition with two religions effectively competing against each other (where the natural log of the effective number of religions is equal to about 0.7), we see the predicted probability an individual participates in a political activist event is just over 60 percent. Overall, this analysis provides supportive evidence that religious competition is positively associated with political activism, signifying that the political process approach's emphasis on highlighting opportunity also helps to explain the development of collective action.

Figure 3.1 presented above illustrates that political theology is associated with positive propensities for individuals to engage in political activism. To visually examine this relationship, Figure 3.4 presents separate predicted probabilities an individual Catholic participated in an activist event based on whether he or she was located in a diocese more likely to have been exposed to politicized theology. As Figure 3.4 demonstrates, Catholics who live in dioceses more receptive to politicized theology are associated with a 12 percent higher predicted probability of engaging in some form of activism than individuals who do not. The analysis provides supportive evidence that political theology is positively associated with political activism and signifies that the political process approach's highlighting of framing, like opportunity, importantly informs our understanding of collective action generally and the behavior of religious institutions more specifically.

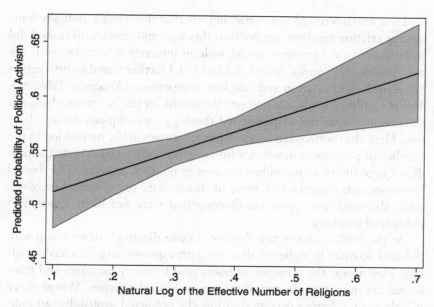

Figure 3.3. Religious competition and political activism

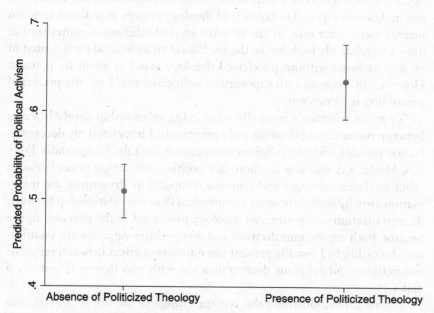

Figure 3.4. Political theology and political activism

I was also interested in ascertaining whether there was a mutually rein-forcing relationship between political theology and decentralization. I did so by running a regression model with an interaction term between the two variables (Appendix Table A.6, Model 1). I further tested an interaction between decentralization and religious competition (Appendix Table A.6, Model 2). Figure 3.5 below presents the results for the interaction between the potential presence of politicized theology and religious decentraliza-tion. Here the (horizontal) x-axis depicts increases in the natural log in the number of permanent deacons, while the (vertical) y-axis depicts the pre-dicted probability an individual engages in political activism. The dashed line represents dioceses with more likely exposure to politicized theology, while the solid line represents dioceses that were not likely exposed to politicized theology.

As the reader can see, the slope of decentralization's relationship with political activism is higher in dioceses with exposure to politicized theol-ogy. This means the presence of politicized theology increases and rein-forces the impact of decentralization on political activism. Where there is little to no religious decentralization, the predicted probability an indi-vidual participates in activism is 44 percent, regardless of whether that individual resides in a region with potential exposure to politicized theol-ogy. However, as decentralization increases, the likelihood individuals who live in dioceses exposed to politicized theology engage in political activism increases at a faster rate. By the time the level of religious decentralization moves to relatively high levels, the likelihood an individual participated in an activist event without politicized theology stand at about 63 percent. However, in dioceses with exposure to politicized theology, the predicted probability is 72 percent.

To assess whether a mutually reinforcing relationship similarly exists between resource mobilization and opportunity, I interacted my decentral-ization variable with the religious competition variable. As Appendix Table A.6, Model 2 demonstrates, there is a positive interaction effect between religious decentralization and religious competition. Presenting this infor-mation visually is slightly more complicated than the relationship between decentralization and politicized theology presented in the previous figure because both my decentralization and competition variables are continu-ous. Accordingly, I visually present the interaction effect between religious competition and religious decentralization with two figures (Figures 3.6 and 3.7).

Figure 3.6 demonstrates the average change in the impact of religious decentralization's impact on political activism given increasing levels of

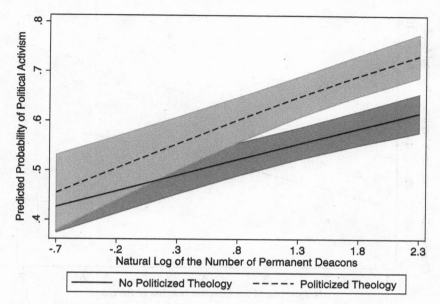

Figure 3.5. Interaction between decentralization and politicized theology

religious competition. Here the (horizontal) x-axis depicts the natural log of the effective number of religions, while the (vertical) y-axis depicts the change in decentralization's impact on the predicted probability of political activism. In other words, the y-axis depicts the degree to which religious competition increases religious decentralization's likelihood of encouraging an individual's political activism. At low levels of religious competition, we can see that the variable has a relatively small impact in increasing the effect of decentralization on political activism. However, as the level of religious competition increases, the impact of decentralization on political activism strengthens. By the time there is a relatively high degree of religious competition, the predicted probability decentralization produces an act of political activism is increased by a further 10 percent.

An alternative approach to visualizing this reinforcing relationship is to graph decentralization's association with political activism at varying levels of religious competition. In Figure 3.7 below, the (horizontal) x-axis depicts the natural log of the number of permanent deacons, while the y-axis demonstrates the overall predicted probability an individual engages in political activism (as opposed to the change in the predicted probability of activism as depicted in Figure 3.6). I display the relationship of increasing levels of religious competition at four different values of religious competition:

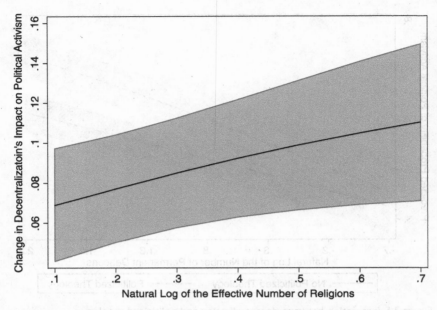

Figure 3.6. Interaction between decentralization and religious competition: marginal impact

where there is no religious competition (log ENR = 0), where there is some religious competition (log ENR = 0.3), where there is significant religious competition (log ENR = 0.6), and where there is a high degree of religious competition (log ENR = 0.9).

Figure 3.7 visually demonstrates the reinforcing impact increasing levels of religious competition have on the positive relationship between religious decentralization and political activism. We see that, even when there is no religious competition (log ENR = 0), decentralization has a positive association with the predicted probability an individual participates in activism. However, we also see visually that increased levels of religious competition further increase the slope of the positive association between religious decentralization and political activism.

The implication here is that decentralization's impacts on individual political activism are strengthened when it is combined with a coordinating political theology and when religious elites have incentives to support secular political movements. Embedding my theory of religious decentralization within a broader political process framework provides a heightened understanding of religion's impact on political activism.

As for the alternative explanations, and as we see illustrated in Figure 3.1 above, political party competition does not have a statistically signifi-

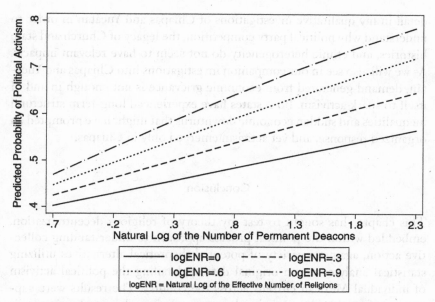

Figure 3.7. Decentralization and political activism at varying levels of religious competition

cant relationship with an individual's activism. This is the case across most of the statistical models presented across the appendix.[14] The qualitative discussion assessing the impact of political party competition in Chiapas and Yucatán (chapter 6) suggests this may be because political party competition creates conditions that counterintuitively discourage activism. This analysis also finds limited support for the contention that legacies of church/state history correspond to individual propensities to engage in political activism. The variable shows up as statistically significant at the 90 percent confidence interval in the primary model, but it is not statistically significant in the majority of the robustness checks.[15] Similarly, we see the deprivation variable has mixed results across the various statistical models.[16] The analysis provides only weak evidence that areas that are marked by higher levels of economic deprivation are characterized by increased propensities to engage in political activism. Finally, Figure 3.1 suggests that the level of ethnic heterogeneity in a community does not have a statistically significant impact with political activism.[17] Accordingly, this analysis finds little support that ethnic heterogeneity should be associated with political activism across Mexico.

I do not find strong evidence of a general relationship between most of my alternative explanations and political activism, and I will go into further detail in my qualitative investigations of Chiapas and Yucatán in order to understand why political party competition, the legacy of Church and state histories, and ethnic heterogeneity do not seem to have relevant impacts. As we will also see in our companion investigations into Chiapas and Yucatán, demand generated from economic grievance is not enough in and of itself to spark activism. Both states have experienced long-term structural inequalities and sudden economic downturns that might have prompted an organized response, and yet activism emerged only in Chiapas.

Conclusion

This chapter has sought to test my theory of religious decentralization, embedded within the political process approach to understanding collective action, against a variety of potential theoretical alternatives utilizing statistical analyses on an original dataset detailing the political activism of individual Mexican citizens across the country. The results were supportive of a general association between religious decentralization, religious competition, and political theology with political activism. I ran a variety of statistical models to assess the robustness of my results, all of which are available for interested readers in the appendix at the end of this book. Taken collectively, we see that the ability of an institution to mobilize resources, the presence of religious theologies that coordinate activism, and opportunities for engagement engendered by religious competition each encourage political activism, and the impact of resource mobilization is reinforced by the presence of framing and opportunity.

To this point, the study has provided support for the presence of a general association between religious decentralization and political activism, but this statistical analysis cannot tell us why that relationship exists. I theorized that decentralization prompts greater reciprocity, club goods production, and the subsequent development of organizational capacities allowing individuals to mobilize. Our confidence in the theory would be greatly enhanced to the degree to which we can see that this general relationship manifests itself in this manner. For this reason, the next chapters examine the pathways connecting religious decentralization to political activism in two distinct cases. First, we examine Chiapas, a Mexican state that has experienced a great deal of political activism, and the burden is to demonstrate that decentralization prompted political activism there through my hypothesized pathway.

FOUR

Religious Decentralization and Political Activism in Chiapas

> You can't imagine how it all came together, in a very nice, very exciting way. . . . In all the communities, something arose from the production of coffee, cooperatives, these types of things. Everything revolved around coffee.
>
> Chiapan Catholic priest (Interview 45, 2012)

The Catholic priest quoted above has worked closely with several indigenous communities in rural Chiapas since the 1960s. During our interview, he emphasized how coffee production gave birth to political organizations such as *Tierra y Libertad* ("Land and Liberty") and *Lucha Campesina* ("Peasant Struggle"). Throughout the region, hundreds of local cooperatives directly created by the institutional Catholic Church produced the structural framework that sparked political engagement. The previous chapter provided support for my hypothesis that religious decentralization is generally and positively associated with political activism. However, I also hypothesized that religious decentralization prompts heightened positive reciprocal interactions, the provision of club goods and services, and the subsequent development of an organizational infrastructure that can be lent to collective action.

I assess this hypothesized causal pathway over the next several chapters through in-depth qualitative investigation of events in Chiapas, Yucatán, and Morelos. The present chapter examines Chiapas. As we will see,

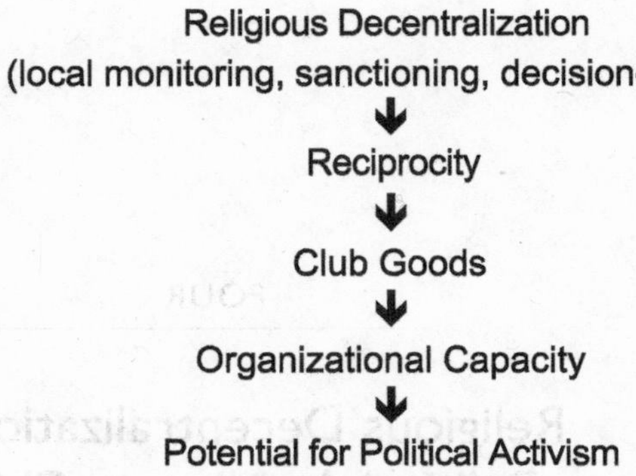

Religious Decentralization
(local monitoring, sanctioning, decision-making)
⬇
Reciprocity
⬇
Club Goods
⬇
Organizational Capacity
⬇
Potential for Political Activism

Figure 4.1.Tracing the
causal chain

throughout the first half of the twentieth century, there was little political activism, and the Catholic Church was not particularly concerned with
supporting the social or political concerns of its indigenous adherents.
However, beginning in the early part of the 1960s, things changed radically, and the Church became a key prompter of political activism. I argue
this occurred because the Diocese of San Cristóbal de las Casas decentralized authority to its laity and subsequently prompted increased reciprocal
interactions, the development of religious club goods, and the growth of an
organizational infrastructure that could then be lent to political activism.
Figure 4.1 illustrates this hypothesized causal pathway visually.

If my argument is correct, we should see this causal process at work
in Chiapas. This chapter is particularly concerned with events from 1960
through the 1980s, and I demonstrate that the Diocese of San Cristóbal de
las Casas did indeed devolve decision-making, monitoring, and sanctioning responsibilities to its laity beginning in the 1960s. Decision-making
was decentralized in Chiapas through lay teachers called catechists and
deacons who decided their own themes for discussion and who reinterpreted Catholic dogma to make it more accessible to indigenous cultural
sensibilities. Monitoring and sanctioning, on the other hand, were decentralized through economic cooperatives directly formed by the Catholic
Church. Here, Catholic laity, not clergy, were given complete responsibility for monitoring the productive contributions to the cooperative and for
sanctioning shirking behavior.

Following diocesan decentralization from the 1960s through the 1970s,
individuals slowly, but increasingly, became willing to *reciprocally* interact
and cooperate with one another within their communities and within productive cooperative organizations directly planned by the Catholic Church
as a strategy for providing material club goods to adherents. The result

was increased material *club goods production* through a variety of goods and services but particularly through the production of coffee which increased substantially in the 1970s and early 1980s. We then see the development and consolidation of *organizational infrastructure* through a large number of producer groups that, beginning in the late 1970s and continuing through the present, directly organized *political activism*. Furthermore, liberation theology served as a frame enabling an "insurgent consciousness" that encouraged political engagement, and the massive influx of Protestant competition throughout the region gave Catholic clergy an incentive to support popular political movements.

The Diocese of San Cristóbal de las Casas

Chiapas is characterized by both low-lying coastal plains and mountainous terrain. The western portion of the state, encapsulated by the Catholic Diocese of Tapachula and the Archdiocese of Tuxtla Gutiérrez, tends to be flatter than the rugged, mountainous territory to the east. This study, however, is preoccupied with the eastern territory consisting of the Diocese of San Cristóbal de las Casas, where 80 percent of the indigenous population resides and where the majority of indigenous activism has occurred (Harvey 1998, 70). Chiapas has historically been isolated from the rest of Mexico, giving it a unique cultural and political trajectory. Its mountains have made it more difficult for the Mexican state to assert authority, and the reforms of the Mexican revolution were unevenly implemented (Womack 1999, 87–96; G. Collier and Quaratiello 1999, 28–29).

Before the 1960s, there was little independent indigenous organizing or political activism. Few interactions and little coordination occurred between indigenous communities that were tightly enclosed, parochial, and compliant to the authoritarian Mexican state (Mattiace 2003, 1–2; G. Collier and Quaratiello 1999, 15; Eisenstadt 2011, 7). Collective action was also potentially inhibited by the sheer diversity of Chiapas's indigenous groups who are characterized by different languages and cultural practices. Thirty-six percent of indigenous language speakers identify as Tzotzil, 34.4 percent as Tzeltal, 17.3 percent as Chol, 4.6 percent as Tojolabal, and 5.1 percent as Zoque.

Throughout the nineteenth and twentieth centuries, these indigenous populations were subjected to aggressive efforts at cultural assimilation and subjugation (Eisenstadt 2011, 20–21). In many cases, they were used as forced labor, "often on the very lands that had been expropriated from them by large land-owners" (Jaffee 2007, 39). Mestizo landowners also held major political power even though indigenous peasants constituted the demographic majority in many parts of the state (G. Collier and Quaratiello 1999, 39). While the Mexican Revolution had started a process of land reform to redistribute land to peasants, the process was extraordinarily slow, particularly in Chiapas. When Mexican revolutionaries came to Chiapas to free peasants of their labor and debt servitude, landed elites successfully staved off many land reform initiatives and even took powerful positions within the PRI party itself (G. Collier and Quaratiello 1999, 28–19).

By 1960, more than half the land was owned by only slightly more than 2 percent of the population (Eisenstadt 2011, 33). The federal government did little to enforce its land reform policies in Chiapas (G. Collier and Quaratiello 1999, 30). Land the government did manage to grant was often marked by conflicting and overlapping claims, and Chiapas had one of the largest backlogs of ungranted land claims in all of Mexico (Eisenstadt 2011, 33). Those indigenous communities that received redistributed territory were given poor quality land, and they were often still forced to sell their product back to large plantations (Nigh 1997, 429; Jaffee 2007, 39; Eisenstadt 2011, 33; G. Collier and Quaratiello 1999, 30).

Furthermore, the Catholic diocese in Chiapas before the 1960s was marked by a hierarchical relationship between priests and parishioners, clergy had little interest in engaging with the cultural traditions of the indigenous population, and the Church aligned itself with landed elites (Trejo 2009, 336; Kovic 2005, 48; Interview 29, 2011; Interview 45, 2012). Priests only occasionally ventured out into the countryside to perform baptisms and marriages (Womack 1999, 128). As one Chiapan priest described, "the few priests in these communities never came to spend time with the communities themselves. They only went to the master's home" (Interview 45, 2012). Another priest mentioned that when he arrived in Chiapas in the 1960s, it was with his camera to "photograph the Indians who dressed strangely. This was the mentality of the Church [at that time]—that we were going to see strange people" (Interview 29, 2011).[1]

Lay responsibilities were limited. There were two hundred catechists, who are lay instructors of the Catholic faith. Their manual for instruction dated back to the sixteenth century, was written entirely in Spanish, and detailed only the basics of the Catholic creed (Womack 1999, 128–30). Priests decided who would become catechists, and these individuals were treated as "passive receptors of evangelization" (Kovic 2005, 49; Floyd 1996, 155). Furthermore, their instruction was "doctrinaire, authoritarian, and [predicated] on the local premises of Indian inferiority" (Womack 1999, 130). Training centers were far removed from indigenous communities, and catechists often had to travel significant distances to receive their training (Interview 31, 2011). Accordingly, these catechists often reproduced vertical power relations within their own communities (Harvey 1998, 72).

However, the situation changed dramatically with the arrival of Bishop Samuel Ruiz García in 1960. Many studies have attributed to the bishop a prominent role in sparking political activism throughout the state, and they have focused on the importance of framing and political theology in allowing him to do so. According to these accounts, Samuel Ruiz radicalized as a result of the poverty he witnessed across his diocese and his participation in the Second Vatican Council in Rome (1962–1965). He embraced liberation theology and encouraged the indigenous adherents of his diocese to mobilize politically. When the Mexican state adopted neoliberalism and instituted severe austerity economic policies during the 1980s, these reforms hit the indigenous peasants of Chiapas hard. Because of the reforms enacted by Bishop Ruiz, the peasants were able to respond, and vibrant political activism emerged during the 1980s and 1990s (Womack 1999; Harvey 1998; G. Collier and Quaratiello 1994; Nash 2001; Mattiace 2003; Kovic 2005). This story has been revised to some extent by the religious economy school by suggesting it was really emerging Protestant competition that explains Bishop Ruiz's support of secular political activism. According to this version of events, the Church was challenged by the aggressive expansion of Protestant competition beginning in the 1960s, and it was forced to help mobilize the indigenous peasants to stem the tide of conversions to Protestantism (Gill 1998; Trejo 2012).

I do not dispute either account. Both are essential to explaining why political activism emerged in Chiapas. However, our understanding of religion's impact on political activism remains incomplete. How did the Church create the substantial organizational infrastructure across indigenous communities that permitted political activism? We cannot understand how the Church mobilized political activism until we understand its institutional decentralization. To make this argument, I first demonstrate that the Catholic Church decentralized monitoring, sanctioning, and decision-making authority to its adherents in the Diocese of San Cristóbal de las Casas. I then demonstrate how decentralization led to increased reciprocal interactions, increased club goods production, and the subsequent development of an organizational base grown at the grassroots that was lent to organizing political activism.

Decentralization in Catholic Chiapas

Gradually throughout the 1960s and into the 1970s, Bishop Ruiz decentralized *decision-making, monitoring, and sanctioning*. Though the Diocese of San Cristóbal de las Casas had originally encompassed the entire state of Chiapas, he divided it into what would eventually become three separate dioceses. One new diocese encapsulated the southwestern zone of Tapachula while another encompassed the northwestern zone of Tuxtla Gutiérrez. Bishop Ruiz took over the now smaller Diocese of San Cristóbal de las Casas, geographically delineated to serving the predominantly poor indigenous communities in the eastern half of Chiapas (Harvey 1998, 69–70; Kovic 2005, 50). Ruiz further subdivided the Diocese of San Cristóbal de las Casas into six pastoral zones to make it more responsive to local needs (Kovic 2005, 50).

Decision-Making

The diocese decentralized monitoring, sanctioning, and decision-making authority to its lay parishioners. This allowed local communities to develop their own autonomously determined agenda for action within the religious institution. A key focus of diocesan reorganization was on giving the laity a democratic voice in the Church's affairs. As several Church officials described, newly formed pastoral assemblies provided parishioners with an opportunity to express their opinion over Church programs, and pastoral councils consulted with the bishop to make decisions (Interview 81, 2011; Interview 56, 2011).

Several Church officials explained during my interviews the continuing, present-day commitment the diocese maintains with regard to processes first put in place in the 1960s. "The decisions of the diocese do not only come from the Bishop. It's the assembly" (Interview 56, 2011). "We have every 12 months a meeting with the pastoral diocesan council that represents the seven pastoral zones. We consult with them to make decisions" (Interview 81, 2011). "One very important thing that Samuel Ruiz did . . . they [pastoral workers] ask all the communities for their opinions. . . . They hear the people—it's democratic" (Interview 56, 2011).[2] Consultation with the laity allowed local communities to form their own religious agenda predicated on local needs.[3]

Furthermore, the Church in Chiapas made itself more accessible to its parishioners by integrating indigenous culture into the liturgy. Through deep consultation with indigenous communities, the diocese encouraged priests and nuns to learn indigenous languages, translate the Bible into those languages, incorporate Mayan beliefs and customs into mass, and reinterpret the Gospel through indigenous communities' unique cultural perspective (Trejo 2009, 338–39; Kovic 2005, 58; Interview 1, 2012; Interview 56, 2011; Interview 46, 2011). Rather than passively experiencing mass, indigenous communities now actively participated in redefining how mass occurred. As one priest described, it is "important to know the language, to know the culture and from there conduct a process of ministry in the communities" (Interview 46, 2011). Such moves made it possible for indigenous individuals to engage effectively within the religious institution.

Beginning in the late 1960s, the diocese allowed communities to democratically select their own catechists (Floyd 1996, 156; Interview 4, 2011; Interview 45, 2012; Womack 1999, 32). Instead of passively instructing students in fundamentals of the Catholic faith, catechists actively developed their own ideas for reflection (Womack 1999, 30, 132–34; Harvey 1998, 73; Interview 4, 2011). One catechist I interviewed explained that his responsibilities included "having the lesson, leading reflection, and sharing our experiences" (Interview 4, 2011). These experiences came to center on demands for land, the mediation of community disputes, and means to promote "the production of coffee and handcraft" (Interview 56, 2011). Indigenous catechists subsequently selected human rights, agricultural production, and political analysis as themes for discussion (Kovic 2004, 195; Trejo 2004, 144). Such devolution of decision-making control was by no means inevitably granted in indigenous Catholic dioceses, as we will see in our companion investigation of Yucatán.

The diocese also created permanent deacons. Like catechists, these individuals teach and decide their own themes for discussion, but they are given additional authority to perform sacramental functions such as baptisms and weddings (Trejo 2009, 339; Interview 56, 2011; Harvey 1998, 74). One must have served as a catechist for five years before becoming a deacon (Interview 81, 2011; Interview 45, 2012),[4] and deacons are considered to be important community leaders. There are a limited number allotted by the diocese, and they are democratically selected by each community after much deliberation (Harvey 1998, 74; Interview 31, 2011). "We have 320 deacons and they are very important in evangelization. . . . They aid in celebrations of baptism, marriage, death rites, prayer for the sick, celebrating the Word of God on Sundays and distributing communion. They are assigned in their own communities, and they live with their families. They are primarily *campesinos* [peasants] in rural areas" (Interview

81, 2011). Together, the eight thousand catechists and three hundred deacons located throughout the Diocese of San Cristóbal de las Casas became
important leaders in their communities by organizing local Bible study
groups and aiding in pastoral decisions. Perhaps most importantly, and as
further described in the next section, these individuals were given complete decision-making authority in directing economic cooperatives, the
Church's key efforts at providing material goods to its members (Mattiace
2003, 18; Kovic 2004, 188–93, 201; Harvey 1998, 74; Interview 56, 2011;
Interview 4, 2011; Interview 81, 2011).

Monitoring and Sanctioning

Beginning in the late 1960s, the institutional Catholic Church directly created economic cooperatives as a deliberate strategy to provide goods and
services to its adherents, and these cooperatives allowed for decentralized
monitoring and sanctioning of the production of material Catholic club
goods. The Diocese of San Cristóbal de las Casas invested substantial effort
in developing hundreds of lay-managed productive communal enterprises
across the region (Trejo 2009, 338). The Church provided the intellec-
tual impetus for their creation and empowered Catholic lay catechists and
deacons to run them (Eisenstadt 2011, 86; Harvey 1998, 71; Trejo 2009).
Church pastoral workers provided the technical and organizational assistance that was necessary to start the cooperatives, and their demographic
composition was overwhelmingly Catholic. "Only Catholics belonged"
(Womack 1999, 32). As one cooperative member noted, "the Church had
a lot to do with it in the beginning because the Church already had its
groups working in evangelization . . . it was these groups that had the idea
of how to reorganize the land" (Interview 17, 2012). These cooperatives
were an important part of the indigenous Catholic community in Chiapas.
    Clerical pastoral workers provided technical and organizational assis-
tance to get cooperatives started, and they put in place practices that guide
the operation of producer cooperatives throughout the region (Trejo 2009,
338; Interview 45, 2012; Interview 17, 2012; Interview 1, 2012; Interview
2, 2012). One priest explained that the role of Church officials in one agricultural cooperative is to provide "education, food supplies, corn, [and
advice regarding] where to get the mills to grind corn and make tortillas"
(Interview 46, 2011). Another Church official elaborated on the early days
of forming these cooperatives. "We had great programs in mind, but the
problem was that [the indigenous communities] could not read or write.
From the beginning, we dedicated ourselves to literacy" (Interview 45,

2012). In order to develop the technical knowledge and proficiency for indigenous communities to run their own organizations, clergy dedicated themselves to teaching "reading, math, [and] Spanish classes" (Interview 1, 2012). Catholic commissions further organized seminars among local producers to teach sustainable farming practices (Hernández Castillo and Nigh 1998, 141).

It is important to be very clear on this point: the institutional diocese planned these cooperatives and encouraged lay catechists and deacons to create them (Eisenstadt 2011, 86; Harvey 1998, 71). Church pastoral workers created their decentralized governance structures and provided the technical assistance necessary to start them. As one Catholic pastoral worker assigned to a Catholic mission related, "the role of the Mission was to be the initiator of cooperatives in the community" (Interview 45, 2012).

At the same time, it was lay Catholics themselves who started and directed the cooperatives, primarily though catechists and deacons: "Catechists and predeacons ran it" (Womack 1999, 32). "The new organizations that emerged were not controlled by interests loyal to the PRI but by the . . . [network of community deacons and catechists] who had participated in the Indigenous Congress" (Harvey 1998, 79–80). "Catechists led the formation of communal shops . . . catechists also led the creation of cooperatives for communal transportation. . . . Pastoral agents and catechists created inter-community cooperatives to market their own agricultural commodities" (Trejo 2012, 97–98). "Bible study groups served as the organizational basis on which these cooperatives were built, and catechists led this process" (Trejo 2009, 338) "Pastoral workers played a key role in the formation of Quiptic ta Lecubtesel, a productive cooperative run by catechists" (Kovic 2005, 59). "It is important to note that most of the indigenous leaders of the ARIC [an intercommunal cooperative] learned to read, write, and interact with the world thanks to courses developed by the Diocese of San Cristóbal de las Casas. Many of them were first catechists and later representatives of their communities" (Acosta Chávez 2003, 129). Furthermore, one pastoral worker I interviewed suggested the Church had been involved in the formation of a broad range of cooperatives, including agricultural cooperatives, artisanal cooperatives, and that they are generally led by either catechists or deacons (Interview 46, 2011).

Depending on each community's specific needs, cooperatives focused on agricultural production (particularly coffee), transportation, financial savings, health, and women's issues (Trejo 2009, 338; Interview 1, 2012; Interview 2, 2012; Interview 17, 2012; Interview 46, 2011). Though clergy and pastoral workers provided technical assistance, control over cooperative administration was completely given to local laity (Interview 45, 2012; Interview 17, 2012; Interview 30, 2012). Local communities determined their own agenda for the material goods to be provided (Interview 1, 2012; Interview 2, 2012). As one Church pastoral worker put it, "we have always tried to make sure that these social, economic, and even religious organizations are not under the shadow of the Church" (Interview 45, 2012).[5]

Nearly every cooperative member I spoke with suggested the institutional Church played a pivotal role in their respective cooperative's formation[6] but then relinquished authority and allowed its members to manage their own affairs (Interview 17, 2012; Interview 2, 2012). "Now we don't have much relation with the Church, but before there was a lot. The Church helped to found the cooperative" (Interview 30, 2012). Clergy gave the laity a great deal of autonomy in managing these cooperatives once on their feet. Instead of clerical management, they were democratically managed by indigenous communities themselves (Nigh 1997, 428, 431).

Given their decentralized management and the diverse array of products produced across communities (such as coffee, transportation, and artisanal products), cooperatives were managed in a variety of ways. However, successful cooperatives typically had several structures in common. "Participation was highest when the organization was directly addressing the most important needs of the base and when it rotated positions of responsibility among community members" (Harvey 1998, 84). Typically, cooperatives consisted of a general assembly where communities sent delegates to voice their concerns. They also consisted of an executive committee with a president wielding administrative powers. However, the president's authority came with significant institutional oversight and checks on authority (Cámara Repetto and Toloza Pasos 2000, 54). "The final decision remains with the entire community, not the catechists nor the deacons, who are simply expected to carry out the agreements made in assemblies" (Harvey 1998, 73). Catechists and deacons often initially held the leadership posts within cooperatives, but with regular elections these positions could be ceded to other individuals. While the Church played an instrumental role in creating these cooperatives, it fully granted control to members.

Cooperatives were not only present in Chiapas but were a common feature in many similarly decentralized Catholic Christian base communities across Latin America (Levine 1988, 253). They operated along an organizational model borrowed from European cooperativism and emphasized "direct participatory democracy, equity, and mutuality" as well as efficient production using techniques predicated on reciprocity (Hernández Castillo and Nigh 1998, 141–42). While it is easy to conjure dubious images of idealized socialist societies where all freely share and give, cooperatives "adapted themselves to efficient functioning in the capitalist system" using production techniques predicated on reciprocity (Hernández Castillo and Nigh 1998, 141–42). "They are collective organizations based on traditional Indian concepts of reciprocity and communitarian democracy, yet they have clearly defined administrative structures and business-like financial controls" (Nigh 1997, 428).

A key concern for these cooperatives, then, was effective monitoring of member contributions. While a single cooperative may have been composed of many communities, responsibility for monitoring and sanctioning resided with the laity. According to a representative of one regional organization that coordinated the activity of dozens of early cooperatives across Chiapas, there are

> internal agreements of each group. . . . They have their ways to assure production, but it's within each [local group]. One example to ensure that each person is doing his or her part: in each community there is a control, whether it's a daily quota of work to be produced or it's a financial contribution. There are ways to observe this, but it is the responsibility of each community. They correct, advise, and counsel. Members always receive benefits so long as they contribute to the organization. If they don't comply, they are left out. (Interview 43, 2012)

Even though many cooperatives subsequently consolidated into large regional organizations (as discussed below), monitoring continued to be a local endeavor. Not only did monitoring occur locally, but the decisions about how monitoring should occur were also locally determined by indigenous communities themselves. Some communities might have decided the most effective form of monitoring was to set easily observed daily quotas of product that must be produced, while other local cooperatives might have decided that certain financial contributions were appropriate. Other communities embedded an elderly couple with younger workers to ensure work was done. "The indigenous young people . . . have their elderly couple who accompany them in their work. There is a group of elders who work in the cooperative and accompanies these processes" (Interview 46, 2011). Whether through production quotas or direct supervision as individuals went about common work tasks, the community members monitored the productive output of members themselves without relying on external authorities.

Furthermore, the cooperatives scattered across Chiapas typically maintained "vigilance councils" to make sure work was done correctly and to eliminate corruption (C. Simpson and Rapone 2000, 51; Martínez-Torres 2006, 94). Cooperatives also maintained additional membership obligations. Among them, members were required to attend a variety of meetings and technical seminars and to pay membership fees. As many coffee cooperatives adopted organic modes of coffee production, producers also had to cultivate their coffee in exacting and laborious ways (Milford 2012, 6; Jaffee 2007, 91, 126–27; Martínez-Torres 2006, 21).

Sanctioning, on the other hand, involved the parceling of material resources. Individuals producing more product, such as coffee, received a larger portion of the profit from the sale of collectively produced products relative to individuals who produced less (Interview 30, 2012; Interview 43, 2012; Interview 17, 2012; Interview 83, 2012). "Those who work more receive more in the production of what they do" (Interview 30, 2012). "Obviously those who produce more receive more" (Interview 17, 2012). Sanctioning was further characterized by exclusion from a variety of services cooperatives provided for their members, including international marketing, technical assistance, consultations, and variety of health and educational benefits (Interview 83, 2012; Interview 17, 2012; Interview 30, 2012). For the most part,[7] these services were only available to members, and membership required productive or financial contributions (Interview 83, 2012; Interview 1, 2012; Interview 43, 2012). "The services are not for the entire community. They are only for members" (Interview 83, 2012). "Members always receive benefits so long as they do not leave" (Interview 43, 2012). As one clergy member instrumental in the development of several early cooperatives suggested, "if there are rights, there must be obligations" (Interview 1, 2012).[8]

Because of the rigorous monitoring and sanctioning, and despite "open door" policies encouraging new members, many choose not to join. In some areas, cooperatives constitute only between 10 and 20 percent of the households of a community. Both members and nonmembers agree the organization asks a lot of its members. "They don't want to [join] because of the work. . . . It seems to me too difficult to work in the organization; they ask a lot of work" (Jaffee 2007, 125–26). The cooperatives effectively weeded out free riders through their decentralized monitoring and sanctioning capabilities. The decentralized governance of these cooperatives was a critical component to their success. As one organizer emphasized, cooperatives generally fail when they are governed in a centralized manner.

To work, communities must have autonomous control (Interview 71, 2012). To reiterate that point, a Jesuit mission established several early cooperatives but placed them under the auspices of a government agency. Because the cooperatives were not characterized by decentralized and autonomous control, they failed (Early 2012, 170–71).

Reciprocity, Club Goods, and Organizational Infrastructure

Reciprocity

With effective monitoring, sanctioning, and decision-making in place in productive cooperatives by the late 1960s and early 1970s, my theoretical expectation is that this opened the door for individuals to become more comfortable engaging in increasingly cooperative reciprocal interactions. Furthermore, priests, catechists, and deacons were ideally positioned to signal initial intentions to cooperate in the early stages of decentralization and helped prompt cooperative reciprocal interactions that slowly but surely took shape from the late 1960s onward.

According to pastoral workers assigned to Altamirano and Las Margaritas in the 1960s, many indigenous individuals were initially skeptical of the Church's new productive cooperatives, most could not read or write, and no one wanted to volunteer for anything. "When we began to visit the communities, they didn't accept us easily . . . this was a normal reaction. . . . At first when everything started, the word we always heard was 'I don't know,' or 'I can't.' This situation was in all the groups. Nobody wanted to volunteer" (Interview 45, 2012). These problems were overcome by the sustained patience and tenacity of pastoral workers who also taught the basic administrative, Spanish, arithmetic, and technical skills to the indigenous laity to run their own cooperative organizations, skills that would later be essential to help organize civic participation (Kovic 2005, 79–80; Interview 45, 2012; Interview 1, 2012; Interview 42, 2011). It was clergy who repeatedly initiated attempts to prompt larger cooperation and who steadfastly took on the difficult work of providing basic instruction to indigenous communities.

As related earlier, deacons and catechists often held leadership positions at the inception of the cooperatives. These were the lay individuals, who, in the past, had developed reputations as trustworthy individuals. "We have discovered that they have the best projection across the community. This means that they are not people who are going to do something on the side with the money. . . . It's trust, that's not all of it, but mostly this is why they are in charge" (Interview 46, 2011). Because these prosocial individuals had a history of cooperating in situations where self-interested individuals might defect, they engendered reciprocal interaction within their communities. While cooperation was slow to form, progress was made as pastoral workers and lay catechists and deacons took initial steps to provide religious club goods. To use an analogy, they supplied the spark to prompt cooperation.

Though the cooperatives were initially small and local in character (Levine 1988, 253), they expanded and eventually encompassed many communities. In doing so, they increased the level of reciprocal interactions across small villages and towns. As discussed by my interview respondents, these cooperatives linked communities and indigenous groups across the state. "There are about 40 communities [in the cooperative], and they are distributed across different regions . . . of Chiapas" (Interview 17, 2012). "We are in 22 municipalities of the state" (Interview 43, 2012). The cooperatives have also networked various indigenous groups. "We work with different dialects . . . we have representatives directly in each region according to the dialect" (Interview 43, 2012).[9]

As a result, individuals from various municipalities became increasingly willing to interact with each other. As one government observer put it, "I think the Church has helped create consciousness in the indigenous communities through the trust it has created" (Interview 42, 2011). While it was once the case, for example, that small villages would not permit their daughters to marry outside the community, one pastoral worker directly attributes the influence of these lay-run organizations to fostering more intercommunal marriages (Interview 1, 2012). "There is solidarity between communities now. It used to be that in some of the smaller areas, they would not allow their daughters to see or marry someone from outside. Now that has changed. There is a lot of cooperation between groups in various ways. For me, it was the organizations that have changed and formed the relations between communities" (Interview 1, 2012). "Many others volunteered, men and women, or the assembly elected them, and they did their part, on one committee or commission, then another, then another, taking turns at the chances for communal appreciation. In time they all learned something about everything they had in common, and learned their value to each other" (Womack 1999, 19).

A brief vignette provided by Christine Kovic's study of a Chiapan Catholic community in Guadalupe may help further illustrate:

·What impressed me was the way the Guadalupe Catholics committed themselves to Buena Vista and to many other communities,
offering their time, moral support, spiritual guidance, and material donations. In addition to the many trips to Buena Vista, Guadalupe residents traveled to a number of hamlets . . . at the same
time, indigenous Catholics from other communities regularly visit
Guadalupe to preach, join in worship, and exchange information on
local events. . . . On the material level, Guadalupe Catholics rely on
networks for mutual aid, and their links with others in their community are an economic necessity, a sort of safety net, in the fragility of
their everyday lives. On a social level, these networks connect them
to others with a shared vision for justice and dignity. In the long run,
these ties may lay the groundwork for political mobilization. (Kovic
2005, 150–51)

Specifically assessing the impact of producer cooperatives in the 1960s
and 1970s, Shannan Mattiace concludes that they "were not explicitly cultural, but they organized Indians across community boundaries, allowing
Indians of different ethnicities to see themselves as members of a larger
community" (Mattiace 2003, 19), and Guillermo Trejo notes that "within
these emerging communal groups and networks, people developed new
bonds of trust, solidarity, and cooperation and learned basic organizational
skills. . . . [T]his social capital served as the organizational infrastructure
for the emergence of peasant indigenous protest movements across Indian
Mexico" (Trejo 2004, 144).

The result was that "people were participating for the first time as
citizens. In some cases as many as 40 percent of villagers occupied some
office or other, while community assemblies became the center of decision-
making" (Harvey 1998, 64–65). One independent organization formed to
provide cheap transportation, thereby breaking the community's reliance
on expensive transportation provided by a local political boss. "They saw
that it would be good to . . . buy their own bus through the efforts of the
community . . . and in this way it advanced and cooperation between the
people grew" (Mattiace 2003, 44). Finally, "cooperative structures allow
individuals and communities to direct their own collective affairs, accu-
mulating 'social capital,' or what might better be termed 'organizational
capital' which can be directed toward diverse projects and development"
(C. Simpson and Rapone 2000, 46).[10]

Club Goods

We have seen thus far that the Diocese of San Cristóbal de las Casas completely decentralized control over its material club goods production in the 1960s and early 1970s, and that this led to heightened levels of reciprocity across the indigenous regions of Chiapas during the late 1960s and through the 1970s. As individuals increasingly engaged in reciprocal interactions, my theoretical framework next hypothesizes that religious club goods production should increase. This is, indeed, what we see in Chiapas. For example, one account analyzing the financial success of cooperative networks in Chiapas noted this success relied on a preexisting network of mutual reciprocity, or what some scholars might describe as "social capital." "The organization and networking of small-scale farmers—the level of social capital they have built—is the key element that allows them to tap into market opportunities and to intensify their production in a sustainable manner" (Martínez-Torres 2006, 2).

These economic cooperatives began providing robust material rewards for their members, and many individuals were drawn by the benefits the cooperatives increasingly provided. A pastoral worker told me how there was a cooperative project involving the production of pork, "and I heard that 1 or two [families] didn't want to enter into it when it started. They had their reasons, . . . but since then they have joined . . . because they see the benefit of the work, they see the gain" (Interview 1, 2012). "The Church tells you that you have to help . . . but on the other hand it's also seeing the benefits that the organization starts to provide in the management of the land . . . it's seeing the fruit of the organization that prompts more cooperation and more work" (Interview 17, 2012).

The benefits of cooperative participation were large. In addition to providing excludable goods such as profit shares, technical and marketing assistance, and health benefits, cooperatives also used "their own labor and capital to capture profit previously lost to such middlemen as truckers, money lenders, brokers, and in-country processors" (C. Simpson and Rapone 2000, 46). For example, coffee cooperatives broke the conventional coffee production chain filled with middlemen and intermediaries who appropriated much profit (Frank, Eakin, and López-Carr 2011, 73; Nigh 1997, 432), and they shielded members from the worst effects of variability in world coffee prices (Jaffee 2007, 55–56).[11]

Throughout the 1970s and 1980s, producer cooperatives became economic engines of their communities, thrived (Rus et al. 2003, 12), and grew substantially. The production of coffee provides one example. By 1990, the total acreage of coffee cultivation increased by 900 percent when compared to 1970 within the highlands of Chiapas (Martínez-Torres 2006, 54–55). One priest described the vibrant success of cooperatives in his region and pointed to

> the work that is done by the women of the Word of God, from the cooperative of cafes that have had an economic impact . . . the deacons and catechists have a coffee cooperative that has had transcendent success . . . there were several cooperatives that collaborated with the economies of the communities. Right now, there is a cooperative of artisans who have a wonderful embroidery that sustains a group of women in the cooperative. There is another cooperative of honey and another of coffee. (Interview 46, 2011)

These cooperatives have had important economic implications. Mexico, for its part, has become the world's largest single supplier of organic coffee (Jaffee 2007, 91). While precise statistical information on coffee production is often contradictory and unreliable (Nigh 1997, 430; Daviron and Ponte 2005, 171), "most organic coffee imported in North America originates from Latin America, especially Mexico. There are no precise figures for the total area of certified organic coffee in the world, but industry observers estimate it at over 205,000 hectares. Latin America accounts for more than 85 percent of this area, and Mexico alone accounts for 45 per cent" (Daviron and Ponte 2005, 171–72). This production is dominated by Mexico's indigenous peasants. "About two-thirds of the producers who grow less than two hectares of coffee—virtually half of all Mexican coffee farmers—are indigenous people" (Jaffee 2007, 40). "The pioneer growers of organic coffee in the global economy have proven to be mostly indigenous peasants from the mountain ranges and ravines across the poor southern Mexican states of Chiapas and Oaxaca" (Martínez-Torres 2008, 99).[12] As we will see in the next section, the effective production of coffee was well underway by the mid-1970s, and it was the pretext of effective coffee production that built the organizational resources for Chiapan collective action.

Figure 4.2 below visually recaps the chain of events in Chiapas thus far. We have seen that decentralization began in Chiapas in the 1960s through the early 1970s with the arrival of Bishop Samuel Ruiz García to Chiapas and as monitoring, sanctioning, and decision-making responsibilities were devolved through the development of lay catechists, deacons, and productive cooperatives managed by these lay catechists and deacons. As cooperatives expanded, they offered greater reciprocal interactions both

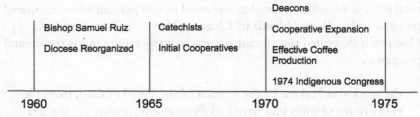

Figure 4.2. Chiapan timeline of events: 1960–75

within and across indigenous communities, and by the mid-1970s they were important suppliers of material goods and resources to participating Catholic adherents in the region, particularly through the production of coffee. In the next section, we will see that these processes directly contributed to the development of organizational infrastructure that was utilized for indigenous political activism in Chiapas.

Organizational Infrastructure

Through decentralization, reciprocity, and club goods provision, Chiapas was primed for the development of an organizational infrastructure that could be applied to political activism, and the indigenous communities of the region demonstrated their nascent capabilities to organize in 1974. The governor of Chiapas had asked Bishop Ruiz's assistance in organizing an Indigenous Congress to curry favor with the indigenous population. The ruling PRI political party of Mexico was still unpopular following its violent suppression of a student movement in 1968, and the governor's request was part of a larger effort by the government to ingratiate itself with the public. It was not the intent of the governor to create a forum for indigenous communities to express their grievances (G. Collier and Quaratiello 1999, 61; Harvey 1998, 76–77).

Ruiz agreed so long as the congress was organized by the indigenous themselves (G. Collier and Quaratiello 1999, 61; Harvey 1998, 77; Womack 1999, 31). He chose six organizers (Catholic priests and members of religious orders) to promote the event throughout the diocese, and by this point lay pastoral agents of the Church were ideally positioned to coordinate the congress. "Throughout the 1960s and 1970s, catechists and deacons had slowly become the most powerful and respected local community leaders in Chiapas's indigenous regions—especially those that also functioned as leaders of ejido unions [transcommunal cooperatives] and the emerging popular movements" (Trejo 2004, 236).

These six organizers sent groups of indigenous Catholic catechists out into the countryside who pulled on their own Catholic cooperative organizational networks. The catechists met with representatives of small individual indigenous communities and explained that the purpose was to represent their interests (Womack 1999, 148). While organizing the conference, these catechists "talked with 400,000 people in a thousand communities" (Early 2012, 124). Many communities agreed to participate and in turn developed their own internal coordinators and organizers, also drawing on their newfound Catholic organizational networks, to coordinate activities within and across indigenous communities (Womack 1999, 148–49). The resultant congress was "dominated" by Catholic catechists (Trejo 2012, 97). It was the first assembly of its kind that allowed the 1,250 indigenous delegates from 327 communities to voice concerns, questions, indignation, criticism, and solutions (G. Collier and Quaratiello 1999, 62–63; Womack 1999, 31–32; Harvey 1998, 78).

Much to the consternation of state officials and landed elites (Womack 1999, 32), the delegations used the congress to voice their displeasure with the government and the slow pace of land reform, and they also called for less discrimination against indigenous communities. These themes reflected topics of discussion commonly covered in catechist-led discussion groups. It was with the congress that the indigenous populations realized their potential to politically organize.

The congress marked a watershed in indigenous organization and further inspired heightened political activism. The entire diocese had become characterized by highly decentralized local units, closely and actively engaged in the production of material club goods and well-networked by ties linking productive cooperatives across communities. The stage was set for the emergence of politicized groups throughout the region. Soon after, catechists began consolidating the vast array of Catholic food production, transportation, health, and service cooperatives into large, regional, and more explicitly politicized producer organizations independent of the Mexican corporatist state (Harvey 1998, 74, 78–79; Womack 1999, 32; Nash 2001, 95–96, 114).

The potential of these regional Catholic organizations to produce political change grew first from their ability to provide basic goods and services to their members. A brief examination of two of these organizations that formed in the late 1970s and early 1980s, La'Qu'iptik (alternatively "La Quiptic") and the subsequent Union de Uniones (Union of Unions),[13] helps to reinforce the point. In both cases, organizers (primarily Catholic catechists) were interested in prompting independent peasant organization, but they realized such organization had to be grounded on providing tangible material benefits to individual producers (Kovic 2005, 59).

La Quiptic was constructed primarily by indigenous Catholics, directed by catechists, and was constituted by eighteen communities near the town of Ocosingo (Acosta Chávez 2003, 118–23; Harvey 1998, 79; Kovic 2005, 59). Its organizational structure was modeled after the decentralized structure of the diocese and was nicknamed the "little brother of the Word of God" (Early 2012, 279). Coffee served as the pretext for successful organization. Politicized Catholic communities sent delegations throughout the region to explain how successful organizing, predicated on decentralized cooperative modes of production, could lead to better terms for the supply and transportation of coffee (Harvey 1998, 84). Organizational life in remote communities like Guadalupe Tepeyac and San Marcos (later Zapatista strongholds) subsequently grew around coffee cooperatives, and it was through economic development that these regional organizations grew. The "capacity for independent political action depended less on denunciations and confrontations and more on the economic viability of peasant organizations . . . economics became the key to political emancipation" (Harvey 1998, 87).

La Quiptic had to deal with a serious problem when the federal government issued orders to evict twenty-six communities to facilitate logging operations. Between 1973 and 1978, deacons and catechists across the diocese organized a contingent of communities through La Quiptic that successfully halted many of these operations. While some families were relocated, they received "promises of government support, credit, and subsidies in new settlements" as a result of Quiptic's mobilization efforts (Harvey 1998, 79–80). Slowly, additional successes materialized, and one of my interview respondents spoke of the aftermath of the Indigenous Congress during the late 1970s with noticeable enthusiasm:

> This is when the grand movement began . . . because it was now not only in one place but at the level of the state. . . . You can't imagine how it all came together, in a very nice, very exciting way. Two large organizations emerged here in the community . . . Lucha Campesina (Peasant Struggle) and Tierra y Libertad (Land and Liberty). In all the communities, something arose from the production of coffee, cooperatives, these types of things. Everything revolved around coffee. (Interview 45, 2012)

These producer cooperatives formed considerable organizational infrastructure. Many were constituted by thousands of members representing dozens of communities across the state. Communities often represented their interests to a cooperative, as discussed previously, by sending delegates to a representative assembly. Furthermore, cooperatives typically functioned best when rotating leadership, and new executive committees were elected periodically (Hernández Castillo and Nigh 1998, 142; C. Simpson and Rapone 2000, 51). In this way, individuals gained organizational experience, communities developed the ability to express and aggregate their interests through a larger institutional body, and cooperative networks enabled rapid information dissemination from a regional center to outlying communities.

Furthermore, cooperatives such as La Quiptic amassed organizational resources in pursuit of their members' economic agendas. As alluded to earlier, coffee producers in Chiapas depended on intermediaries, who charged considerable fees, to bring their product to market. To break this dependence, cooperatives developed "their own economic infrastructure, including credit unions, processing plants, and retail networks" (Harvey 1998, 129). Others produced their own coffee-processing, toasting, and packing facilities, along with their own means to secure financing (Hernández Castillo and Nigh 1998, 142). As they became more powerful and increasingly capable of mobilizing resources and activism, they negotiated concessions from the Mexican government. La'Qu'iptik, for example, used mobilization against federal relocation programs to negotiate coffee transportation subsidies from the state. It also obtained permission to form a comprehensive Union of Unions to further consolidate the interests of various regional cooperatives and to increase their power to press the state with demands (G. Collier and Quaratiello 1994, 75). Accordingly, Quiptic merged with Lucha Campesina, Tierra y Libertad, and other cooperative organizations in 1980 to form the Union of Ejido Unions and Associated Peasant Groups of Chiapas. This large conglomeration represented at least 150 separate communities and 10,000 families. It became the first and strongest independent peasant power in the region (Womack 1999, 34; Harvey 1998, 84; Rus et al. 2003, 41; G. Collier and Quaratiello 1999, 76).

As they grew larger, more economically viable, and consolidated into the Union of Unions, the possibilities for political activism expanded. "The Union of Unions . . . armed with independent credits and special market access . . . quickly became an organizing force" throughout Chiapas (G. Collier and Quaratiello 1994, 75–76). Other large regional politicized producer organizations such as the CIOAC (Independent Confederation of Agricultural Workers and Peasants) and OCEZ (Emiliano Zapata Peasant Organization) collaborated to produce marches and demonstrations (G. Collier and Quaratiello 1994, 76). Catechists and deacons were the primary catalysts in constructing powerful intracommunity organizations that directly sponsored new protest movements (Trejo 2012, 99).

These grassroots organizations orchestrated massive protests of indigenous peasants and engendered greater concessions from the political elite (Womack 1999, 34; Harvey 1998, 84; Mattiace 2003, 41; G. Collier and Quaratiello 1999, 70, 76). Political activism developed far beyond the initial input of the Church. Local cooperative organizations continued to grow, consolidate, and become regional political powers. In 1981, the Union of Unions organized a march on Tuxtla Gutiérrez by three thousand peasants to protest evictions (G. Collier and Quaratiello 1999, 76), and the Union successfully negotiated with the government for transportation and credit concessions for its member communities (Mattiace 2003, 41; Harvey 1998, 83; Womack 1999, 34). "The most important growers of organic coffee in the global economy, mostly indigenous peasants from the mountains across the poor southern Mexican states of Chiapas and Oaxaca, became the most organized sector of Mexico's revitalized peasant movement in the 1980s and 1990s" (Martínez-Torres 2006, 1).

We see now the process through which decentralization prompted political activism in Chiapas. Whereas Figure 4.2 demonstrated the timeline of decentralization, reciprocity, and club goods provision, Figure 4.3 demonstrates the timeline indicating the development of an institutional infrastructure applied to political activism. Indigenous individuals demonstrated their burgeoning capacities for mobilization with the 1974 Indigenous Congress. As cooperatives continued to expand and effectively produce public goods throughout the 1970s, larger regional producer organizations emerged with increased organizational capacities. By the late 1970s and early 1980s, these organizations directly sponsored wide-ranging political activism across Chiapas. While the previous chapter demonstrated a general relationship between religious decentralization and political activism across Mexico, this chapter has demonstrated the mechanisms of how decentralization develops political activism.

The Zapatistas

While the purpose of this book is not to recount the origins or repercussions of the Zapatista rebellion, the uprising was of such consequence, and its organizational origins so intertwined with decentralization by the Catholic Church, that some discussion is necessary. Given the local and decentralized character of the diocese, it is unsurprising that the large consolidated producer organizations fractured. By 1983, the Union of Unions

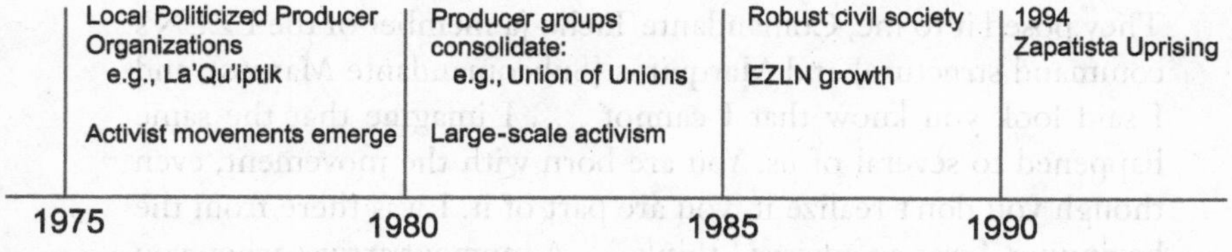

Local Politicized Producer Organizations e.g., La'Qu'iptik	Producer groups consolidate: e.g., Union of Unions	Robust civil society EZLN growth	1994 Zapatista Uprising
Activist movements emerge	Large-scale activism		

| 1975 | 1980 | 1985 | 1990 |

Figure 4.3. Chiapan timeline of events: 1975–95

had trouble holding together its various local factions. While it had won concessions from the government, more radical elements accused it of col-lusion and left the organization. Some groups looked for better economic and credit opportunities (Womack 1999, 36; Eisenstadt 2011, 87). Many began to feel that peaceful protest was useless (Manaut, Selee, and Arnson 2006, 136–37), and a large current of thought moved well beyond the dio-cese's vision of peaceful resistance.

Throughout the 1980s, prominent Catholic laity allied themselves with social workers in the Forces of National Liberation (FLN), a radical and violent leftist political group. Soon the influential deacon of deacons and high-ranking lay members of other predominantly Catholic organizations became members of the FLN. They encouraged members of their commu-nities in the Lancandón jungle to arm themselves (Womack 1999, 35–37), and they did so while continuing to carry out social programs in the name of the diocese. The FLN would later go on to spawn the armed Zapatista Army of National Liberation (EZLN) that led the 1994 rebellion. Despite his progressive stance, and although he initially contemplated the utility of armed force, Bishop Ruiz eventually resolved decisively on the desirability of incremental reform over social revolution (Harvey 1998, 71; Early 2012, 285–87).

The experience of Chiapas shows the unexpected consequences of decentralization to an institutional hierarchy, as the Church risked losing control of its members (Kalyvas 1996, 31). Political activism took forms far afield from those originally envisioned by the Diocese of San Cristóbal de las Casas. In a sign that the direction of some activist groups had spiraled beyond the Church's expectations and wishes, the diocese formally broke with the radical and violent FLN in 1988, six years before the Zapatista uprising (Womack 1999, 199–201). Local priests severed ties with commu-nities they had worked with for decades, often painfully. One priest I spoke with emotionally recalled his decision to leave the community he had min-istered to for years after being approached to support the Zapatistas:

They posed it to me, Comandante Tacho [a member of the EZLN's command structure] and Marquitos [Subcomandante Marcos], and I said look you know that I cannot . . . I imagine that the same happened to several of us. You are born with the movement, even though you don't realize it, you are part of it. I was there from the beginning, I was an adviser I think. . . . A moment arrives when you realize that you cannot continue, above all when . . . certain decisions mean life or death. . . . Many [in the Church] said I cannot anymore, because it's going to do more harm than good. (Interview 45, 2012)[14]

By the end of the 1980s, there were a variety of independent organizations, violent and nonviolent, representing the interests of indigenous *Chiapanecos*. Some of these organizations were perceived as having been co-opted by the state, others managed to continue to work independently, and others prepared for war. Armed insurgency was not what the Church had originally envisioned for Chiapas.

Notwithstanding reticence from the institutional diocese, the EZLN was strongly affiliated with Catholic networks that developed in the region. After the Union of Unions split, radical members sought a means to protect themselves from violent evictions perpetrated by individuals affiliated with the state. The Zapatista Army of National Liberation (EZLN) formed partially as a self-defense group to prevent such evictions. The movement moved rapidly through networks created by the Union of Unions and its affiliated institutions, and between 1989 and 1992 the number of members in the EZLN doubled (Harvey 1998, 164–67, 197). The federal government formally ended land reform in 1992, and any hope indigenous communities possessed for obtaining collectively held land from the state ended. When combined with violent repression from the Chiapan state government, the implementation of neoliberal economic policies, the collapse of coffee prices, and new formidable organizing potential, the stage was set for rebellion. Utilizing the element of surprise, thousands of armed members of the EZLN seized control of several cities throughout Chiapas, including San Cristóbal de las Casas, on January 1, 1994. However, the Mexican army pushed the Zapatistas back into the mountains within a matter of days, resulting in the death of several hundred combatants (Vanden and Prevost 2015, 100–101).[15]

Despite its unintended consequences, diocesan decentralization continues today in the Diocese of San Cristóbal de las Casas. Bishop Samuel Ruiz retired in 2000, but his successor, Bishop Felipe Arizmendi, has maintained the broad form of Ruiz's pastoral plan (Interview 81, 2011; Interview 56, 2011).[16] The Vatican, concerned about political radicalism in Chiapas and recognizing the power of decentralization, restricted the appointment of new permanent deacons in 2002, though Pope Francis reinstated the practice in 2014 (Interview 56, 2011; Interview 31, 2011; Interview 46, 2011; Thompson 2002; Yardley and Villegas 2016). Even during the Vatican's restriction, the diocese remained served by more than three hundred permanent deacons. The Zapatista rebellion of 1994, of course, changed the contours of civil society. International NGO's took substantial interest and poured a great deal of resources into the region, started their own organizations, and became part of the network of Chiapan civil society. While some of this international interest has subsequently waned, grassroots indigenous political activism endures.

The Political Process Approach

Religious decentralization helps us to understand how the Diocese of San Cristóbal de las Casas helped to develop organizational capacity that facilitated political activism across Chiapas. However, to understand why that activism devoted itself to progressive causes and why Catholic religious elites consented to mobilizing activism through the Church, we must understand the frames and opportunities that also helped develop collective action.

Many academic sources have detailed the important role liberation theology played in framing religious adherents' perspectives and prompting collective action across Chiapas (Womack 1999; G. Collier and Quaratiello 2005; Harvey 1998). Here I summarize the important impact of framing in coordinating expectations and in helping develop a relatively cohesive trajectory for activism. However, I also point out that the presence of progressive Catholic theology on its own is not sufficient to prompt political activism absent decentralization. With decentralization, on the other hand, indigenous communities reinterpreted liberation theology for their own purposes, and the result was a new indigenous theology that helped to guide political activism.

Similarly, Guillermo Trejo has already provided a convincing account of the role of Protestant competition in encouraging Bishop Samuel Ruiz García to support secular political movements, and I briefly summarize that account here. However, Protestant competition, like progressive Catholicism and decentralization, is not sufficient on its own to prompt political

activism. The political process approach informs us that framing, opportunity, and resource mobilization are all necessary for collective action to
find fruition.

A Framing Political Theology

Church decentralization created a well-networked system of catechists,
deacons, and productive cooperatives throughout the Diocese of San Cristóbal de las Casas. However, why did that organizational potential apply
itself to progressive political causes? What prevented that organizational
potential from remaining dormant? Here, consideration of the ideological
frames that coordinated activity will be instructive.

The Catholic Church in Chiapas was undeniably informed by progressive Catholicism. Though initially marked by conservatism, Bishop Samuel
Ruiz García was one of the few Mexican bishops to be influenced by liberation theology. "[Ruiz] arrived when he was 35 years old. He arrived with a
traditional way of evangelizing. . . . [However], he learned that the Church
has to develop programs to look after health, land rights, and to go against
poverty" (Interview 56, 2011). Much of this was due to Ruiz's participation
at the Second Vatican Council from 1963 to 1965, where he was exposed to
the burgeoning ideological undercurrents of liberation theology (Harvey
1998, 72).

Ruiz took on the agenda of liberation theology and came to feel that the
Church should make indigenous communities aware of their marginalized
situation, question their position in the social order, and help build capacities to change that order (Womack 1999, 23). All throughout the diocese,
catechists were charged with the mission of consciousness-raising and pro-
moting both community and political participation (Womack 1999, 28–
31; Harvey 1998, 83; G. Collier and Quaratiello 1999, 75–76). Catechists
led Bible studies within their own communities emphasizing this message
(Womack 1999, 132).

Some might argue diocesan decentralization in Chiapas was the direct
result of liberation theology's mandate for clergy to share authority. However, we should keep in mind that the liberation theology movement consisted of both ideological and organizational principles. As Kalyvas reminds
us in his study of the European Catholic Church, "hierarchy and control
are organizational rather than ideological attributes" (Kalyvas 1996, 30).
While the ideology of liberation theology sought to shift the consciousness of Catholic adherents and question the social order, the organizational
principles called for a greater role for the laity (C. Smith 1991, 25).

The Church does not automatically become decentralized when clergy subscribe to the ideological aspects of progressive Catholicism. "There are countless cases" where progressive clerical elements in the Catholic Church failed to turn their liberation-inspired ideals into reality (Levine 1988, 252). Failure typically occurred when clergy attempted to politicize Catholic communities from the onset rather than becoming embedded within marginalized groups, working closely with them, and allowing them to develop their own particular character (Levine 1988, 252). Years of paternalistic relationships between priests and laity can make it difficult for bishops and priests, even those committed to the ideal of liberation theology, to decentralize control. "Liberationist discourse has often remained alien to its intended clients. Even with the best intentions, liberationist activists have had problems shedding directive and paternalistic roles" (Levine 1995, 121).

Frequently, liberation theology was unsuccessful in prompting political activism, and this was often in cases when the institutional Church neglected to grant decentralized control. "It is common to encounter the anomaly of 'progressive' priests . . . [promoting] a liberationist agenda in authoritarian ways" (Levine 1988, 257). These authoritarian priests emphasized the theological component of liberation theology, but not the organizational component. Roderic Camp similarly notes that while "popular and even academic perceptions . . . reinforce the belief that only those bishops and archbishops who tow [*sic*] a conservative or traditional line are authoritarian" in reality "process takes precedence over ideology" in determining a particular bishop's management style (Camp 1997, 268). Ideological biases in the Catholic Church do not automatically translate into particular forms of diocesan administration (Camp 1997, 269).

Importantly, as one of my interviewees insisted, the Church in Chiapas did not force its agenda on communities. "Don Samuel didn't act as a patron but rather as a facilitator of the creativity and decisions of the people" (Interview 28, 2011). The diocese did not determine the demands of the indigenous communities, but it did work to facilitate their agenda (Interview 28, 2011). The diocese centrally decided to reorient catechism so that it was "communitarian, reflective, evocative, stirring the community, [and] dissolving the Word of God into it" (Womack 1999, 30–31). Catechists were instructed by the hierarchy to encourage adherents to reflect on their experiences and socioeconomic position (Harvey 1998, 64). However, the Church in Chiapas was careful to break away from the previously paternalistic nature of catechism and to encourage indigenous communities to form their own reflections on their socioeconomic status. It saw its role as accompanying indigenous communities rather than leading them (Harvey 1998, 63, 75).

While initially missionaries and priests wrote syntheses for catechists to use in their lessons, indigenous catechists quickly designed their own lessons to lead autonomous reflective discussions within the community. They developed their own themes for discussion and examined their ethnic status, the extremely low wages they were paid to work landowners' land, their relationship with the government, and their relationships with mestizo business and landowners (Harvey 1998, 73; Womack 1999, 132–34).

The book of Exodus, in particular, had a powerful impact. It detailed "a political story of struggle against oppression and corruption, a divine promise of liberation, [and] a humanly organized escape" (Womack 1999, 30). Pastoral workers recognized the parallels between the Exodus of the Jewish people from Egypt and the plight of indigenous peasants who faced discrimination and misery in Chiapas. Catechists learned Exodus from Church pastoral workers, and they then adapted it on their own to make it resonate with their home indigenous communities' own experiences (Kovic 2005, 53; Womack 1999, 132; Harvey 1998, 63). The most common reading was from chapter 22, verses 22 through 27 (Kovic 2005, 110). Here, the book provides injunctions against taking advantage of the powerless, including a stipulation against charging the poor interest for loans. These passages surely tapped into latent populist rage held by indigenous individuals accustomed to discrimination, exploitation, and predatory business arrangements from landed mestizos. God assures his followers he is compassionate and vividly describes how he will destroy those who exploit them. After the presentation, catechists organized individuals into groups to apply the readings to their own situations (Kovic 2005, 110).

Accordingly, such catechism helped to foment an "insurgent consciousness" among the indigenous communities of Chiapas. As a result of lectures planned by indigenous catechists and deacons who encouraged communities to think about their own social and political problems, the indigenous communities became conscious of their socioeconomic status. The book of Exodus gave them the inspiration to believe it was possible to overcome it. "God wants us to get out to freedom like the ancient Jewish people. . . . [But] they had to get out and fight to gain their freedom . . . we have to struggle against poverty, hunger, and injustice" (Womack 1999, 31).

Communities formed agreements on how to defend themselves from exploitation, and these were "the result of dialogue rather than preestablished doctrines and were interpreted by the dioceses as theological statements" (Harvey 1998, 73). Certainly, reassessment of the status quo was an ideological imperative centrally planned and coordinated by the diocese. However, it was up to individual communities to come up with their own reactions to that status quo and to design their own responses to it. This was facilitated by newly decentralized decision-making granted to catechists and deacons. The result was a new political theology that emerged at the grassroots seeking social justice through political engagement. When combined with the organizational capacity that resulted from decentralization, the result was an extraordinary potential for political activism. In much the same way my statistical analysis in the previous chapter found decentralization and liberation theology reinforced and strengthened each other's impact on political activism, decentralization and liberation theology nurtured each other to produce political activism in Chiapas.

Finally, following the outbreak of the 1994 Zapatista revolt, a variety of Mexican scholars, in an attempt to deny the legitimacy of the Zapatista rebellion as an autonomous movement, argued that leftists and the progressive Catholic Church manipulated indigenous communities into rebellion (Harvey 1998, 8–9). These arguments noted that Bishop Ruiz had invited leftist political elements to assist in the work of preparing delegates for the Indigenous Congress (Womack 1999, 173–74). Furthermore, the organization La Quiptic arose with the aid of leftist organizers (Harvey 1998, 79–80).

Consistent with the manner in which he had reorganized his diocese, Bishop Samuel Ruiz had indeed recruited individuals who could help organize at a base, grassroots level (Harvey 1998, 81; Womack 1999, 174). He met with representatives of the leftist Proletarian Line (also known as Popular Politics) in 1976. The organization appealed to Ruiz because it did not call for armed action, and it had a history of successful grassroots organizing (Womack 1999, 33–34, 175; Harvey 1998, 82; G. Collier and Quaratiello 1999, 75). Several local priests were supportive and allowed leftist organizers access to catechist-organized meetings (G. Collier and Quaratiello 1999, 75; Womack 1999, 34).

At this point, however, the organizers of the Proletarian Line tried to wrest control of the cooperatives away from the deacons and catechists who ran them. These efforts were successfully fended off (Womack 1999, 34; Harvey 1998, 82–83; Early 2012, 280). The communities had final say over whether they would accept the organizing efforts of the leftist outsiders. As one prominent community member recalled: "In general, we thought it would be dishonest to turn the communities over to people who, though apparently very well intentioned, were outsiders . . . we would not close the doors, but neither would we turn the communities over to them" (G. Collier and Quaratiello 1999, 75). The leftist organizers served at the behest of the indigenous communities.

Guillermo Trejo similarly concludes that, rather than guerilla leftists influencing the character of Chiapas, it was "the unparalleled wealth of the communal organizational networks, mostly built by Bishop Samuel Ruiz and his dioceses . . . [that] were the real magnet that attracted urban gue- rilla groups into the highlands, north and east of Chiapas" (Trejo 2004, 207). Instead of outside influences prompting Chiapan civil society, it was the prior existence of said civil society that drew in leftist elements.

Protestant Competition

Religious competition can encourage religious leaders to abandon tradi- tional alliances with socioeconomic elites, and theories linking Protestant competition to political activism seemingly explain Chiapas well. In 1970, Protestants made up 5.8 percent of the Chiapan population. By 1990, they made up 16.3 percent, and by 2000, Protestants made up 21.9 percent of the population (J. Dow 2005, 830). One Catholic official I spoke with estimates that now 27 percent of the population is Protestant (Interview 81), and this rise in Protestant competition to the Catholic Church temporally coincides with the onset of Catholic support for political activism in Chiapas.

More systematically, Guillermo Trejo provides rigorous statistical evidence examining Mexico's indigenous populations and demonstrates indigenous Mexican municipalities with higher levels of Protestant com- petition are positively associated with protest (Trejo 2009). My own sta- tistical analysis conducted in the previous chapter provides further sup- portive evidence of a similar relationship across Mexican Catholics more generally. Trejo details the evangelizing efforts of Protestant missionaries in Chiapas throughout the midpart of the twentieth century and suggests they offered a variety of material, cultural, and ecclesial rewards that made them attractive to indigenous populations and prompted mass conversions from Catholicism. He argues it was then this Protestant competition that compelled the Catholic Church to offer its own rewards to make it more competitive with Protestants (Trejo 2009, 337).

An argument could be made that Protestant competition in Latin America compels decentralization by the Catholic Church as a strategy to compete with Protestants' ability to rapidly train and deploy clergy (Gill 1999, 29–33). On the other hand, the Catholic Church possesses a variety of strategies to compete with Protestants, and religious competition does not necessarily prompt decentralization. In certain locations, the Catholic Church might mimic Protestant worship styles, lobby the state for advantages against its competitors, or increase its own evangelical outreach through additional priests and nuns in the face of Protestant competition (Trejo 2009; Hagopian 2009, 44; A. Smith 2016). In much the same way we saw decentralization was not an automatic consequence of progressive Catholic theology, organizational imperatives for Catholic decentralization did not naturally flow from the presence of Protestant competition. As we will see in the next chapter, for example, Protestant competition did not prompt religious decentralization in Yucatán.

My account complements the explanations proffered by Gill (1998) and Trejo (2009) that argue for the importance of religious competition in prompting religious leadership to support secular political causes. Trejo convincingly argues that religious competition provided clergy in Chiapas with incentives to respond to Protestant competition, to pay greater attention to the concerns of their adherents, and subsequently to support political movements that might antagonize economic or political elites. Explanations emphasizing the importance of religious competition help us understand the conditions under which religious authorities will support secular political movements, enabling an opportunity for collective action through the religious institution. My contribution is to explain how religious decentralization prompts the development of an organizational infrastructure at the grassroots.

Conclusion

In this chapter, I assessed the mechanisms linking decentralization to political activism using the case of Chiapas. According to my theory, religious decentralization prompts heightened levels of reciprocal interactions within communities, the subsequent ability of the religious organization to offer increasingly valuable goods and services to its members, and finally to an organizational capacity that can then be utilized to provide public goods such as political activism.

I found that decision-making authority was firmly devolved to the Catholic laity in a variety of ways. Control over doctrinal and ecclesial functions had been highly decentralized compared to the traditional structure of the Catholic Church. The indigenous laity of Chiapas were given the power to interpret scriptures to fit their own unique perspectives and socioeconomic experiences. Ecclesial authority was devolved substantially through lay catechists and deacons who had the authority to reinterpret scripture and to provide a variety of liturgical functions that had previously been performed only by clergy.

The Diocese of San Cristóbal de las Casas developed the deliberate strategy to produce material club goods for its members through hundreds of local economic cooperatives scattered across Chiapas. Here, laity had complete decision-making authority regarding how to manage the cooperatives and to decide what types of goods and services should be produced, how monitoring should occur, and the types of sanctions that were appropriate for shirkers. Monitoring and sanctioning responsibilities had also been completely devolved. Monitoring was decided locally and occurred through production quotas, membership fees, and direct supervision during common work tasks. Sanctioning involved the exclusion of valuable club goods and services from noncontributors.

I then linked decentralization to political activism. I found decentralization greatly fostered levels of cooperation both within and between communities. Religious adherents and clergy may have a key role in prompting cooperative interactions in the early stages of institution-building. I found that individuals became increasingly willing to interact within these decentralized cooperatives. Small towns that barely interacted would now allow intercommunal marriages, and indigenous individuals developed a pan-indigenous identity. Economic cooperatives became extremely effective at producing valuable goods and services for their members and became economic engines of their communities. An organizational infrastructure organically developed in the form of increasingly consolidated producer organizations that then directly sponsored a variety of protest movements. Networks of catechists and deacons were essential in building the Indigenous Congress. However, we also saw that decentralization can create unanticipated consequences. It sparks political activism, but that activism can take a form far afield from what clergy anticipated. The organizational network that developed because of diocesan decentralization was directly utilized by the Zapatista armed movement that engaged in a rebellion against the Mexican state in 1994.

At the same time, I also found that framing and opportunity structures played important roles. Framing created a common theological frame that coordinated actors' actions and that, importantly, made indigenous individuals aware of their situation and gave them inspiration for overcoming it. Religious competition was critical because it gave religious clergy an incentive to lend their institutions out to secular causes, creating an opportunity for secular political activism through the religious institution.

However, neither framing nor opportunity was sufficient on its own to prompt activism. Priests all across Latin American where unable to prompt activist movements when they implemented progressive Catholicism in a hierarchical manner. Furthermore, though Protestant competition played an important role in prompting the Catholic Church in Chiapas to support secular movements, Protestant competition did not prompt a similar response in Yucatán.

The investigation now turns to Yucatán, a case like Chiapas in many respects but that experienced far lower levels of indigenous political activism. Within the next chapter, I demonstrate that religious decentralization did not occur. Accordingly, it has not served as a basis for reciprocal interactions, the provision of material club goods from the Catholic Church, and it lacks the organizational infrastructure that is necessary to prompt collective action from the grassroots.

FIVE

Activist Malaise in the Centralized Archdiocese of Yucatán

Everything comes from the top.
(Interview 22, 2012)

Before the 1980s, Yucatán had been economically dependent on the exportation of henequen, a natural fiber used to produce rope. Though synthetic fibers replaced henequen on the international market by the middle of the twentieth century, Mexico's ruling PRI political party subsidized henequen production to sustain jobs and to buttress its political support in the region. With the economic crises that hit Mexico and most of the rest of Latin America during the 1980s, the Mexican state was forced to implement neoliberal economic policies and roll back its support of henequen. Tens of thousands of Yucatec workers either lost their jobs or were forced into early retirement. Though popular accounts of indigenous movements in Latin America pointed to neoliberal restructuring as a cause of indigenous discontent, these processes did not prompt a similar response in Yucatán.[1] Why did Yucatán not see the emergence of political activism by its indigenous populations, and why did the Catholic Church not support such a movement as it had in Chiapas?

Yucatán is located on the northernmost portion of the Yucatán peninsula, at the farthest eastern reaches of Mexico, and it is bordered by the

Gulf of Mexico to its north and west.[2] Throughout the nineteenth century, Yucatán's only land connection to the rest of Mexico was through the practically impassible wilderness to its south. It was only accessible by sea (Rugeley 2009, 10). Much like Chiapas, Yucatán's geographic isolation from the rest of Mexico subsequently has given it a unique cultural and political history at the periphery of Mexican national politics (K. Martin and González 2008, 170). In both states, the indigenous population has been historically marginalized. "Large haciendas broke up ethnic communities in the latter quarter of the nineteenth century, forcing indigenous peoples to work as peons . . . on their former lands" (Mattiace 2009, 139), and many indigenous individuals were forced into debt servitude (Fallaw 1997, 552–53). Yucatán's history is somewhat differentiated from Chiapas in that it declared independence from Mexico in 1841 but was permanently reincorporated in 1848 during the tumult of the Caste War, a civil war that engulfed much of the peninsula. Political maneuvering led Hispanic elites to simultaneously arm and antagonize indigenous communities across Yucatán, resulting in several decades of conflict (Gabbert 2004, 91; Rugeley 2009, 40, 59; Mattiace 2009, 139). While Yucatán's experience during the 1840s was distinctive, both states experienced indigenous revolts during the nineteenth century.

Also like Chiapas, elaborate mechanisms of exploitation sapped the indigenous communities of productive incentive, and Hispanic elites developed racist stereotypes of indigenous peasant "listlessness and stupidity" (Rugeley 2009, 17). Furthermore, as the PRI political party consolidated control over Mexico during the 1930s and 1940s, the Mexican government created indigenous corporatist institutions in both Chiapas and Yucatán whose purpose was to assimilate indigenous communities into a broader mestizo identity (Mattiace 2009, 139). The Mexican government also organized individuals in both states into peasant confederations that discouraged independent organizing.

Quite unlike Chiapas, there is little contemporary indigenous political activism, or activism of any kind, across Yucatán. The Mexican government, in the form of the National Commission for the Development of Indigenous Peoples (CDI), has been more engaged with efforts to write indigenous rights into the state's constitution than indigenous communities themselves. This largely explains why Yucatán was the last of Mexico's southern indigenous states to incorporate indigenous rights into its constitution (Mattiace 2009, 140). According to a representative from the Mexican government:

There wasn't a lot of participation. We had to try . . . almost oblige them to participate. There weren't people who supported us, to say "we want our rights [written] into law." On the contrary, *we* fought so that *they* could have them, but we didn't receive any response [from the indigenous communities]. This is why it took so long, from 2007 to 2011, for statutory law to be made. (Interview 8, 2011)

In this chapter, I demonstrate that the Catholic Archdiocese of Yucatán has not decentralized governance in a similar manner as the Diocese of San Cristóbal de las Casas in Chiapas. Clergy in Yucatán maintain tight ecclesial control, and there are no cooperatives or comparable structures that decentralize the management of material club goods. Yucatán has not subsequently developed reciprocal interactions, effective club goods production, or an organizational infrastructure through the Catholic Church.

This chapter also examines several factors that might alternatively explain political activism across Chiapas and Yucatán, including the potential impacts of economic deprivation, political party competition, legacies of Church and state conflict, and ethnic diversity. I find that none of these alternative explanations account for variation in political activism between the two states, and the findings from my qualitative investigation also helpfully inform the more general findings of the quantitative tests conducted in chapter 3.

The Centralized Archdiocese of Yucatán

My investigation finds that the Archdiocese of Yucatán has not decentralized decision-making, monitoring, or sanctioning authority to its laity. Because of this, we should not see the causal chain linking religious institutional structure to political activism that we saw in Chiapas. More specifically, we should not see the development of reciprocal interactions facilitated by the Catholic Church within and across communities in Yucatán, we should not see the extensive development of religious club goods by the Catholic Church in the region, and accordingly there should not be a grassroots organizational structure provided by the Catholic Church to draw on to facilitate secular political activism.

Decision-making in the Archdiocese of Yucatán is somewhat dispersed, but only within the confines of the Church's hierarchical clergy. Though the archbishop maintains final decision-making authority in all matters (Interview 11, 2012), the priests I interviewed explained that the archdiocese gives them a great deal of latitude to implement pastoral goals and to manage the day-to-day operations of their parishes (Interview 23, 2012; Interview 11, 2012; Interview 63, 2011; Interview 51, 2011). While priests follow the general guidelines of the pastoral plan (a broad framework for achieving the archdiocese's ministerial goals), a local priest has the freedom to adapt it to his own environment. The archdiocese recognizes that the pastoral needs of a metropolitan center such as Mérida are very different from small communities of only several hundred people (Interview 11, 2012). "The Bishop isn't a feudal lord who says 'this is my land, do what I want.' He listens to priests . . . his team of people who help him make decisions" (Interview 11, 2012).[3]

Furthermore, the archdiocese appeared to have made a commitment to increase avenues of participation for its laity under Archbishop Emilio Carlos Berlie Belaunzarán in 1995.[4] Yucatán's Catholic hierarchy has emphasized greater participation of the people in their own parishes, and a key development in this regard has been the creation of pastoral councils who advise the parish priest. Each parish has its own council of laity intended to help a priest make decisions such as where and when mass should take place (Interview 69, 2011; Interview 11, 2012).

While this appears participatory, laity are not given substantive decision-making authority across the archdiocese. The pastoral plan is drawn up by a select number of individuals in the hierarchy. Local priests are given freedom to choose the best way to implement it, but "everything comes from the top" (Interview 22, 2012). Laity have the right under canon law to assemble and advise clergy, but they do so under the direct supervision of a parish priest (Interview 63, 2011; Interview 22, 2012). At no point, one priest stressed, do laity convene together to identify or formulate solutions to problems (Interview 22, 2012).

While individuals follow instructions given to them from a priest, they do not make decisions themselves. "The parishioners do what the priest tells them to do, . . . but they lack leadership. Laity lack initiative in this sense. What the priest says, they do with good charity but always just what the priest says" (Interview 23, 2012). One lay person explained to me that, "there are people here that, yes, they give when the priest asks them to, not because they want to, but for obligation . . . because our religion requests it" (Interview 48, 2011). One priest also made it clear he ultimately makes the decisions in the parish. "What [the council] tells me is fine, but I decide what's going to happen. The decision is mine" (Interview 51, 2011). Thus, while parishioners are given the right to organize and advise in pastoral councils, they have few capacities to make substantive decisions.

In Chiapas, lay catechists were given authority to select themes for discussion for local lessons. This created a forum wherein individuals could discuss their social and economic problems and formulate solutions for them. In Yucatán, lay catechists receive instructions from the priest and implement those instructions throughout the pastoral sector (Interview 26, 2011). The priest guides the themes for discussion (Interview 11, 2012). According to one lay catechist I spoke with, the archdiocese decides the theme to be discussed each month and the types of activities that are going to be done. The parish priest then decides how this is to be taught locally (Interview 39, 2012).

Also unlike Chiapas, where deacons share decentralized ecclesial authority and direct economic cooperatives throughout the countryside, Yucatán's much fewer number of permanent deacons are entirely concentrated in metropolitan Mérida (Interview 11, 2012). One priest mentioned that he hoped his Eucharist ministers might one day become permanent deacons. In the thirty years that he has been a priest, however, he's only been able to work with one permanent deacon (Interview 11, 2012). While there has been some talk of establishing a deaconate school in the south of the state, this has not materialized. The archdiocese has not promoted the development of deacons across the diocese, despite priests away from Mérida noting a need for them (Interview 23, 2012).

As discussed in the previous chapter, the Catholic Church in Chiapas made a concerted effort to incorporate Mayan beliefs, customs, and languages into the liturgy of the Church, making it easier for local populations to participate in it. In the Archdiocese of Yucatán, however, this has not been the case. The archdiocese has not made a resolute push to incorporate Maya culture into its pastoral plan. This has resulted in fewer avenues for participation than in the Chiapan Church by indigenous communities.

Some priests express a need to adopt indigenous liturgical elements into the Church, suggesting that incorporating Maya elements into the liturgy "is not syncretism but an expression of symbolic faith with Maya elements" (Interview 11, 2012). However, the Archdiocese of Yucatán has not made the kind of concerted effort the Diocese of San Cristóbal de las Casas has in this regard. "There are priests that don't speak Maya, there are priests that have not engaged with Maya traditions. We have not given the indigenous what Catholic liturgy and doctrine gives to us. . . . Here in Yucatán it's more traditional" (Interview 23, 2012). Another priest, while acknowledging that he would like to learn Maya, admitted that he has not done so (Interview 63, 2011). Other priests express outright hostility to such an idea:

There is a whole current of thought in academics, in government—a whole current of *indigenista*. . . . They are considered to be of a purity that is superior to decayed Western society. . . . Our great Maya— the marvelous Maya—made human sacrifices, so it's nonsensical to believe that they are pure because they are ancient. . . . There were marvelous things in indigenous cultures but also horrible things, just like in our society. So the first thing is not to fall in *indigenismo*. . . . What I want for them is to be Christians, believe in Christ, and be saved. (Interview 51, 2011)

As a further marker of decentralization in Chiapas, the Church completely decentralized monitoring and sanctioning responsibilities through economic cooperatives. Lay and clerical pastoral workers provided technical assistance and a common decentralized model of local governance. Unlike the Diocese of San Cristóbal de las Casas in Chiapas, the Archdiocese of Yucatán has not promoted similar producer cooperatives. In fact, the hierarchy has actively discouraged such cooperatives, and it has provided no similar initiative throughout the Yucatán peninsula.

The few cooperatives that do exist have formed outside the auspices of the Church. I spoke to one individual who has led an effort to create them. Though devoutly Catholic, he suggested the two largest obstacles to his work have been the government and the institutional Church, both of which have put up impediments to forming economic cooperatives in Yucatán. The people do not have the proper training to run them, and many cooperatives do not have the resources to function properly. Accordingly, the work of forming and sustaining cooperatives has been difficult (Interview 71, 2012). Similarly, a small core of progressive priests operating an agricultural school (Escuela de Agricultura Ecológica) in the southeastern town of Maní encouraged the development of an economic cooperative. However, the archdiocese has actively sought to hinder their efforts by shutting the project down, and it has also succeeded in intimidating priests to abandon the project. Consequently, the focus and impact of the economic cooperative is too localized to have the capacity to link communities and foment a regional political movement. Furthermore, the relatively few cooperatives in Yucatán are small and isolated. They have not been able to produce significant economic benefits for their members (Mattiace 2009, 151–52).

Because the Archdiocese of Yucatán has not decentralized monitoring, sanctioning, and decision-making authority to its laity, it has not provided a platform prompting increased reciprocity, club goods provision, or an organizational infrastructure that can be applied to political activism through the Catholic Church. With regard to reciprocal interactions, there is little solidarity across communities in Yucatán or within the larger municipalities (Interview 8, 2011). Reciprocal networks do not exist. It was common for me to encounter skepticism on the part of interview respondents regarding whether they could count on other members of their communities to cooperate rather than pursue their own individual interests. While there is some degree of solidarity within the smallest villages (Interview 8, 2011; Interview 26, 2011),[5] there is little solidarity in larger communities, and there is also very little solidarity across communities (Interview 8, 2011). Many respondents focused on the egoism of the people in accounting for the lack of civic participation in the peninsula (Interview 25, 2011; Interview 37, 2011; Interview 38, 2011; Interview 48, 2011; Interview 49, 2011; Interview 10, 2011; Interview 70, 2011). As one respondent suggested, "throughout the whole state, we tend to be quarrelsome. We don't know how to work in a team . . . we are a selfish people who do not allow others to grow" (Interview 25, 2011). Such a view expresses little confidence that others can generally be expected to cooperate.

Furthermore, reciprocity does not appear to be a norm. When asked why individuals in Yucatán don't participate civically, one participant stated that the people don't trust each other. When individuals do get into a group, they wonder how others will try to exploit them (Interview 70, 2011). Another interviewee added, "people do not usually get involved. . . . The people . . . are very individualistic and hardly get together to do things for others. There isn't the development of an altruistic spirit that teaches people to collaborate" (Interview 49, 2011). "Many people say 'and why would I help you? Why help.' . . . We are selfish. You look to yourself, your kids, your wife, and your family, but you do not see beyond" (Interview 48, 2011). Finally, one interviewee summed up the attitude of the people as follows: "they only want to receive, receive" (Interview 37, 2011).

The Catholic Church in Yucatán subsequently has provided few material club goods for its members and has not facilitated the emergence of an organizational network. There is, accordingly, little institutional infrastructure to facilitate resource mobilization. Associational activity across the state is highly limited. There are few regional organizations to network individuals across the state and marshal resources for collective action, and "there are no large-scale associations in Yucatán centered on an ethnic identity of 'Maya'" (Cocom 2005, 146). What little organizational activity emerged often developed out of the Mexican state's sanctioned peasant organizations and disintegrated quickly after specific demands were met (Mattiace 2009, 145–46). My interviewees similarly expressed general agreement that there are few organizations across Yucatán (Interview 8, 2011; Interview 26, 2011; Interview 37, 2011; Interview 41, 2012; Interview 48, 2011; Interview 50, 2012). "It's very little—there are very few civic associations here" (Interview 37, 2011).[6]

The Archdiocese of Yucatán has not encouraged the development of decentralized monitoring and sanctioning through cooperatives or through any other analogous institutional mechanism. Cooperatives have not, subsequently, served to entice participation in the production of material club goods. They also have not contributed to reciprocal interactions across the archdiocese or the development of an organizational network. Subsequently, the Catholic Church has not contributed to political activism across the state.

Framing and Protestant Competition

Under Archbishop Manuel Castro Ruiz from 1969 to 1995, the Archdiocese of Yucatán was one of the most conservative dioceses in all of Mexico. It was "dominated by a conservative hierarchy, uninterested and—indeed—openly hostile to the formation of translocal social movements" (Mattiace 2009, 148, 150). However, the archdiocese has pursued a less ideologically conservative course under Archbishop Emilio Carlos Berlie Belaunzarán than what had been pursued under his predecessor. Nevertheless, because this more progressive stance has not also been accompanied by decentralization, political activism has not developed.

While liberation theology never became pronounced throughout the peninsula, framing opportunities did exist to encourage political engagement. The Archdiocese of Yucatán has been slowly marked by increasing encouragement of civic participation and democratic engagement. Over the last fifteen years, there has been a significant expansion of avenues for lay participation through pastoral assemblies.[7] The pastoral plan implements many of the progressive pastoral recommendations made by the Second Vatican Council (Interview 51, 2011). Indeed, the Church in Yucatán has even sought to foster heightened democratic participation through workshops on democracy.

"They recently gave a course over democracy, according to the guidelines of the Church, a workshop on democracy that doesn't have anything to do with political parties but more generally with making sure the people have what they need to develop their criteria and to make a conscious choice, a free choice. . . . It's been difficult because for many years the people have been manipulated" (Interview 11, 2012). As another priest explained, "there is always a message . . . to participate" (Interview 51, 2011).

The diocese has slowly become characterized by what Roderic Camp describes as the "Chihuahua Tendency" where members of the hierarchy advocate for "political rights, electoral integrity, and democratic change" but are not "progressive on other pastoral and spiritual issues" (Camp 1997, 272). Such movement frames certainly have the capacity to promote a great deal of civic engagement, as vast protests and activities in Chihuahua against the PRI political party in the 1980s can attest (Chand 2001, 160–69). However, because this frame has not also been accompanied by decentralization, political activism has not developed.

For example, participation within one parish in Yucatán continues to be bogged down by lay apathy despite efforts to prompt engagement (Interview 63, 2011). The priest, who himself had worked with liberation theologians in the 1970s and 1980s, complained about his attempts to prompt more participation within the pastoral council and to prompt civic engagement more broadly. He has found the laity are generally unwilling to participate. "It is difficult to get people to participate. . . . Sometimes, they say why am I going to say something, or do something, if things are going to be the same. They don't believe in the change" (Interview 63, 2011). At the same time, he mentioned that he makes most of the decisions as to how parish operations will operate. "If you are the priest, you have to decide what to do with everything . . . one of the things the Mayan culture has is to be more submissive. It is a little difficult to make them to awaken and say, 'I'm not in charge but I have to work.'" He has further found the laity are generally unwilling to participate and attributes this reluctance to the years in which laity have lacked a legitimate voice in parish affairs. However, encouraging the laity to participate is not the same as giving it decentralized authority. Without a sustained effort by the archdiocese to the latter, it is difficult to effectively prompt the former.

Furthermore, Yucatán, like Chiapas, has experienced considerable Protestant growth, particularly from the 1970s to the 1990s. In 1970, Protestants made up 3.4 percent of the Yucatecan population. By 1990, they made up 9.3 percent. During that time, Yucatán was second only to Chiapas among Mexican states in gains made among Protestants as a percentage of the population. By the year 2000, Protestants made up 11.4 percent of the Yucatecan population. Only Chiapas (21.9 percent), Campeche (17.9 percent), Quintana Roo (15.7 percent), and Tabasco (18.6 percent) had a higher percentage of Protestants than Yucatán (J. Dow 2005, 830).

The growth is clearly visible to the people of Yucatán: "Lately the sects have grown a lot . . . in the small and poor communities" (Interview 8, 2011). "What used to reign was Catholicism . . . now we have about 15 different Churches and about 7 or 8 different kinds of religions" (Interview 9, 2011). "From about the 1980s until now a mountain of religions have arrived" (Interview 37, 2011). A Baptist minister I spoke with mentioned that "in Yucatán it is clear that the evangelical people continue growing [in numbers]" (Interview 24, 2012).

Catholic clergy gave varied responses to why they believed Protestantism had grown so rapidly. One explanation focused on aggressive attacks on Catholic theology by Protestant religions (Interview 11, 2012; Interview 23, 2012). Other theories implicated the US Nixon administration for sending money to Protestant missionaries to combat the perceived leftist flavor of liberation theology (Interview 22, 2012; Interview 63, 2011; Interview 69, 2011).

However, the most common responses I received tended to note the failure of the Catholic Church to effectively reach people while also emphasizing the ability of Protestant sects to offer *material* club goods and services (Interview 11, 2012; Interview 51, 2011; Interview 63, 2011). As one member of the clergy in Yucatán explained, "I believe there are many factors [for the rise of Protestantism], but the most determinative is the omission of the Catholic Church . . . the ineffectiveness of the Catholic Church that couldn't reach out. What happens is the faith becomes weaker and more fragile" (Interview 51, 2011). Another priest mentioned that "we continue with traditional evangelization that doesn't reach everyone" (Interview 11, 2012). The same priests also noted the ability of Protestant sects to provide goods and services to their members. "There are many things. There are gifts, promises, you go to a poor family and you give them bags of food and clothing . . . they are going to receive something" (Interview 63, 2011). Many respondents pointed to the resources that could be marshaled by Protestant sects and somewhat cynically suggested that these groups were taking advantage of the "ignorance" of the poor (Interview 11, 2012; Interview 51, 2011).

As a result, it is not surprising that the most common response for effectively combating Protestantism was to strengthen evangelization efforts and to build a sense of community. "We created pastoral centers that bring the people together. We also use a little of [Protestant] methods through popular devotion . . . we try to arrive to them through popular devotions. The people like processions, having their images blessed, and having their homes blessed" (Interview 11, 2012).

One priest told me that "the Protestants have their choir, their music and everything," but "the strategy is not to compete against them" (Interview 51, 2011). Instead, remedies to combat threats from Protestantism focused on strengthening outreach programs and building a sense of community. "What we want to bring is formation and communion to the community so that they feel part of the church and part of something, like a family" (Interview 11, 2012).

Furthermore, though Protestant denominations did offer material rewards to members, the Pentecostal denominations in Yucatán may have emphasized spiritual rewards and gifts more than the material rewards that mainline Protestant denominations had modestly offered in Chiapas. Accordingly, the Archdiocese of Yucatán sought to compete with Protestants by offering spiritual rewards rather than material ones. It may have had less incentive to encourage political mobilization due to the particular nature of Protestant competition in Yucatán (Trejo 2009, 340). While Protestant competition causes clergy to reevaluate its commitment to the social needs of the laity, this may not necessarily always take the form of encouraging political advocacy. The degree to which it does is likely highly dependent on a variety of factors, including whether a progressive theology is also present and whether an organizational infrastructure is in place supported by religious decentralization.

In both Chiapas and Yucatán, Protestant competition prompted engagement with Church evangelical practices and strategies to make it more effective. Certainly, the development of Protestant competition prompted a response from the Catholic Church in Yucatán. It became focused on administering to the needs of peasants throughout the countryside. However, though the Catholic hierarchy became more concerned with effectively addressing its flock, this was not sufficient on its own to prompt political activism throughout Yucatán. Protestant competition gives religious elites an incentive to support the social needs of their adherents, but that space must also be accompanied by appropriate framing and resource capacity through decentralization to manifest itself as political activism.

Alternative Explanations

This chapter now considers alternative theories potentially explaining variation in political activism between Chiapas and Yucatán, including the impacts of economic deprivation, political party competition, legacies of Church/state conflict, and ethnic diversity. The analysis suggests that the economic situation for peasants was dire in both states, and that both states also experienced the political opportunity and space necessary for the development of autonomous political movements. Furthermore, the ethnically diverse indigenous populations of Chiapas developed a vibrant political movement, while the ethnically homogeneous indigenous population of Yucatán did not. Accordingly, economic deprivation, political party competition, legacies of Church/state conflict, and ethnic heterogeneity do not explain divergent levels of political activism between Chiapas and Yucatán.

Economic Grievance

Theories of economic deprivation suggest socioeconomic disparities and poverty create frustration, demand for political change, and the development of collective action (Gurr 1970; Snow et al. 1986, 465; Zald 1996, 265). The reader may wonder whether Chiapas suffered economic deprivation while Yucatán did not, creating a demand for sociopolitical change in the former but not the latter. In fact, both states have experienced structural economic hardships for some time, and both faced sudden economic dislocations as a result of neoliberal economic reform. Explanations focusing on grievance subsequently do not explain the patterns of activism we see in Chiapas and Yucatán.

Economic conditions have certainly fostered economic hardship in Chiapas. It ranks toward the bottom of Mexican states in terms of education, household income, infant mortality, and the provision of social services. As of the 1990s, half of the population was malnourished, and nearly 70 percent of the population lived on less than the minimum wage. In the primarily indigenous portions of the state, nearly two-thirds had no indoor plumbing, electrical services, or potable water (G. Collier and Quaratiello 1999, 16; Womack 1999, 11; Manaut, Selee, and Arnson 2006, 135).

One respondent mentioned that before the 1990s, there were few social services available. "[Before 1986] it was difficult to travel . . . and yes, there are still communities . . . that don't have good roads—where there is no light or electricity. There is no potable water" (Interview 4, 2011). Another interviewee stated many regions still lack potable water and concrete floors (Interview 3, 2011). Indigenous communities generally live in conditions of high marginalization (Interview 42, 2011).

By the end of the 1970s, Chiapans were looking elsewhere for economic opportunities, including Cancún and the Mexican Gulf Coast (Rus et al. 2003, 7). The situation was aggravated in the 1980s by refugees from the Guatemalan civil war who underbid Mexican laborers on coffee plantations at rates that even impoverished Chiapans could not compete with (Womack 1999, 21). The debt crisis and the end of agrarian land reform in 1992 presented additional hardships, and the price of coffee plummeted at the end of the 1980s. Small farmers lost up to 70 percent of their income (Womack 1999, 21). The situation was further exacerbated by the 1989 dissolution of the corporatist Mexican Coffee Institute, the government organ responsible for technical, credit, and price stabilization to coffee farmers, as a result of Mexico's neoliberal economic restructuring (Jaffee 2007, 50–51). Farmers lost government support they had grown to rely on when they needed it most.

However, grievance-based accounts explaining the rise of activism in Chiapas as a result of neoliberal restructuring are unsatisfying. Mexican economic restructuring came about nationally as a result of the Latin American debt crisis of the mid-1980s, but we have already seen that indigenous populations organized in protest against the Mexican government in the late 1970s and early 1980s. This activism began before the onset of neoliberal structural adjustment and before the end of Mexican corporatist support of coffee prices in 1989. While economic distress created a great deal of frustration and may have contributed to the popularity of the Zapatista's resort to armed violence in 1994, the indigenous peasants of Chiapas had already mobilized before the onset of neoliberal economic reform and the crash in world coffee prices.

On the other hand, some economic indicators might suggest the situation was better in Yucatán. Its diversified economy is highly ranked among Mexican states in terms of income, employment, and fixed-capital formation (K. Martin and González 2008, 171; Baklanoff 2008, 7–8; B. Turner 2002, 117). Yucatán has been able to capitalize on the explosive development of Cancún by drawing visitors into the interior of the peninsula to see Maya archaeological ruins (Baklanoff 2008, 7–10). Furthermore, Yucatán has been the beneficiary of an "escape valve" of migration from Yucatán to Quintana Roo (Mattiace 2009, 150) as Cancún provided desperately needed jobs and wages in a commutable distance (Diggles 2008, 48; Cruz 2008, 139; Baklanoff 2008, 10–12).

However, the benefits of tourism and economic diversification have not been shared by everyone. Jobs produced in both the tourism and *maquiladora* (sweatshop) sectors are generally marked by "low wages, few benefits or stability, and little opportunity for socio-economic mobility" (K. Martin and González 2008, 165, 171). While tourism flourishes around well-trodden archeological sites such as Chichen Itza, tourists seldom stop at most Yucatecan towns or villages. Most communities see little benefit from the tourist trade (K. Martin and González 2008, 174). One individual I interviewed explained, "if you're in the city there is no need, but if you go outside you will find the reality . . . if you go to the *comisarías* [small towns] or to the ranches you will not find electricity, water, transportation, or telephones . . . the interior is all the same in Yucatán" (Interview 9, 2011).

Furthermore, several statistics suggest the economic situation in Yucatán is dire. In the year 2000, 34.6 percent of the population lived in poverty, ranking Yucatán seventh worst among Mexican states. Of the rural population of Yucatán, 48.4 percent live in poverty, which ranks it fourth worst among Mexican states. Only Chiapas, Oaxaca, and Guerrero suffer worse rural poverty (Székely Pardo et al. 2007, 249, 260). While elements of Yucatecan society certainly have benefited economically from Yucatán's recent economic expansion, poverty remains a serious problem outside urban centers.

Additionally, many Yucatecan laborers, up to 30 and 40 percent of the male population in some communities, commute to Cancún for days and weeks at a time for low-wage positions, leaving behind their families (Heusinkveld 2008, 121, 113). As a respondent from one small village explained: "the majority of the people from here go to the Riviera Maya or Cancún. . . . They only see their family during their day off . . . it's difficult to live like that" (Interview 9, 2011). These patterns put a strain on family life. "Sometimes we see [that the wife here says] 'I cannot take this anymore. Who is going to take care of my children?'" (Interview 63, 2011). The benefits supposedly associated with economic diversification and neoliberal reform have been severely disruptive of traditional village life, offer few possibilities for economic advancement, and have illustrated stark differences in living conditions among economic classes.

Moreover, the dismantling of corporatist economic relationships in Yucatán had profound economic impacts on the region. The production of henequen became an effective instrument for the PRI political party to maintain control throughout the twentieth century. Peasants depended on the PRI for cultivable land, and the party developed peasant leagues that effectively channeled political demands (Diggles 2008, 47). Unfortunately, as synthetic fibers became increasingly available throughout the twentieth century, the international competitiveness of henequen dropped considerably.

Because the PRI's political authority depended on its ability to provide wages through the production of henequen, the Mexican government continued to pour money into the product long after it was no longer a

competitive export. Governmental policy was designed to keep rural peasants loyal to the PRI rather than to respond to external market conditions
(Baklanoff 2008, 6–7), and the Mexican government lost eighty-three cents
on every dollar spent on henequen production (Baños Ramírez 1988, 310).
By the end of the 1970s, Yucatán subsequently became one of the poorest
states in Mexico. It was kept adrift by federal investment in a decaying and
corrupt production system (Moseley and Delpar 2008, 37), but a system on
which peasants were wholly dependent.

Economic crisis forced a retrenchment of Mexico's corporatist political
and economic practices during the 1980s. A huge proportion of the Maya
peasant population relied on the state for its livelihood, but the end of
corporatism sounded the death-knell of their economic support (Mattiace 2009, 144). Throughout the period, subsidies to the region diminished
significantly, the henequen industry was privatized, and land redistribution
was officially ended in 1992 (Mattiace 2009, 145; Diggles 2008, 50; Baklanoff 2008, 7). Over thirty thousand individuals received severance pay
from the Mexican government, while an additional twelve thousand were
forced into early retirement. The traditional economic engine of Yucatán's
economy was thoroughly dismantled (Baklanoff 2008, 7), and the end of
agricultural subsidies discouraged farming (Kray 2005, 339). Despite dramatic economic dislocation as a result of neoliberal economic restructuring, the indigenous populations of Yucatán did not rise up in protest.

As this discussion demonstrates, there was potential for grievance in
both Chiapas and Yucatán. Both states are extraordinarily poor, particularly
within the rural portion of the population. Both states, furthermore, suffered economic dislocation from the rollback of state corporatism. In both
regions, large sectors of the economy that relied on the state for support
collapsed once the state adopted neoliberal economic policies. While these
forces may have contributed to the development of activism in Chiapas,
similar processes have not had the same impact in Yucatán.

Political Opportunities: Political Party Competition

Two related alternative explanations, political party competition and legacies of Church/state interactions, point to the potentially important role
of political opportunities. Political party competition broadens the range
of interests represented in society, creates greater interest in the political system, and itself may be a sign that authoritarian political leaders are
liberalizing their policies. One might surmise that Chiapas experienced
higher political opportunities for activism relative to Yucatán, alternatively

explaining why activism developed there. What we see, however, is that party competition arrived earlier in Yucatán than in Chiapas. Chiapas also experienced several impediments to activism in the form of heavy repression and attempts to co-opt independent organizations.

Throughout the 1990s, the PRI lost a substantial share of municipalities in Chiapas. Though it held 111 localities in 1994, it had lost 46 either to the PRD or the PAN by 2001 (Inclán 2008, 1326). However, as we have already seen, the opening of political activism in Chiapas predated the opening of political party competition in the mid-1990s, and it was not dependent on the opening of political party competition. Independent organizations arose throughout the 1970s, well before the PRI began losing elections in Chiapas during the 1990s.

Civil society also continued in Chiapas despite heavy repression from the Mexican government. The 1980s were particularly treacherous as five independent organizers were assassinated in 1982. There were also violent evictions, dozens of kidnappings, and the destruction of a small town (G. Collier and Quaratiello 1999, 80). Such repression worsened throughout the 1980s under the governorship of Absalón Castellanos Domínguez (G. Collier and Quaratiello 1999, 80). PRI supporters in the northern sections of the state formed paramilitaries to violently reinstitute PRI rule on defecting communities (Womack 1999, 53, 56).

The PRI also withheld social spending from opposition-controlled districts or individuals suspected of supporting opposition parties. Such clientelistic practices in this "punishment regime" were common throughout the Mexican countryside (Magaloni 2006). Individuals who protested these measures were expelled from their communities (G. Collier and Quaratiello 1999, 125, 130; Rus and Collier 2003, 50). At the same time, the PRI political party rewarded its loyal base. As disputes over land became increasingly common, the government initiated a program in the 1980s and 1990s to buy land and distribute it as ejidos. PRI-dominated communities received preferential treatment in receiving this land (Womack 1999, 20–21).

Similarly, President Carlos Salinas came to office in 1988 determined to fold independent organizations into the PRI (Rus and Collier 2003, 48; Harvey 1998, 1). In that spirit, Salinas launched the National Solidarity Program (PRONASOL) and brought $500 million US dollars to Chiapas for social projects and employment opportunities in the early 1990s (Womack 1999, 11; Rus and Collier 2003, 48). To undercut independent organizing, Solidarity only provided funds to local organizations with official ties to the government (Rus and Collier 2003, 49). Organizations were obliged to follow a variety of regulations provided by the state, resulting in the dissolution of many independent productive organizations. Solidarity became a clientelistic mechanism for reinstituting PRI control, particularly in municipalities that were marked by high levels of defection from the PRI party (Rus and Collier 2003, 49; Magaloni and Diaz-Cayeros 2007, 193–202).[8]

The opening of political competition, which began in earnest in the 1990s after independent political activism had already developed in the 1970s, created a stark political climate in Chiapas. The PRI party manipulated the distribution of state resources to loyal party members and municipalities, increasing the costs associated with collective action. As independent organizations arose, they were subjected to repression and co-optation by the government. However, activism continued throughout Chiapas.

As for Yucatán, electoral competition came in the 1960s, much earlier than in Chiapas. The PAN was able to win the mayorship of Mérida as well as seats within the state legislature (Moseley and Delpar 2008, 37; Diggles 2008, 153; B. Turner 2002, 104). While initially isolated, opposition victories by the PAN throughout Yucatán were common by the 1990s (B. Turner 2002, 104). Compared to the rest of Mexico, the political system was relatively open. The PRI corporatist regime generally opted for co-optation rather than repression of political dissidents, creating potential space for citizens to express their grievances (Mattiace 2009, 139). Corporatist PRI resistance did not represent a major impediment to political participation in the region. "The relative absence of ethnic mobilization in Yucatán during these years was not the result of coercive state politics [or] a lack of political opportunities" (Mattiace 2009, 147–48).

On the other hand, increased political competition between the PAN and PRI political parties in Yucatán has had complicated effects on political activism and political participation.[9] In order to gain votes, both parties have developed extensive organizational means to reach deep into the countryside. I interviewed party leaders from the PAN and the PRI who detailed efforts to engage individuals (Interview 52, 2011; Interview 25, 2011). Both parties are strongly active throughout the state and have a great deal of influence, making it difficult for other community organizers to gain the attention of the people (Mattiace 2009, 150).

Conflicts between PAN municipal governments and the PRI state government that ruled Yucatán throughout the 1990s were intense and have created acrimony within communities (Cruz 2008, 140). The PRI made it difficult for opposition-controlled municipalities to obtain federal funding. Additionally, PRI mayors were often accused of favoring established PRI supporters in the distribution of municipal resources (B. Turner 2002, 119). Municipal and state transfers of party control have created problems in the distribution of funds in Yucatán. One former municipal official from the PAN party explained to me his troubles with the PRI state government. "When we were in power, we were PAN. The [PRI state] government didn't send us all of our resources, and it didn't send them on time. When the resources aren't sent on time, a lot of things get held up . . . it's difficult when the governments aren't the same party" (Interview 9, 2011). Such a situation was typical across Mexico (Magaloni 2006).

The resultant back and forth between the parties makes citizens reluctant to participate. They fear they will suffer economic consequences for having publicly supported a political party or for having advocated a political position once parties change power. One interview respondent claimed that municipal authorities have been known to withhold social services and Mexican PROCAMPO agricultural subsidies from individuals who are too critical of local government, political activists, and members of opposing parties (Interview 9, 2011). Another party official mentioned that it is common for new political groups in power to disproportionately dole resources out to their supporters (Interview 10, 2011). In at least one community in Yucatán, the National System for the Integral Development of the Family (DIF), which distributes federal social assistance at the municipal level, has historically served as an instrument for parceling partisan favors and punishing opposition (Interview 49, 2011). In such an environment, it is likely that keeping quiet is the safest economic course for individuals to pursue.

Certainly, political space has existed in Yucatán for the development of political movements. However, citizens must navigate a complicated political situation wherein state governments may withhold federal funds from troublesome municipalities, and municipal officials may withhold federal funds from troublesome individuals. Such considerations have likely played a dampening effect on political activism in the region. However, Chiapas is marked by partisan competition that is at least as acrimonious as it is in Yucatán, if not more so. Despite such divisive partisan feuds, political activism is vibrant in Chiapas. Accordingly, political party competition does not explain divergent levels of political activism between Chiapas and Yucatán.

Political Opportunities: Legacies of Church/State Interactions

Some accounts suggest where there has been a history of Church/state conflict, religious institutions have less space to foster political activism among the laity (Fetzer and Soper 2005; Chand 2001, 160–62). Both Chiapas and Yucatán were located at the periphery of the Cristero Conflict, and both maintain relatively cordial relationships with the Mexican state. As a result, both have space to speak politically. Though the Church in Chiapas has taken advantage of this space to speak out on political matters, the Church in Yucatán has not.

Within Chiapas, there is little oppression by the government against the Catholic Church, and the region was not affected by the fighting of the Cristero War (Meyer 1978, 108–9). We see, as we would expect, that the Catholic Church in Chiapas had space to act politically. While relationships between the Church in Chiapas and the government are respectful and collaborative (Interview 19, 2011), the Church often criticizes the government publicly. One clergy member I spoke with mentioned that "there has always been respect. . . . But yes, there is excess from people in government, and it's denounced" (Interview 46, 2011). Similarly, another Church official also mentioned that "in general there is respect. There are [times] where we relate to the government the necessities that the people have and urge a solution. This is not for political reasons but for the good of the people" (Interview 81, 2011). Indeed, clergy in the Diocese of San Cristóbal de las Casas often critique government policies (Interview 19, 2011).[10] As was demonstrated in the previous chapter, the diocese also played a decisive role in prompting political activism by the laity.

Yucatán has had similar space. However, the Archdiocese of Yucatán has not been as vocal about criticizing the Mexican state. Several priests I spoke with suggested that the relationship between the government and the Church is one of prudential respect (Interview 11, 2012; Interview 23, 2012; Interview 24, 2012). For example, one priest related that relations between the Church and state are "separated, but now there are no confrontations. On the contrary, the Church always looks for the support of civil authorities and politicians for things that the Church cannot finance itself" (Interview 11, 2012).

Priests painted a picture of collaborative exchanges between the Catholic Church and the state. "They give us support for activities, and [the relationship] is close and prudent" (Interview 23, 2012). At the same time, these exchanges tend to be through informal personal networks rather than through formal institutional channels. "There are links, but they are personal and not between institutions. . . . The current municipal president is from the PAN party.[11] . . . He asks advice and I give him a little. Of course he does whatever he wants" (Interview 51, 2011). An official I spoke with from the federal government's welfare arm (DIF) suggests that "we have big connections with the Catholic Church through the Director and me. The two of us work in the Catholic Church here" (Interview 49, 2011).

Despite this apparently cordial relationship, priests in Yucatán are cautious when speaking publicly about politics (Interview 23, 2012; Interview 11, 2012; Interview 51, 2011). This is not because they fear retaliation by the state, but because of the polarized political climate in Yucatán. "You have to be very careful now, because of the elections. The people are very sensitive, and anything you say can offend or be interpreted as favoring a particular party" (Interview 23, 2012). Furthermore, Mexican politicians are not above using priests to gain votes. "During political campaigns, the candidates look for the sympathy of Catholics. . . . For example, in one of the communities I oversee, the Municipal President . . . offered 15 new benches for the Church to gain support for the party before elections. . . . As the majority are Catholics, it's a way to win" (Interview 11, 2012). Another priest stated that "the little chapel that we are making right now—they offered to help the work on it even though I didn't ask for it. I try to keep distance" (Interview 51, 2011). As a result, priests' pronouncements on politics appear to be limited to subtle policy references and toward encouraging political participation generally. One priest explained that he tells his parishioners to "vote for the party that agrees with [their] convictions and conscience" (Interview 11, 2012).

Though some theories suggest religious institutions that have not been marked by Church/state conflict have more room to prompt political activism, such theories appear to do little to explain variation in political activism between Chiapas and Yucatán. There is little conflict between the local governmental authorities and either the Diocese of San Cristóbal de las Casas or the Archdiocese of Yucatán. Mexico's contentious historical relations do not appear to have severely afflicted relations between Church and state in either setting, and neither is marked by a repressive relationship with civil authorities. Despite this space, the Church in Yucatán is hesitant to speak out on political matters and, as demonstrated throughout this chapter, the Church has not prompted political activism by laity.

Ethnic Characteristics

Finally, one might point to differentiation in ethnic characteristics in Chiapas and Yucatán to explain variation in indigenous political activism between the two states. Much literature suggests that ethnic heterogeneity has a negative impact on the provision of public goods (Putnam

2007; Alesina, Baqir, and Easterly 1999; Habyarimana et al. 2007; Baldwin and Huber 2010). Differing ethnicities may not share common tastes for the type of public goods to be provided, they may not have high other-regarding preferences, and monitoring and sanctioning may be difficult in ethnically diverse settings where individuals may not even speak the same language. Accordingly, we might not expect that the seven major ethnic groups in Chiapas, each sharing distinct linguistic and cultural traits (Harvey 1998, 70), effectively collaborated to produce political activism. At the same time, the ethnically homogeneous indigenous population of Yucatán has not produced political activism.

Indigenous populations make up a larger proportion of the overall population in Yucatán than in Chiapas. An indigenous language is spoken by 37.3 percent of the inhabitants of Yucatán, compared to 24.6 percent of Chiapas's inhabitants (CDI 2000). More importantly, and as discussed in the previous chapter, Chiapas's indigenous population is ethnically heterogeneous, while Yucatán's is ethnically homogeneous. Yucatán's primary indigenous language is almost universally spoken among its indigenous population, as over 99 percent of individuals speaking an indigenous language speak ancestral Maya (CDI 2000; Cifuentes and Moctezuma 2006, 212). If common ethnic and linguistic traits produce common preferences or facilitate monitoring and sanctioning, it should be easier for political activism to emerge in Yucatán.

To explain why the indigenous population of Yucatán did not organize around indigenous identity, an argument could be made that ethnic identity was not as developed in Yucatán as it was in Chiapas. Despite continuing traditional customs that are highly differentiated from mestizo society, including maintaining their own distinct language and dress (Mattiace 2009, 142), the indigenous populations in Yucatán generally resist being labeled as Maya and disassociate themselves from the accomplishments of ancient Maya civilizations (Mattiace 2009, 141; Fallaw 1997, 574). Furthermore, many reject the political message of the Zapatistas in Chiapas (as it has evolved after 1994) and do not want to be associated with that movement's political ideology (Castañeda 2004, 38). The reluctance of the Maya in Yucatán to organize as an ethnic identity dates back at least to the attempts of Lázaro Cárdenas to mobilize the region's indigenous population in the 1930s (Fallaw 1997, 574–75).

However, the indigenous populations of Chiapas did not initially organize as an explicitly "indigenous" or ethnic movement either. Throughout the twentieth century, the PRI political party had intentionally sought to downplay ethnic identity across Mexico's indigenous populations, and this had the effect of stifling demands predicated on indigenous identity. The PRI organized separate peasant (CNC) and indigenous (INI) organizations. These bodies were not encouraged to interact or collaborate even though the vast majority of indigenous individuals were also peasants (G. Collier and Quaratiello 1999, 69). While members of the peasant organizations were granted special subsidies, access to equipment, and better access to land reform, the indigenous state-sponsored organizations focused on assimilating the indigenous into mestizo society, offered few rewards for individuals to adopt an indigenous identity, and subsequently "fomented class identity at the expense of ethnic identity" (Eisenstadt 2011, 8). The federal government discouraged collective action between indigenous communities by channeling federal resources through local government, increasing the parochial and isolated nature of individual communities (G. Collier and Quaratiello 1999, 35–36).

Because of the way the PRI had successfully downplayed ethnic identity, when political activism emerged in Chiapas, it was not as a cohesive ethnic movement. As indigenous groups began to mobilize in the 1970s, they advocated for land, health, and education rather than for their rights as an ethnic indigenous minority (G. Collier and Quaratiello 1999, 63). "Community cohesion in the lowlands was given not by strict adherence to native traditions, but by a shared organizational militancy" (Harvey 1998, 64–65). Eisenstadt argues persuasively, for example, that the indigenous of Chiapas are more united by their interests in land reform and their socioeconomic status than by their ethnic heritage (Eisenstadt 2011, 82). The Zapatista rebellion "began primarily as a peasant rebellion, not an exclusively Indian rebellion" (G. Collier and Quaratiello 1999, 7), and the Zapatistas at the onset of the rebellion made no ethnic demands (Eisenstadt 2011, 5).

In short, the movement that emerged in Chiapas was also not ethnic in character. Ethnic demands did come, but not to a large extent until after the Zapatista uprising in 1994. By that point, activism oriented toward achieving peasant demands had been in place for at least twenty years. There is little reason why a similar peasant movement could not have emerged among Yucatán's indigenous population, and it would have been easier to coordinate as it would not have had to traverse many different languages or ethnic customs.

As the previous chapter discussing Chiapas demonstrated, decentralization within the Catholic Church set the stage for the development of political activism across that state's diverse indigenous population. Such decentralization encouraged the production of commonly consumed institutional goods and resources across ethnic boundaries. As the cooperatives in the state expanded, they provided excludable club goods to dozens of indigenous communities, and a common organizational infrastructure emerged across ethnic lines. The effect of this was so powerful that political activism emerged despite the difficulties associated with coordinating collective action across ethnic boundaries.

The analysis provides suggestive, though not explicitly tested, evidence that multiethnic collective action may be strongly facilitated to the degree to which multiple ethnic communities produce commonly consumed excludable club goods. Varshney (2002) similarly finds that strong associational ties can also overcome negative outcomes associated with ethnic diversity. My research points to avenues in which nonstate local institutions might influence ethnic relations, particularly when these institutions encourage the production of commonly consumed club goods and services governed in a decentralized manner and across ethnic identities, and I return to this point in the concluding chapter of this book.

Conclusion

My theoretical approach is embedded in the political process approach where framing, opportunity, and resource mobilization are important to political activism. Both Chiapas and Yucatán experienced opportunities for activism through the Church as a result of intense Protestant competition. Both experienced theological frames encouraging secular political engagement. However, while the previous chapter demonstrated that the Diocese of San Cristóbal de las Casas decentralized authority, this chapter has shown that the Catholic Church in Yucatán is centralized. Laity are given little decision-making, monitoring, or sanctioning responsibilities. Important decisions come from the Church hierarchy, while laity have little substantive decision-making authority. Economic cooperatives are actively discouraged by the Church hierarchy in Yucatán, and no similar provision for producing club goods by the Church has been put in place. As a result, there are few reciprocal interactions among indigenous communities throughout the region, little club goods production, and virtually no organizational base that can serve to mobilize resources across Yucatán.

The chapter assessed a variety of alternative explanations that might explain why political activism was pronounced in Chiapas but not in Yucatán. Both regions experienced economic grievance, rank among the poorest of Mexican states, and suffered severe economic dislocation with the transition to neoliberal economic policies. Furthermore, political party competition was robust in both regions. Additionally, there was severe political repression of independent organizing in Chiapas, and yet these impediments to opportunity still did not prevent Chiapas from engaging in high levels of political activism. Accordingly, theories predicated on grievance and political party competition do not seem to explain political activism across Chiapas and Yucatán.

Moreover, while legacies of Church/state interaction might have impeded political activism in the center of the country, both Chiapas and Yucatán were spared the worst of the Cristero conflict, and both continue to maintain relatively cooperative relations with state officials. Finally, while there is much empirical evidence suggesting ethnically diverse communities have difficulty producing public goods, it was the ethnically heterogeneous communities of Chiapas that developed political activism, while the ethnically homogeneous communities of Yucatán did not. The results of the investigation suggest the character of nonstate institutions can play an important role in circumventing the negative association between ethnicity and public goods provision.

I have examined the impact of religion on political activism in heavily indigenous and historically peripheral areas of Mexico. To assure that nothing specific to these regions drives results of the analysis, the next chapter examines Morelos, a nonindigenous state in central Mexico. Just as in Chiapas, I find that religious decentralization prompted greater levels of reciprocity, club goods production, and the development of an organizational infrastructure that facilitated secular political activism. Morelos provides a further opportunity to examine what happens if a religion recentralizes after decentralization.

SIX

Decentralization and Recentralization in the Diocese of Cuernavaca

[In CEBs, you] meet once a week. . . . [You] sing hymns, read from the Bible . . . you're going to do it on your own—There's not going to be a clergy person there. There won't even be a nun.

(Interview 61, 2012)

In Chiapas, decentralization prompted reciprocity, club goods provision, and the development of an organizational base that could facilitate collective action. We further saw that in Yucatán, the absence of decentralization meant there was little reciprocity, club goods provision, or organizational structure available from the Catholic Church. However, both Chiapas and Yucatán contain large indigenous populations, and the reader may wonder whether any broader insights from that comparison might accordingly be limited. Furthermore, we saw that both Chiapas and Yucatán developed at the periphery of Mexican national politics, and the reader may also wonder whether that may have in some way influenced the processes linking decentralization to political activism. Finally, institutions change. What happens when a formally decentralized religious institution recentralizes its governance structures?

An examination of the Diocese of Cuernavaca, located in the Mexican state of Morelos, provides an opportunity to address these questions. Morelos is the second smallest state in Mexico by land and among the smallest in population. However, it has one of the highest concentrations of independent civic organizations in the country (González Vázquez 2001, 7). A variety of political movements swept across the state beginning in the 1970s. Workers associated with the automobile industry and other industrial sectors organized a vibrant movement that successfully produced independent unions. Teachers' and textile workers' groups also managed to amass tens of thousands of protesters in the early 1980s to denounce economic austerity and to defend social justice. Furthermore, there have been pronounced peasant movements throughout the countryside (Concha Malo et al. 1986, 249; Mackin 1997, 32; González Vázquez 2001, 7), and many observers attribute the growth of civic movements in Cuernavaca to Sergio Méndez Arceo, bishop of the Diocese of Cuernavaca from 1952 to 1982 (Concha Malo et al. 1986, 249; Mackin 1997, 32; González Vázquez 2001, 7; Healy 2008; Videla 1984).

Cuernavaca, Morelos's largest city, is only fifty miles south of Mexico City and near the very center of the nation's political, economic, and cultural power. Unlike Yucatán and Chiapas, Morelos has not developed at the periphery of Mexican politics. It is a state that is "centrally on display" (Videla 1984, 99).[1] Furthermore, and also quite unlike Chiapas and Yucatán, Morelos possesses a small indigenous population (Mackin 1997, 32). Less than 3 percent of the population aged five or over identifies as indigenous, and in Cuernavaca, less than 2 percent of the population does so.[2] This chapter examines Morelos as a shadow case in order to "provide brief points of comparison for the case(s) of primary interest" (Gerring and Cojocaru 2016, 407). By examining a state located near the center of political power and without a large indigenous population, the present chapter demonstrates the mechanisms that linked decentralization to political activism in Chiapas work similarly in a very different setting.

Bishop Sergio Méndez Arceo initiated religious decentralization in Morelos in the 1950s. The Church granted decision-making authority to the laity through Christian base communities (CEBs) that created small Catholic groups of between ten and twenty people. Individuals within these groups conducted their own Bible studies and established their own themes for discussion. The diocese, even before the Second Vatican Council, made a concerted effort to open lines of dialogue to the laity and give them a voice in parish affairs. Monitoring and sanctioning were provided by cooperatives and economic support networks that were created by the Church and its religiously committed lay agents. Moreover, progressive Catholicism created an ideological current encouraging activism, and Protestant competition created an opportunity for activism through the religious institution. Catholic clergy displayed a willingness to break from traditional practices and borrowed from Protestant evangelical techniques to better engage with their adherents, often to the dismay of traditional Catholics.

The Diocese of Cuernavaca is also an intriguing case because it provides an opportunity to examine the consequences of religious *centralization* after decentralization. Following the retirement of Bishop Sergio Méndez Arceo in 1982, the Vatican posted a successive line of conservative bishops in the Diocese of Cuernavaca who have actively worked to recentralize the diocese. Despite their efforts, the decentralized framework of lay activism has remained remarkably intact over thirty years. At the same time, decades of neglect and antagonism by the institutional Church have taken a toll, primarily through the loss of recruitment opportunities offered by the institutional diocese. The result has been a gradual erosion of CEB influence in civic affairs, although they continue to have a strong presence. Finally, this chapter provides an opportunity to discuss the operation of Christian base communities which have had some degree of influence across Latin America.

From Revolution to Acquiescence

Morelos was one of the cradles of the Mexican Revolution (1910–20), and its influence on Mexican popular imagination was so profound that the aforementioned Zapatistas in Chiapas took their name from Emiliano Zapata who led an agrarian revolt from Morelos. He and his followers (the original Zapatistas) promulgated the 1911 Plan de Ayala calling for the redistribution of land from wealthy land owners to peasants. Zapata amassed extraordinary support in launching his insurrection, and Morelos was a hotbed of revolutionary activity (Salinas 2018; Hart 2005, 1). However, Morelos was devastated by the war. By the beginning of the 1920s, its population had contracted by 40 percent. Zapata was assassinated in 1919, and Morelos's peasants looked for a new compromise with the federal government. Perhaps surprisingly, they found a willing partner.

President Alvaro Obregón sought to bring stability to Morelos and initiated a land reform program that expropriated private property and redistributed it to peasants as small, collectively farmed plots of land (ejidos) (Salinas 2018; Hart 2005, 219–20). "In return the local people were staunchly loyal to the federal government . . . by 1927 statistics indicated that Morelos had changed more from agrarian programs than any other state" (Womack 1968, 374). Tensions rose during the 1930s after Plutarco Calles created what would become the PRI and centralized political control. However, further aggressive land reform from President Lázaro Cárdenas during the 1930s eased conflict. The peasants of Morelos (and across Mexico) acquiesced to centralized state authority in exchange for land, credit, patronage, and various forms of federal farming assistance (Salinas 2018; Peña 1981, 105–6; Hart 2005, 230).

By the 1940s, the PRI effectively controlled the countryside. The state created a giant corporatist infrastructure to represent and control the peasantry, and independent organizing outside officially state-sanctioned organizations did not exist. The revolutionary movement was all but dead, having been "institutionalized" and co-opted by the PRI. "The majority joined the political apparatus or kept quiet" (Warman 1980, 192). By the early 1950s, "almost all the Zapatista old-timers passed on . . . the few survivors were mostly too aged for more than a quiet sit in the morning sun . . . between 1946 and 1958 only three strikes formally occurred in Morelos, involving only ninety-four workers" (Womack 1968, 384–85). While Morelos had been at the center of the Mexican Revolution, by the time Bishop Sergio Méndez Arceo arrived to Morelos's Catholic Diocese of Cuernavaca in 1952, there was little to no independent organizing whatsoever. The PRI effectively controlled civil society through its single-party dictatorship, and Morelos was devoid of the framing, opportunity, or resources that might enable political activism.

Decentralization in the Diocese of Cuernavaca

Sergio Méndez Arceo arrived to Cuernavaca as its bishop in 1952. He was conservative, disciplinarian, and marked by authoritarian tendencies during his first several years in the diocese (Mackin 1997, 34–35). Like nearly everywhere else in the Catholic Church, mass occurred in Latin, was recited by the Catholic priest, and was largely inaccessible to most Catholics. Furthermore, before the 1960s, Morelos was by no means a hotbed of political resistance. Instead, the state's economy was dominated by the production of corn, beans, sugar, and white rice, and Cuernavaca was a "sleepy village of only 220,000 inhabitants" (Mackin 1997, 32, 76).

Efforts to make the liturgy more accessible to parishioners began one year before the arrival of Méndez Arceo in 1951 when Benedictine monks experimented with the Spanish mass on a small scale (Mackin 1997, 34–35). One of these monks, Gregorio Lemercier, and another radical priest named Ivan Illich would exert a great deal of influence on Méndez Arceo and the manner in which the Diocese of Cuernavaca operated (Mackin 1997, 35, 39). As a result of these influences, the bishop took the first steps toward decentralizing the diocese in the late 1950s. Like Samuel Ruiz García in Chiapas, Méndez Arceo worked to make the religion more accessible to his parishioners, and mass was revolutionized. Ten years before the Second Vatican Council transitioned the Church to a vernacular mass, the Diocese of Cuernavaca employed a Spanish mass in the 1950s (Mackin 1997, 33–36). Furthermore, innovations were made in the main cathedral. Rather than facing the wall, the altar was moved to face parishioners. Clergy would no longer perform particular liturgical ceremonies with their backs to everyone else as had been common before Méndez Arceo's renovations (Interview 61, 2012).

To further engage his parishioners, Méndez Arceo and his collaborators introduced the "mariachi mass" in the mid-1960s where musical celebrations were performed in popular Mexican styles (Suarez 1970, 23–24). Finally, and perhaps most radically, Méndez Arceo distributed Protestant Bibles to his parishioners so that they could take them home and use them to form their own small Bible study groups (Mackin 1997, 63; Videla 1984, 39). Méndez Arceo, like Samuel Ruiz García, attended the Second Vatican Council. He brought the radical voice of Gregorio Lemercier, and together they sought to drive change at Vatican II (Mackin 1997, 37–38).

Christian base communities (*comunidades eclesiales de base*, or CEBs) are often associated with liberation theology, although they typically were "distinctly modest, nonpolitical, and nonrevolutionary" (Levine 2012, 133). CEBs became prominent fixtures across many Catholic dioceses in Latin America, and they were particularly pronounced in Morelos. These CEBs were small groups, consisting of ten to thirty individuals with a common community or occupational linkage, stressing an association with the institutional Church (Videla 1984, 93; Levine 2012, 132–33). Members met at least once a week in someone's home and discussed the Bible and their shared concerns (Levine 1988, 251). They were encouraged by clergy to reflect on the teachings of the Bible and to develop their own themes for discussion. Indeed, these were largely self-directed, as one of my interview respondents explained:

[In CEBs, you] meet once a week. It doesn't have to be Saturday or Sundays. It could be on Tuesdays if you want. You could . . . have it at one family's house one week, and then do it someplace else. [You] sing hymns, read from the Bible . . . you're going to do it on your own—There's not going to be a clergy person there. There won't even be a nun. (Interview 61, 2012)

Accordingly, the role of priests within these communities changed. They transitioned from an authoritative role that imparted theological doctrine to an "advisory" role that encouraged autonomous religious reflection by the laity (Videla 1984, 98). In meetings with clergy and even with the bishop (outside of mass), parishioners were allowed to set the agenda for discussion (Videla 1984, 97). In this way, CEBs were a substantial break from the traditional and hierarchical form of Church control as they "underscored equal access to knowledge (through the Bible) and equal participation in managing group affairs" (Levine 2012, 134).

Though small communities of believers had been studying the Bible on their own in Cuernavaca since the early 1960s, the diocese formally introduced CEBs in 1966, two years before the Second Latin American Episcopal Conference (CELAM II) endorsed them. While many of these groups would eventually become politicized, "the groups that were started in Cuernavaca were [initially] not very political" (Mackin 1997, 63). They were formed to strengthen religious communities rather than to become igniters of political activism (Levine 1988, 255).

Somewhat differently from Chiapas, Méndez Arceo did not create permanent deacons in Cuernavaca. While the Chiapan deaconate program developed during the 1970s, Méndez Arceo was nearing his mandatory 1982 retirement, and his focus was on shoring up the innovations he had made in the face of a likely conservative successor. Still, the Diocese of Cuernavaca and one of its clergy, Ivan Illich, provided a major ideological impetus for the deaconate program as it would come to be practiced across Latin America (Suarez 1970, 151–54). Illich had a radical idea for the future of the deaconate and for the nature of the clergy of the Church. "The priest of the future . . . will be a member of the laity ordained for the ministry, and the ministry will be exercised in an individual's free time rather than as a job. The deaconate will be the primary institutional unit of the Church, planted within the parish. I hope that the Church will weaken as an institutional social force" (Suarez 1970, 151).[3] Though Méndez Arceo did not have sufficient time to develop his own deaconate program, his diocese was one of its birthplaces.

The CEBs, on the other hand, grew dramatically. By the middle of the 1970s, more than seven hundred were scattered throughout the diocese. Political analysis came gradually and centered on the perspective of the poor. "The key to this new mode by the Church is that the base Christian groups use their own resources and organization to solve their problems. They exchange their own experiences and feelings over reality. They help each other mutually and mitigate the sensation of economic, social, and political insecurity that each member of society suffers" (Videla 1984, 94).

As the previous quote suggests, a key focus of the CEBs was on the "*lucha para la vivencia*," the fight for a living (Interview 7, 2012). As in Chiapas, religiously committed laity created a wide range of cooperatives that were embedded directly within the CEBs. These groups were designed to aid in the economic development and sustenance of CEB members, and they included savings, consumer, and production cooperatives (Interview 7, 2012). They were predicated on mutual responsibility and reciprocity. Their small size facilitated monitoring and sanctioning. According to Bishop Arceo, "the key to this new mode of doing Church is that the grassroots Christian groups depend on their own resources and organization to solve their own problems" (Videla 1984, 94). The groups gave excludable benefits to their members as they worked to achieve specific economic ends. "It gives a benefit to our families when we sell our products—it's something else that helps to sell the products" (Interview 7, 2012). Within these community groups, cooperative members shared among themselves, but the fruit of the labor was restricted to contributors (Interview 7, 2012).

The consumer cooperatives in Morelos were similarly dependent on reciprocity. In one such cooperative arrangement, families rotated monthly to make bulk purchases at better prices benefiting the community. One family would pay a substantial amount of money one month to provide basic consumer goods for members and then would benefit in subsequent months as other families did the same (Interview 7, 2012). Like rotating credit associations, these cooperative groups were seemingly susceptible to opportunism by families who could "defect" by taking advantage of those families who had made previous purchases and defaulting on their obligations to make purchases once their turn came. The fact that families were willing, however, to stake relatively large sums of money spoke to the confidence that members had in other members of the CEBs that their contributions would not be exploited (Hechter 1987, 107–11; Putnam 1993, 168–69; Vélez-Ibañez 1983; Interview 7, 2012).

Similar economic cooperatives were common in decentralized Christian base communities throughout Central and South America (Levine 1988, 253). The CEBs prompted a wide range of common cooperative economic endeavors across Latin America. "The federation of peasant cooperatives in Paraguay, . . . soup kitchens in Chile, various groups of popular education in Peru, or committees for the defense of peasants in the northeast of

Brazil have been born from these [Christian base] communities, through the reflection of the lessons and values of the Bible" (Videla 1984, 99).

Within Cuernavaca and throughout many other locations in Latin America

> the people come together and in most cases work cooperatively to remedy problems, obtain services and accumulate resources . . . over and over again [there is] discussion of how people got together to build schools and houses and clinics, gather funds to support teachers and nurses, established production and consumer cooperatives . . . [these topics] were obviously of greatest interest to the members of the CEBs as they dealt with very concrete matters which made a big difference in how they lived. In this sense the people in the CEBs are promoting their own development at the grassroots and this is all the more important because of the general absence of this tradition of self-help in most regions of Latin America. (Bruneau 1980, 542)

Political Activism in Cuernavaca

The CEBs directly contributed to the political activism that emerged in Cuernavaca in the 1970s (Mackin 2003, 508; Videla 1984, 22; Concha Malo et al. 1986). In 1969, the Union Training Center in the State of Morelos (*Centro de Formación Sindical en el Estado de Morelos*—CEFOSEM) was formed by independent organizers with the support of the Catholic Church (Mackin 1997, 79). This organization consisted of a coordinated movement by workers in Cuernavaca's automotive and industrial sectors to challenge the corrupt union structure embedded within the Mexican state. Its members sought to form their own democratically elected union leadership. Importantly, CEFOSEM grew from the Christian base communities. Much of its leadership came from members of these Catholic groups (Healy 2008, 51–52), and the mode of instruction within CEFOSEM was predicated on the "See-Judge-Act" methodology common to CEBs (Mackin 2003, 506–7). This methodology encouraged analysis and action and was utilized throughout Latin American Christian base communities as a strategy to "see in the most objective way possible; to judge events in the light of the gospel, and to act in consequence" (Hartch 2014, 132).

The development of the independent labor movement in Morelos also illustrates the potential of religious decentralization to create unanticipated political consequences. Though he was actively involved in the liberation theology movement (Videla 1984, 24), Méndez Arceo was still considered at the turn of the 1970s to be something of a friend to big business. The bishop saw himself as an intermediary between workers and industrialists (Mackin 2003, 508), and he had been known to critique the work ethic of laborers. One quote from the bishop speaking to the organizers of the CEFOSEM school is telling: "Yes, go ahead. Struggle to get a better salary. But also, do your duties as workers because I know you are lazy and irresponsible. You break the machines" (Healy 2008, 52).

As a result, independent organizers in the labor sector, despite having developed in the CEBs, lacked confidence that the bishop sided with them. After Bishop Méndez Arceo spoke with striking textile workers, for example, laborers responded skeptically that he was only trying to get them to go back to work (Interview 61, 2012). He was challenged, by the same organizations that religious decentralization had helped to spawn, to spend more time with the workers and to get to know their point of view (Interview 61, 2012; Healy 2008, 52). It was only after doing so that Méndez Arceo eventually came to give the diocese's unconditional support to the independent labor movement (Mackin 2003, 508). The bishop had set the seeds for his own radicalization unintentionally by enabling the political activism of his laity through religious decentralization.

As the 1970s continued, CEFOSEM became a powerful force demanding workers' rights through strikes and marches. The labor movement found political support through the network of CEBs. These CEBs provided food and moral support to strikers, collected donations, and spread information about the workers' cause (Healy 2008, 52). Perhaps most striking is the fact that many of these CEB members were not themselves auto workers. "Many communities [CEBs] were linked to the workers' struggle from the outset, and their presence in strikes and rallies was considerable: 'we see them on guard during strikes, we see them in marches, in rallies, in the various activities of the organization. . . . They are always helping, supporting, and driving the fight'" (Puertas 2015, 175). By 1976, however, the state, its official unions, and local law enforcement had organized a repressive response to the movement. The subsequent dispersing of marches, disruption of organizational networks, and blacklisting of organized laborers forced many out of Cuernavaca to seek work and eventually quelled the labor movement (Healy 2008, 63; Mackin 1997, 83). While the movement was stifled by the end of the decade, it successfully managed to remove the state-sponsored union in exchange for an independent and democratic one (Mackin 1997, 83).

Such political movements were not limited to the industrial sectors. By the end of the 1970s and 1980s, textile workers' and teachers' movements mobilized to become significant political forces in the region. They organized hunger strikes and marches forty thousand strong in Cuernavaca's central square in 1981. By 1982, the movement had grown to include protests against Mexico's economic crisis and austerity policies (Healy 2008, 63–64). Just as in the case of the industrial and auto workers, CEBs played critical supporting roles to these movements by providing the organizational and social base of their support and by providing willing participants to protest (Concha Malo et al. 1986, 249–51). They played similarly important roles in community development and peasant groups (Concha Malo et al. 1986, 251–56). For example, peasant CEB members were directly responsible for the formation of the Morelos Peoples' Union that successfully prevented the expropriation by the state of land for an airport (Puertas 2015, 176). Additionally, these communities also received political refugees from South and Central America during the political tumult of the 1970s and 1980s. One organization I spoke with formed from the CEBs to educate the people about international problems (Interview 15, 2012), and the CEBs are also active in environmental issues (Interview 14, 2012).

Political Theology and Protestant Competition

As discussed throughout this book, organizational potential alone is not sufficient to prompt a political movement. Activism also requires appropriate framing and opportunity. Within the religious realm, framing involves the development of a political theology that actively encourages engagement with political concerns. Not only was Sergio Méndez Arceo an adherent of liberation theology, he was one of the early innovators of the movement. The antecedents for Méndez Arceo's advocacy of progressive Catholicism were established with his interactions with a Benedictine monk named Gregorio Lemercier. One year before Méndez Arceo's arrival to Cuernavaca, Lemercier had already experimented with liturgical changes, including conducting mass in Spanish. Arceo arrived with an authoritarian and conservative mindset, but Lemercier influenced his thinking. Furthermore, Arceo eventually participated in the Second Vatican Council where he interacted with other progressive clergy from Latin America and Europe, and he himself was a reformist force. For example, he served on the committee that recommended mass be conducted in vernacular languages (Mackin 1997, 33–52).

Méndez Arceo also sponsored the Intercultural Documentation Center

(CIDOC) in Cuernavaca run by Ivan Illich. The CIDOC regularly invited thinkers associated with liberation theology to speak and give seminars throughout the 1960s, and "Cuernavaca was put on the map as a place to go to get the latest thinking in the liberation theology movement" (Mackin 1997, 59). Additionally, Méndez Arceo attended the Council of Latin American Bishops (CELAM) meeting in 1968 in Medellín, Colombia. Because it was poorly attended by Latin American bishops, the council was dominated by progressive clergy. As a result, the conference produced ambitious progressive goals for the Latin American Church, declaring that social institutions can create "structural sin" and that the Church would adopt a "preferential option for the poor" (Mackin 1997, 66–67).[4]

Sergio Méndez Arceo was at the forefront of liberation theology. He instituted many of the reforms recommended by the Second Vatican Council before it took place. He was, in fact, an architect of some of those reforms. His sponsorship of the CIDOC and the work of Ivan Illich put Cuernavaca at the center of the liberation theology movement, and he attended the CELAM conference in Medellín where the Latin American Church elaborated its preferential option for the poor. These ideas were disseminated throughout the Diocese of Cuernavaca and clearly had an impact on the trajectory of political activism as activists utilized the "See-Judge-Act" methodology promoted by the Christian base communities.

At this point, readers may note the importance of individual leadership in prompting changes in both the Diocese of Cuernavaca under Bishop Méndez Arceo and in our previous discussion of Bishop Samuel Ruíz. Weber suggested charismatic leaders provide followers with the courage to overcome the limits of everyday existence through an emotional release associated with following their leadership (T. Dow 1978, 83–84). Certainly, as noted earlier in this book, charismatic clergy can play an important role as "political entrepreneurs" by coordinating their adherents' interests around particular goals (Taylor 1990, 234; Popkin 1988, 20; Hall 1986, 276–80; Djupe and Gilbert 2006, 119). In this way, they importantly develop and disseminate ideological frames essential to collective action.

Furthermore, the Diocese of Cuernavaca experienced a religious opportunity for activism as a result of Protestant competition. Competition has prompted a break with traditional practices and informed some of the strategies Méndez Arceo took on to evangelize his laity. Protestantism has made inroads throughout the diocese since the 1950s, and it has grown at an annual rate of just over 6 percent between 1970 and the year 2000 (J. Dow 2005, 830).

Like Protestant missionaries, the Catholic Church in Cuernavaca began ministering to its parishioners in their own language. CEBs took on Bible study in small groups, a popular Protestant evangelical practice. The bishop also received special permission from the Vatican to distribute *Protestant* Bibles as the Catholic Church did not have sufficient numbers to distribute to the CEBs (Mackin 2003, 505). By the end of Méndez Arceo's tenure as the Bishop of Cuernavaca, the diocese had distributed more than seventy thousand Bibles across five hundred small communities and Bible study groups (Videla 1984, 79).

As in both Chiapas and Yucatán, the existence of Protestant competition created urgency within the Catholic Church to change its pastoral practices. It aggressively mimicked Protestant forms of evangelization and, in doing so, also brought on the ire of "the more traditional and rural sectors of the diocese with his wide-ranging reforms to the liturgy and cathedral in the late 1950s and 1960s" (Mackin 2003, 506). The Catholic Church renewed the terms of its relationship with impoverished laity and made the Church more accessible to them. It was open to change and to changing its relationship with its traditional allies. When combined with the precepts of liberation theology along with the mobilization potential afforded by diocesan decentralization, the result was a vibrant movement of political activism.

Retrenchment

John Paul II took on the mantle of pope in 1978 and sided with conservatives within the Vatican who believed that liberation theology needed to be reined in (Levine 1988, 254; Levine 1995). Although bishops were often given special permission to continue at their posts past the age of seventy-five, the Vatican informed Méndez Arceo he would not be permitted to remain as Bishop of Cuernavaca (Mackin 1997, 96–97). The bishop and his supporters subsequently made the CEBs as independent as possible from the institutional Church. They gained funds from foreign lenders to develop an organizational headquarters centered in Cuernavaca that would continue to coordinate and support the development of the CEBs throughout Morelos (Mackin 1997, 95). These measures proved necessary.

Méndez Arceo correctly perceived that his successor would enact a retrenchment of his initiatives, and indeed the next Bishop of Cuernavaca, Juan Jesus Posadas Ocampo, recentralized the authority of the hierarchical Catholic Church. "There came, as a strategy of the Vatican . . . a bishop who was very reactionary—that came to break the structure that Don Sergio had generated" (Interview 7, 2012). "The new bishops have done everything possible to revert what Méndez Arceo did" (Interview 61, 2012). The bishop slowly and quietly reassigned progressive priests while bringing in conservative priests. He closed Sergio Méndez Arceo's seminary, cancelled the diocese's monthly meetings with laity, and criticized the independently organized CEBs for being divisive and political. The diocese also sought to ignore and isolate the CEBs from the institutional Church hierarchy (Mackin 1997, 98–104; Interview 7, 2012).

In some respects, however, the conservative hierarchy's strategy was ineffective. Immediately upon Méndez Arceo's retirement, the CEBs enacted a massive independent membership drive that swelled their ranks from seven hundred to over nine hundred groups (Mackin 1997, 104). By the end of the 1980s, the diocese and the CEBs had developed their own modus vivendi. The diocese was content to marginalize and isolate the CEBs away from the institutional Church, and the CEBs viewed themselves as independent of it (Mackin 1997, 104–5). The CEBs have continued supporting independent political movements in Morelos. They are actively involved in human rights and they contribute to a wide variety of social movements (Mackin 1997, 83; Interview 7, 2012; Interview 14, 2012; Interview 61, 2012).[5]

At the same time, the passage of time has slowly diminished their impact, and the withdrawal of formal Church support can make it more difficult for CEBs to recruit members (Levine 2012, 132). Years of neglect by the institutional Church, the inevitable aging of original CEB membership, and the passing of Méndez Arceo in 1992 have taken a toll on their effectiveness. "There is still a network, but it's not what it once was. They continue pretty much on their own, without much, or any, support from the diocese" (Interview 61, 2012). "There are fewer communities. Many [CEBs] work at the margins of their parishes. The priests didn't want them. It had passed from style" (Interview 7, 2012).

A CEB organizer I spoke with mentioned that civic associations in Cuernavaca are now increasingly dominated by political parties or businesses. My own (nonrepresentative) interviews suggest that current associations in Cuernavaca tend to be spearheaded by expatriates from other countries with paid Mexican staff (Interview 47, 2012; Interview 6, 2012; Interview 58, 2012; Interview 59, 2012), run by economically well-off retirees (Interview 35, 2012), or receive government funds (Interview 34, 2011; Interview 60, 2012). At the same time, several of the groups I spoke with had either developed directly from the CEBs or were supported in their political goals by them (Interview 15, 2012; Interview 7, 2012). Though they have diminished, they are still a pronounced political presence in Morelos.

Conclusion

This chapter has examined the Diocese of Cuernavaca located in the Mexican state of Morelos. In contrast to Chiapas and Yucatán, only a small proportion of Morelos's population is indigenous, and Morelos has developed almost literally in the shadow of Mexico City, the political and economic center of the country. I find that the mechanisms of political activism operate very similarly to how they operated in Chiapas. The Catholic Church in Morelos decentralized governance by making mass more accessible to adherents, giving adherents increased decision-making capacities, and decentralizing monitoring and sanctioning responsibilities through Christian base communities that produced economic goods and services for members. The infrastructure created by these CEBs was directly lent to workers', teachers', and peasant movements across Morelos to support political activism. Morelos similarly experienced a liberation theology frame that helped coordinate activity, and, like Chiapas, it experienced high levels of Protestant competition that created an opportunity for activism through the religious institution.

Morelos is also interesting because it recentralized following religious decentralization. We see that decentralization creates the development of an organizational infrastructure in which governance responsibilities belong to the laity. Because of this, if the religion decides to recentralize control, this organizational base, to some degree, is insulated from such a decision. An organizational base has already developed organically that is capable of operating independent of whether religious elites in the religious institution want it there or not. A similar result was observed by Stathis Kalyvas when he noted the Catholic hierarchy's failed attempts to rein in the development of Christian Democratic parties after the Church had mobilized Catholic adherents to protect itself from liberal attack (Kalyvas 1996).

However, this is not to say the organizational infrastructure is not negatively impacted if clergy decide to recentralize and break ties with the institutions that developed out of decentralization. Though the organizations survived and even thrived for a time after the institutional diocese abandoned liberation theology, the institutions slowly lost opportunities for recruitment through the Church, and almost certainly the loss of legitimacy bestowed by the hierarchical clergy closed the willingness of some of the community in Cuernavaca to view these organizations as working on behalf of representative Catholic interests. Without it, though they remain active, the independent political organizations spawned by diocesan decentralization have slowly lost their effectiveness. While they remain active, they are composed of increasingly older individuals and experience difficulty replenishing their ranks.

SEVEN

Wider Reflections on Religion and Grassroots Collective Action

We need to participate for the common good. Sometimes we hear:
a good Catholic is not interested in politics. This is not true: good
Catholics immerse themselves in politics.

Pope Francis, September 16, 2013

A religious community . . . should take a clear stand against
oppression and injustice and should strive to change the situation
without engaging in partisan conflicts.

Thich Nhat Hanh, *Interbeing:*
Fourteen Guidelines for Engaged Buddhism

Come forward as servants of Islam, organize the people
economically, socially, educationally, and politically and I am sure
that you will be a power that will be accepted by everybody.

Muhammad Ali Jinnah

Traditional, naïve, and popular accounts might suggest certain types of
religious traditions, such as Protestantism, aid the development of political
activism while others, such as Catholicism or Buddhism, inhibit it (Weber
1930; Lipset 1959, 92–93; Huntington 1993; Clark, Golder, and Golder
2012, 221–27). Catholicism may have been seen as incompatible with
political engagement in nineteenth-century Europe, but it was a powerful force for political change in mid-twentieth-century Latin America and
Eastern Europe. Though Buddhism has buttressed authoritarian regimes

in South Korea and China, it has been at the center of democratic resistance in Myanmar, Tibet, and Thailand. Finally, while Muslims across Western Europe have had difficulty politically organizing and pressing demands from European states, Islam has engendered massive political movements and democratic agitation across the Middle East. Each of these religious traditions has inhibited political activism, but each has also enabled it. To understand the relationship between religion and political activism, it is not sufficient to look for differences between broad religious traditions. We must understand why the same religious institution might facilitate secular political participation in one setting but not in another.

To explain these differences, this book has advanced a theory of religious decentralization. Where religious institutions are characterized by decentralized monitoring, sanctioning, and decision-making, they are capable of facilitating grassroots political activism. Though my explanation is derived from a rational choice institutionalist approach, I understand collective action is also most likely when religious institutions produce a coordinating theological frame, when structural conditions created by religious competition encourage religious elites to support political activism, and when decentralized institutional structures allow religious institutions to develop organizational capacities necessary for collective action. Accordingly, my approach is nestled within a broader framework that takes the political process approach to understanding collective action seriously.

In elaborating my argument, this book speaks to a number of literatures in political science, sociology, and economics, and it provides a broad framework for combining insights from both the political process and rational choice approaches to understanding collective action. It also provides a general theory applicable to many types of local institutions and explains how communities can develop capacities for collective action at the grassroots. Finally, it gives us some tentative insight into the complex relationship between ethnic diversity and collective action.

Within this concluding chapter, I provide a brief summary of the findings of my study. Decentralization is generally associated with individual propensities for political activism across Mexico, and I also found decentralization led to greater reciprocity, club goods production, and to the development of an organizational infrastructure facilitating political engagement in Chiapas and Morelos. In Yucatán, on the other hand, the absence of decentralization meant this causal chain did not develop. I furthermore found evidence that political theology and religious competition are associated with political activism, and that they both reinforce religious decentralization's impact on political activism. Combining the rational choice and political process approaches to understanding collective action provides insight into how variation in frames, opportunity, and resource mobilization enables collective action. Finally, I discuss the implications of the study and potential avenues for future research. My theoretical framework is applicable to religious institutions beyond Roman Catholicism, the study of local voluntary associations more generally, and it provides some suggestive understanding of the relationship between ethnic diversity and public goods provision.

Religious Institutions and Collective Action in Mexico

I took a two-pronged and multimethod approach to understanding the relationship between religious institutions and collective action, and I did so utilizing both quantitative statistical analyses and qualitative case studies. Quantitative analyses are useful for examining general associations between two variables, while qualitative analyses help us understand how those two variables are linked to each other. I hypothesized adherents residing within decentralized religious institutions would generally be associated with increased propensities for engaging in political activism. Decentralized institutions better reflect the agenda of individuals at the grassroots and also allow for more efficient monitoring and sanctioning. As a result, adherents have more confidence their personal contributions will be reciprocated by others, and they make increasing contributions to the religious institution. Because more individuals pour their own resources into the institution, the value of the club goods it can offer to its adherents grow. This prompts a feedback cycle of greater involvement and increasingly valuable club goods, and the organizational framework and heuristic norms of reciprocal cooperation emerge that can buttress political activism. I further hypothesized that a framing politicized religious theology and religious competition prompting opportunity should also be positively associated with political activism. Finally, I considered alternative explanations and hypothesized economic deprivation, political party competition, legacies of Church and state conflict, and ethnic diversity might each share some type of relationship with political activism across Mexico.

I tested these hypotheses statistically using nationally representative individual-level survey data drawn from the Mexican National Survey of Political Culture and Citizen Practices, and I added data from a variety of additional sources detailing the demographic characteristics of Mexican citizens and institutional characteristics of the Catholic Church. Collectively, the statistical models give strong support for the contention that framing, opportunity, and resource mobilization affect political activism. I found religious decentralization, political theology, and religious competition were each positively associated with individuals' political activism across Mexico. Moreover, the positive impact of religious decentralization on political activism was significantly increased to the degree it was accompanied by exposure to political theology, suggesting the effect of an organizational infrastructure facilitating political activism is increased when it is accompanied by a coordinating political theology. Religious competition also strengthened religious decentralization's impact on political activism. On the other hand, I found little support across my statistical models for any influence between political party competition or ethnic heterogeneity with political activism, and only limited support for the influence of ethnic deprivation and legacies of Church/state conflict.

As for my qualitative comparison, I found the Catholic Diocese of San Cristóbal de las Casas in Chiapas decentralized decision-making by creating pastoral assemblies, translating the Bible into indigenous languages, incorporating indigenous customs into mass, and allowing indigenous individuals to reinterpret passages of the Bible to fit their own socioeconomic contexts. Furthermore, it created hundreds of indigenous permanent deacons and catechists who took on sacramental roles within the Catholic Church and who also formed economic cooperatives. The management of these economic cooperatives, including coffee cooperatives, was completely decentralized. Monitoring was undertaken by adherents themselves through means such as quotas, the direct supervision of work as individuals went about their daily tasks, and membership dues. Individuals who did not contribute were excluded (sanctioned) from the goods and services produced by the cooperatives.

Decentralization in turn prompted reciprocal interactions. Though the indigenous communities scattered throughout Chiapas had previously been characterized by low levels of interaction, decentralized management opportunities brought indigenous communities together in unprecedented ways. Intercommunal cooperatives expanded dramatically, increasing the ability of cooperatives to provide goods and services for their members. The cooperatives became economic engines of their communities, often through the production of coffee. The organizational infrastructure that developed from these Catholic cooperatives was directly supplied to political activism. Within Chiapas, we also saw the important impact of framing. Liberation theology advocated that the Church adopt a preferential option for the poor, and it also helped laity throughout the diocese to develop an "insurgent consciousness" by framing their socioeconomic status as an injustice and letting them know it was possible to change it. Such efforts helped to coordinate efforts across the diocese and created a demand for change. Protestant competition, furthermore, gave Catholic leadership an incentive to move the Church away from its traditional alliances with political and economic elites and to be more attentive to the majority of its adherents.

On the other hand, we saw that there was little decentralization in the Archdiocese of Yucatán, and clergy maintained final decision-making authority. There was also little lay responsibility for monitoring or sanctioning. There were very few cooperatives, nor were there any analogous efforts by the Church to provide goods and services to members of the laity. The result was few reciprocal interactions across the Archdiocese, few club goods produced by the religious institution, and little organizational capacity for political activism. Though liberation theology was never as influential in Yucatán as it was in Chiapas, the Archdiocese of Yucatán was slowly marked, much like the rest of the Mexican Church, by growing engagement with democratic reform and political participation. This frame has shown the potential to create powerful political activism through the Catholic Church in other regions of Mexico, but it did not produce such engagement in Yucatán. Protestant competition was also pronounced and clearly prompted changes in the evangelization strategies of the Catholic Church, creating a potential opening for the Church to support political activism. However, these forces have not developed political activism. The resource capacity for activism has not been built through decentralization at the grassroots level.

Furthermore, my shadow case of Morelos (the Catholic Diocese of Cuernavaca) demonstrated that the same processes connecting decentralization to political activism in Chiapas also functioned in a different region of Mexico. While Chiapas is a heavily indigenous state that developed at the periphery of Mexican national politics, Morelos is centrally located with a relatively small indigenous population. Within the Diocese of Cuernavaca, we saw decentralization through innovations to the liturgy and Christian base communities (CEBs). The CEBs grew rapidly and were also largely responsible for the development of economic cooperatives throughout Morelos. These cooperatives, like those in Chiapas, were completely managed by the laity and were direct mobilizers of political activism that emerged in Morelos beginning in the 1970s and 1980s in the automobile, labor, teachers', and peasant movements. Morelos is also interesting because the Church recentralized following decentralization and cut ties with the CEBs. Though they continued to thrive for some time, decades of neglect from the institutional Church have slowly eroded the effectiveness of the CEBs.

The study likewise examined the influence of several alternative explanations. Both the rational choice and political process approaches to collective action share some degree of skepticism that economic deprivation automatically prompts political activism, and the results of this analysis do little to suggest otherwise. Economic grievance does not appear to explain differences in political activism between Chiapas and Yucatán. Both experienced rural poverty, and both were also harshly affected by neoliberal reform. While political activism emerged in Chiapas, economic grievance was not sufficient to prompt collective action in Yucatán. The statistical analysis, furthermore, offered only limited evidence that economic grievance is associated with individual propensities for political activism. It is not typically associated with political activism across the majority of the statistical models presented in the appendix, although it did have associations in some models in the expected direction.

Political party competition is an important marker of whether there are open political opportunities for political activism. This is particularly true in the Mexican political context as the PRI slowly saw its electoral dominance erode across Mexico during the 1980s, 1990s, and into the twenty-first century. Yucatán, for its part, had a relatively open political party system, and party competition came to the state early. Vibrant political activism also emerged in Chiapas despite high levels of violent repression. Much like the statistical analysis assessing the relationship between political party competition and political activism across Mexico, I find political party competition does not explain variation in political activism between Chiapas and Yucatán. The qualitative comparison provides some suggestive evidence, though, as to why there was no significant relationship in the statistical models. Openings of political party competition in Yucatán may have incentivized victorious political parties to punish independent activists or individuals allied with opposing political parties, particularly by restricting access to state welfare programs. While political party competition may encourage political activism in some settings by creating new avenues for disenfranchised sectors of society to articulate their interests, it may discourage activism in others when victorious parties withhold state funds from individuals and municipalities in an effort to punish political competitors.

Additionally, where there is a history of contentious relationships between the Church and the state, religious elites may not have a great deal of space to mobilize political activism. Mexico was marked by armed conflict between supporters of the Catholic Church and the Mexican state during the early part of the twentieth century. This conflict was more pronounced in the center of the country, and some observers suggest there was less space for the Church to spur collective action in the geographic center than at the periphery of Mexico. Both Chiapas and Yucatán, for their parts, developed at the periphery of Mexican national politics, and neither suffered the ravages of the Cristero War. Both maintain cordial relations with the Mexican state. The Catholic Church in Chiapas has shown more of a willingness to be critical of the government than has the Church in Yucatán. In neither instance, however, can such a difference be attributed to historical legacies of Church/state interactions. The quantitative analysis provided only very weak support for the proposition that the legacy of the Cristero War is associated with political activism, and the qualitative comparison does little to bolster support for it.

Finally, numerous empirical studies suggest there is a negative relationship between ethnically diverse communities and their capacities to coordinate collective action. Yet Chiapas, a region with many indigenous languages and indigenous cultural identities, managed to foment a vibrant movement of political activism. In ethnically homogeneous Yucatán, on the other hand, collective action has not emerged. The results mirror those of the quantitative comparison across Mexico which also failed to find a relationship between ethnic heterogeneity and political activism, and I return to the implications of my finding for the study of ethnic diversity and public goods provision below.

Broader Implications and Avenues for Future Study

While this study informs our understanding of the relationship between the Catholic Church and political activism in Mexico, its theoretical and empirical implications are broader. Theoretically, I provide a framework for combining political process and rational choice approaches to collective action, insight into how nonstate institutions more generally prompt political activism, and suggestive clues as to how nonstate and local institutions might facilitate club goods provision in ethnically diverse areas. The work should further prove applicable to many different types of religious traditions as well as to other nonstate voluntary associations such as community groups, professional associations, and some local unions and NGOs.

A Framework for Understanding Collective Action

This study provides an approach for combining political process and rational choice perspectives to understanding collective action. Scholarship applying the political process model suggests collective action can emerge to the degree framing, opportunity, and resource mobilization are present. Appropriate ideological frames create an "insurgent consciousness" that encourages political engagement. Opportunities for activism arise as a result of structural changes that inspire elites to seek new partners and open new possibilities for activism. Finally, there must be resources and an existing organizational infrastructure to support activism. The rational choice approach, for its part, has examined the forces that encourage individuals to overcome the free-rider problem and engage in political activism. From this perspective, collective action cannot emerge unless individuals are properly incentivized to participate rather than free ride.

As I have argued throughout this book, both the political process and rational choice approaches have provided important insights into our understanding of collective action. However, the political process approach does not explain how grassroots capacities for resource mobilization develop in the first place. The rational choice approach, on the other hand, is less helpful in understanding how individuals coordinate their efforts. Though these two approaches typically are not engaged with each other, they are quite complementary. When combined, we understand the ideological frames that coordinate activity, the structural opportunities that create openings for activism, and the institutional structures that overcome free-rider problems and create grassroots mobilizing potential.

While religious decentralization explains why religious institutions develop capacities that can potentially be utilized for collective action, the perspective cannot fully explain why that capacity gets applied to political activism without elaborating the frames that coordinate adherents' actions. Furthermore, it is difficult to understand why religious elites allow their institutions to be utilized for political activism, potentially damaging relationships with socioeconomic and political elites, without understanding changing incentives imposed by the encroachment of other competing religions. Examination of framing, opportunity, and resource mobilization provides a fuller understanding of why religious institutions engage in secular political activism.

I should note here decentralization comes with serious liabilities for the leadership of any institution, and leadership may subsequently be reluctant to employ it (Kollman 2013). Though the upside can be increased levels of collective action, the risks involve loss of control as activism moves in unanticipated directions (Kalyvas 1996). While decentralization led to increasing levels of political participation in Chiapas, it also led to avenues of activism completely unanticipated and undesired by the Catholic clergy. For this reason, the Vatican enacted a ban on the creation of permanent deacons in Chiapas, and this ban was in place for more than a decade before it was lifted by Pope Francis in 2014. While decentralization can be an effective way to create political pressure and mobilization, leaders of institutions may be wary of deploying it for fear of losing control.

Because my theory is embedded within a broad framework to understanding collective action, it should be amenable to understanding many other types of nonstate institutions, including other religious institutions. As just one example, the framework should be applicable to understanding Islamic political engagement across the Middle East and Africa. My expectation would be that decentralized variants of Islam accompanied by appropriate framing and opportunity should be associated with heightened propensities for political activism. Previous work in predominantly Muslim countries suggests individuals who participate in Muslim voluntary associations are more likely to engage in secular political activism (Sarkissian 2012), and previous work has also suggested the effective provision of religious goods and services are key components enabling radical Islamic activity in groups such as Hamas in Palestine, Hezbollah in Lebanon, and the Taliban in Afghanistan (Berman 2011). My theory of religious decentralization could be tested by assessing whether decentralization prompts greater reciprocity and then to the club goods production and organizational involvement that has already been demonstrated as associated with enhanced propensities for Muslim political engagement.

While I have engaged with progressive Catholicism within this study, the approach should also prove useful in examining conservative and fundamentalist forms of religious political advocacy. Where there are strongly conservative theological frames, conditions creating opportunity, and decentralization creating mobilization potential, my expectation is that we would see conservative movements of collective action prompted by religious institutions. This framework could be used to study the political influence and mobilizing potential of conservative evangelical religious groups in the United States and Latin America, fundamentalist Islamist movements across the Middle East and Africa, and the influence of Buddhist nationalist groups such as Bodu Bala Sena in Sri Lanka.

As a further example, a great deal of scholarship has examined progressive Catholicism in Latin America, but less theoretically driven interest has been given to conservative Catholic advocacy. The Church consistently opposes abortion, and this opposition has had an impact on public policy in the region. For example, abortion is illegal in all circumstances in Nicaragua, El Salvador, the Dominican Republic, and across several Mexican states. It only recently was legalized under limited circumstances in Chile, and abortion is only permitted to save the life of the mother in Argentina and Brazil (Htun 2003, 9, 33–34; Campos Machado 2016; Kozak 2017). My theoretical framework might usefully be employed to understand how conservative Catholic advocacy develops at the grassroots in the region.

Finally, this study has some implications for our understanding of the relationship between religious institutions and authoritarian regimes. Religious institutions provide locations for the development of political activity, and they color their adherents' perception of the legitimacy of the government (Sarkissian 2015, 16). Accordingly, religious institutions potentially constitute serious threats to authoritarian rulers because they are one of the few organizations that can mobilize activist engagement against the regime (Koesel 2014, 159). As this book has argued, decentralized religions are more likely to provide the organizational capacity necessary to do so.[1]

Nonstate Institutions and Collective Action

Following Robert Putnam's (1993) lead, much literature extolling the virtues of "social capital" has pointed to the importance of dense associational activity in prompting both collective action and all manner of positive governmental outcomes. Such associational activity includes nongovernmental and voluntary group activity in organizations such as unions, neighborhood associations, professional associations, NGOs, and, of course, religious institutions (Boulding 2014, 13). One of the contributions of this book is that it helps us understand how dense networks of communal associations develop in the first place, and the dynamics of decentralization should be exportable to other forms of voluntary associations. Vibrant and dense associational activity facilitating collective action should be more likely to develop when local voluntary associations of all stripes are characterized by decentralized monitoring, sanctioning, and decision-making and when these organizations provide desirable excludable club goods to their members. While I have focused on religious institutions because of their ubiquity, I would predict that such decentralization in any of these groups should help build local capacities for action and facilitate collective action.

There are some important scope conditions to consider, however. The theory is oriented toward explaining grassroots voluntary activism that emerges at a local level. It is not meant to understand the behavior of organizations embedded within or manipulated by the state. If the state provides incentives to members of the institution to engage in collective action, members are no longer responsible for supplying their own club goods and instead have incentives to free ride off the state. The state can use the financial dependence of the organization to manipulate activism coming from it for its own purposes.

To illustrate the point, this framework would not likely be useful to explain collective action in unions deeply integrated into corporatist states, such as labor organized in Mexico during authoritarian PRI rule. This is because selective incentives and sanctions provided by the state such as individual bribes more likely explain collective action in these settings. These organizations are "embedded in a web of bureaucratic and legal codes which allows those in power to monitor and regulate collective activities . . . civil society institutions are more an instrument of state control than a mechanism of collective empowerment" (Wiktorowicz 2000). If the state provides incentives for individuals at the base to mobilize, we do not have an example of grassroots collective action because communities do not develop the capacities for activism themselves. The theory also does not explain mobilization within groups that are not truly voluntary. For example, unions who compel membership or dues as a condition of employment are less amenable for study under this framework because associational membership is no longer voluntary on the part of participants.

The framework may also prove useful in explaining the emergence of groups that coalesce into political parties. For example, the initial appearance of Christian Democratic parties in Europe was likely the unwitting result of the Catholic Church's decentralization to laity as it sought to mobilize popular resistance to protect itself from liberal governments (Kalyvas 1996). At the same time, my theory is not applicable to explaining collective action generated by established and bureaucratized political parties. This is because these parties may be closely affiliated with the state, or they have incentives to generate mobilization from the top down for the purpose of winning or maintaining office (Karp and Banducci 2007; Rosenstone and Hansen 1993; Hansen 2016).

Similarly, the theory is more applicable to explaining locally developed and grassroots organizations than it is in understanding how organizations with strong ties to international donors might prompt political activism. Though they constitute nonstate and voluntary associations, NGOs often rely on organizational infrastructure and funds to encourage activism from external sources, such as from international donors. These types of international NGOs, of course, are often important mobilizers of collective action (Boulding 2014), but they mitigate free-rider problems from an external source and are less pertinent to my theory explaining the development of internal grassroots development. To the extent NGOs derive their resources from settings that are external to the communities they assist in mobilizing, they are less likely to be explained by my theoretical perspective.

Furthermore, this study is oriented toward explaining the emergence of collective action and is less engaged with explaining how social movements evolve or in examining changes in protest repertoires. Sidney Tarrow describes a "protest cycle" in which political opportunities create early activists. Early activists in turn create additional opportunities for new groups to organize and engage in activism, and they experiment with new and innovative tactics (repertoires) of activism. Successes are often brief as elites develop strategies to counter the activists' actions, but movements potentially produce permanent expansions of opportunities to organize (Tarrow 1998; Tilly 1995). Certainly, my analyses into Chiapas and Morelos touch on several of these dynamics, but my ultimate theoretical concern is in tracing the development of organizational capacities for activism rather than mapping events onto the political protest cycle. Analyses focusing on protest cycles and repertoires of collective action are important lines of investigation (Bishara 2015; Fu 2017), but outside my delineated scope of inquiry.

Ethnic Diversity and Collective Action

Finally, much scholarship has demonstrated a negative association between ethnic diversity and the capacity of communities to produce public goods, and my study has interesting potential implications for this research. Differing ethnicities are thought to possess divergent preferences for the types of public goods to be produced, lack common cultural experiences, and experience greater difficulty monitoring and sanctioning across ethnic boundaries (Habyarimana et al. 2007).

However, this book provides suggestive evidence that local institutions may overcome these barriers under certain conditions. The indigenous population of Chiapas is incredibly diverse, many different indigenous languages are spoken, and many different cultural customs are observed. Despite this great diversity, disparate indigenous groups were able to effectively coordinate their efforts, build an organizational infrastructure, and produce political activism across the region. Yucatán, despite being characterized by a great deal of linguistic and cultural similarity among its indigenous population, has not seen the same result.

During my field research, I was struck by the degree to which the movement in Chiapas was truly multiethnic. Anecdotally, I attended Church-sponsored pastoral gatherings in San Cristóbal de las Casas and in Bachajón on November 24, 2011, and December 3, 2011, where individuals representing a variety of indigenous groups speaking many different languages gathered in common cause advancing a variety of political demands centered on land, political repression, and environmental protection. Given findings of much of the literature examining ethnic diversity and public goods, the Church's ability to organize these types of major assemblies alone is a major accomplishment, to say nothing of its role in sparking a multiethnic activist movement across the region.

It was by no means inevitable that it would be able to do so. The indigenous populations of Chiapas generally lived in isolation from each other during the first half of the twentieth century. Particular ethnic identities were generally confined to particular local villages, and observers of indigenous Chiapas at the time thought there was "little possibility of interethnic cooperation or organization" (Mattiace 2003, 11). However, decentralization by the Diocese of San Cristóbal de las Casas in the latter part of the century put two thousand lay catechists to work, many of them indigenous individuals of different ethnic groups embedded within their communities. These catechists representing various indigenous groups would meet with each other regularly and began to cooperate with each other in response to social and political problems. It was they who helped form the "pan-ethnic regional cooperatives" across the diocese that, as I have described, provided a variety of valuable club goods. Catechists were well-positioned to recruit translators to coordinate activity across these various groups (Womack 1999, 31; Mattiace 2003, 14).

My findings are suggestive that nonstate local institutions may enable collective action in ethnically diverse settings when they encourage the common production of mutually desirable but *excludable* club goods across ethnic boundaries. Like Ashutosh Varshney's study of ethnic violence in India, the study finds that negative relationships associated with ethnic diversity can be substantially mitigated to the degree that ethnic communities are characterized by the kinds of dense interethnic networks that developed in Chiapas (Varshney 2002). However, my study provides potential insight into how these dense intraethnic associational linkages develop in the first place. In particular, if multiple ethnic communities are encompassed within the same social institution (like religious institutions), and if that institution displays decentralized governance enabling effective club goods provision, this may help overcome collective action problems commonly associated with ethnic diversity.

Future work could test this hypothesis systematically, and it would be a corrective to the current state of the literature. While a great deal of recent work has preoccupied itself with the question of the relationship between ethnic heterogeneity and public goods provision at an individual level, ethnic political mobilization has often been examined instead as a byproduct of political elites' incentives rather than the incentives of individuals at the grassroots. Theories of ethnic outbidding contend politicians often possess electoral incentives to support the interests of particular ethnic groups above others. This process is seen as exacerbating ethnic tensions as minority ethnic groups become demonized and politicians mobilize ethnic sentiment in support of their own political agendas (Horowitz 1985; Kaufman 1996; Chandra 2005; Siroky and Hale 2017; McCauley 2017). Much like the literature examining the incentives of religious elites to mobilize activism, these explanations ignore the incentives of ethnic participants themselves to politically mobilize along ethnic lines. Further research should disentangle the incentives of elites to mobilize activism to the capacity and demand of communities at the grassroots to actually engage in it. While ethnic outbidding of course speaks less to how ethnic cooperation emerges and more to why ethnic groups find themselves in conflict, the example suggests much of this literature could benefit from understanding the incentives of individual ethnic group members to organize at the grassroots.

Empirically, Latin America presents a relatively untapped environment to examine the relationship between ethnic heterogeneity and public goods provision. While plenty of research has examined the underprovision of public goods in the region, most of it has addressed it from an angle emphasizing social and economic inequality rather than ethnic diversity (Soifer 2016, 1344). Researchers can take advantage of a great deal of both within country and cross-country variation to examine the relationship between ethnic diversity and public goods provision. For example, countries like Guatemala, Bolivia, and Peru have an extraordinary diversity of indigenous cultures, whereas countries like Chile, Honduras, and El Salvador have substantially less. Further, even within countries there is a great deal of variation in local levels of ethnic diversity. Mexico provides a case in point. Some states and localities are overwhelmingly homogeneous and ethnically mestizo in character, while there are also many indigenous communities where several different languages are spoken.

Latin America thus provides a potentially fertile laboratory for examining ethnic diversity and collective action. While some heavily indigenous countries have experienced a great deal of political mobilization among ethnic lines, such as Brazil and Bolivia, other ethnically diverse countries such as Peru have experienced little indigenous political mobilization (Yashar 2005; García 2008, 217; Korovkin 2006). Future research might explicitly engage with whether decentralization in local institutional structures, like religious institutional structures, has an impact in prompting collective action in ethnically diverse communities.

Conclusion

This book has sought to understand why religious institutions facilitate secular political activism in some settings, but not others and has argued that they are more likely to do so when they are decentralized. For that organizational potential to find expression as activism, decentralization must be accompanied by politicized theologies that encourage engagement. It must also be accompanied by religious elites with incentives to back activist causes. My statistical analyses utilizing nationally representative Mexican survey data and my qualitative assessments of political activism in Chiapas, Morelos, and Yucatán provide support for this framework. When framing, opportunity, and resource mobilization come together through religious institutions, the results are striking.

This was the case in Chiapas, where coffee and God unleashed political activism in a state that had previously experienced little collective action. Religious decentralization by the Catholic Church created reciprocal interactions and religious club goods provision, particularly in the production of coffee, and created an organizational infrastructure that could be applied to political activism. Liberation theology provided the framing, while Protestant competition provided the opportunity. As a result, the indigenous communities of Chiapas divined their own political interventions. "Now, the entire indigenous population, or the majority, can be found organized in some way or another, for production, for economic issues, for the defense of their rights, or for politics. . . . Before it was thought that one could manipulate the information and the will of the people, but now it's very different" (Interview 5, 2011). As another Chiapan interviewee succinctly put it, "many of these organizations are now involved in the struggle for power" (Interview 42, 2011).

Appendixes

Appendixes

Table of Contents

APPENDIX TABLE A.1A

Descriptive Statistics
(Excluding 2001)

TABLE A.1A. DESCRIPTIVE STATISTICS (EXCLUDING 2001)

Variable	Observations	Mean	Std. Dev.	Min.	Max
Activism	9211	0.56	0.50	0	1
Count Activism	9211	1.94	2.63	0	14
Decentralized	9163	0.87	1.79	−0.69	5.83
No Decentralization	9163	0.46	0.50	0	1
Moderate Decentralization	9163	0.46	0.50	0	1
Heavy Decentralization	9163	0.09	0.28	0	1
Religious Competition	9280	0.36	0.24	0.01	1.58
Political Theology	9280	0.40	0.49	0	1
Party Competition	8884	3.10	0.55	1.93	5.52
Church/State Legacies	9280	1.75	3.17	0	12
Deprivation	9266	0.82	0.07	0.53	0.95
Ethnic Heterogeneity	9280	1.10	0.23	1	3.03
Good Economic Status	9280	0.21	0.41	0	1
Bad Economic Status	9280	0.37	0.48	0	1
Gender	9280	0.46	0.50	0	1
Age	9280	40.35	15.24	18	97
Practicing Catholic	9280	0.82	0.38	0	1
Low Religiosity	9045	0.26	0.44	0	1
Moderate Religiosity	9045	0.39	0.49	0	1
High Rreligiosity	9045	0.12	0.33	0	1

Descriptive Statistics
(Including 2001)

TABLE A.IB. DESCRIPTIVE STATISTICS (INCLUDING 2001)

Variable	Observations	Mean	Std. Dev.	Min.	Max
Activism	13108	0.50	0.50	0	1
Count Activism	13108	1.65	2.46	0	14
Decentralized	13285	0.78	1.72	−0.69	5.83
No Decentralization	13285	0.47	0.50	0	1
Moderate Decentralization	13285	0.46	0.50	0	1
Heavy Decentralization	13285	0.08	0.26	0	1
Religious Competition	13463	0.36	0.24	0.01	1.58
Political Theology	13463	0.35	0.48	0	1
Party Competition	13067	2.96	0.55	1.55	5.52
Church/State Legacies	13463	1.77	3.20	0	12
Deprivation	13437	0.82	0.07	0.53	0.95
Ethnic Heterogeneity	13463	1.10	0.23	1	3.03
Good Economic Status	13463	0.19	0.39	0	1
Bad Economic Status	13463	0.38	0.49	0	1
Gender	13463	0.44	0.50	0	1
Age	13463	40.72	15.37	18	97
Catholic	9280	0.82	0.38	0	1
Low Religiosity	9045	0.26	0.44	0	1
Moderate Religiosity	9045	0.39	0.49	0	1
High Rreligiosity	9045	0.12	0.33	0	1

Fixed Effects Logistic Regression (Discussion)

To make the discussion as accessible as possible to a wide audience, I presented visual depictions of the results of my fixed effects logistic regression models within the main text of the book. In Appendix Table A.2, I present the full statistical model results from which these visual depictions were derived, including raw coefficients, standard errors, and a variety of other relevant information including measures of fit. Figure 3.1 in the book manuscript visually depicts the results demonstrated below in Model 1, which is a conditional fixed effects logistic regression model examining Mexican Catholics with diocese and year fixed effects along with standard errors clustered on dioceses.

TABLE A.2. FIXED EFFECTS LOGISTIC REGRESSION (PRIMARY MODEL)

Variables	Model 1 Logit Fixed Effects
Decentralized	0.34***
	(0.11)
Religious Competition	0.82**
	(0.39)
Political Theology	0.54**
	(0.25)
Party Competition	0.04
	(0.09)
Church/State Legacies	−0.03*
	(0.02)
Deprivation	−1.13
	(0.80)
Ethnic Heterogeneity	0.09
	(0.29)
Good Economic Status	0.20***
	(0.07)
Bad Economic Status	−0.08
	(0.07)
Gender	0.20***
	(0.06)
Age	0.03***
	(0.01)
Age Squared	−0.00***
	(0.00)
Low Religiosity	0.14*
	(0.08)
Moderate Religiosity	0.19**
	(0.08)
High Religiosity	0.29***
	(0.11)
Year	−0.12*
	(0.07)
Observations	7,073
Number of Dioceses	0.83***
Log-Likelihood	−4415.38
AIC	8862.77
BIC	8972.59

Standard errors in parentheses
***$p < 0.01$, **$p < 0.05$, *$p < 0.1$

Random Effects Logistic Regression (Discussion)

In addition to running fixed effects regression models, I also checked the robustness of my primary model results by running it as a random effects model. I present the random effects model here in Appendix Table A.3. The substantive results of the model are similar to the fixed effects models presented in Appendix Table A.2. In a pattern that will be noticeable throughout this appendix, the exception is that Church/state legacies do not pop up as statistically significant, while relative deprivation does.

TABLE A.3. RANDOM EFFECTS LOGISTIC REGRESSION

Variables	Model 1 Logit Random Effects
Decentralized	0.10**
	(0.04)
Religious Competition	0.41*
	(0.22)
Political Theology	0.30***
	(0.11)
Party Competition	−0.00
	(0.06)
Church/State Legacies	−0.02
	(0.02)
Deprivation	−1.12**
	(0.52)
Ethnic Heterogeneity	0.08
	(0.16)
Good Economic Status	0.21***
	(0.07)
Bad Economic Status	−0.08
	(0.06)
Gender	0.20***
	(0.05)
Age	0.03***
	(0.01)
Age Squared	−0.00***
	(0.00)
Low Religiosity	0.13*
	(0.07)
Moderate Religiosity	0.19***
	(0.07)
High Religiosity	0.31***
	(0.10)
Year	−0.09***
	(0.03)
Constant	177.17***
	(56.99)
Observations	7,098
Number of _Dioceses	85
Log-Likelihood	−4725.02
AIC	9486.04
BIC	9609.66

Standard errors in parentheses
***$p < 0.01$, **$p < 0.05$, *$p < 0.1$

Count Models (Discussion)

As also mentioned in the main text, the measure of activism used in the figures in the book is a dichotomous "yes/no" variable assessing simply whether an individual participated in any activist event. This included whether an individual marched, organized, signed petitions, and so on. Alternatively, and to further determine the degree of an individual's activist involvement, I also counted the types of activism an individual participated in. In Appendix Table A.4, I present several statistical models using a count of activist activities as my dependent variable.

In Model 1, I present a fixed effects Poisson regression model with an individual's total number of activist events used as my dependent variable. Model 2 similarly uses Poisson regression, but with a random effects model. Because Poisson regression results can be problematic if there is overdispersion in the data, I also run my results as a fixed effects negative binomial regression (Model 3).

Furthermore, we might also consider running the data as an ordinal logit model. On average, individuals participated in 1.6 activist events, with a standard deviation of about 2.5. Rather than analyzing our dependent variable as a count of different types of activities, we might also consider assessing individuals who engaged in categories of no activism (0), some activism (1), and heavy activism (2). To develop this measure, individuals who had not participated in any activist events were coded as 0, individuals who had participated in between 1 and 4 activist events were coded as 1 (these were those individuals who had participated within one standard deviation of the mean number of protest activities), and finally individuals who had participated in 5 or more activist events were coded as heavy participants with a score of 2.

As can be seen from examining the models, the results generally adhere to the substantive results from the primary models. The only notable differences are that neither Church/state legacies nor relative deprivation stand out as statistically significant. Political party competition, however, is statistically significant in the Poisson models.

TABLE A.4. COUNT MODELS

Variables	Model 1 Poisson Fixed	Model 2 Poisson Random	Model 3 Negative Binomial	Model 4 Ordinal Logit
Decentralized	0.14***	0.08***	0.12***	0.07*
	(0.02)	(0.02)	(0.04)	(0.04)
Religious Competition	0.32***	0.27***	0.35*	0.38**
	(0.09)	(0.08)	(0.18)	(0.19)
Political Theology	0.43***	0.32***	0.45***	0.26**
	(0.06)	(0.05)	(0.12)	(0.10)
Party Competition	0.06***	0.05***	0.04	0.04
	(0.02)	(0.02)	(0.04)	(0.05)
Church/State Legacies	0.00	−0.00	0.00	−0.02
	(0.01)	(0.01)	(0.02)	(0.02)
Deprivation	−0.26	−0.22	−0.20	−0.73
	(0.18)	(0.18)	(0.38)	(0.47)
Ethnic Heterogeneity	0.06	0.02	0.00	−0.05
	(0.06)	(0.06)	(0.12)	(0.14)
Good Economic Status	0.11***	0.11***	0.12***	0.20***
	(0.02)	(0.02)	(0.05)	(0.06)
Bad Economic Status	−0.11***	−0.11***	−0.10***	−0.13**
	(0.02)	(0.02)	(0.04)	(0.05)
Gender	0.17***	0.17***	0.16***	0.23***
	(0.02)	(0.02)	(0.04)	(0.05)
Age	0.03***	0.03***	0.03***	0.03***
	(0.00)	(0.00)	(0.01)	(0.01)
Age Squared	−0.00***	−0.00***	−0.00***	−0.00***
	(0.00)	(0.00)	(0.00)	(0.00)
Low Religiosity	0.09***	0.10***	0.09*	0.12*
	(0.03)	(0.03)	(0.05)	(0.07)
Moderate Religiosity	0.09***	0.09***	0.09*	0.18***
	(0.03)	(0.03)	(0.05)	(0.07)
High Religiosity	0.22***	0.22***	0.19***	0.39***
	(0.03)	(0.03)	(0.07)	(0.09)
Year	0.00	0.01	−0.00	−0.04
	(0.01)	(0.01)	(0.02)	(0.03)
Constant	–	−21.75	0.41***	
		(20.23)	(0.03)	
Observations	7,083	7,098	7,098	7,098
Number of Dioceses	84	85	85	85
Log-Likelihood	−16162.88	−16608.75	−12980.5	−7016.64
AIC	32357.77	33253.5	26165.01	14071.27
BIC	32467.61	33377.11	26865.5	14201.75

Standard errors in parentheses
***$p < 0.01$, **$p < 0.05$, *$p < 0.1$

Ordinary Least Squares Regression (Discussion)

To further test the robustness of my primary results, I also assess my dichotomous activism variable with fixed and random effects Ordinary Least Squares regression (or a linear probability model). While running dichotomous variables through a typical OLS analysis is problematic for a variety of reasons, the exercise here is simply to further test the robustness of my statistical results. The results for the fixed and random effects OLS models are generally quite similar, substantively, to their logit counterparts presented in Appendix Tables A.2 and A.3.

TABLE A.5. ORDINARY LEAST SQUARES REGRESSION

Variables	Model 1 OLS Fixed Effects	Model 2 OLS Random Effects
Decentralized	0.08***	0.02**
	(0.02)	(0.01)
Religious Competition	0.17**	0.08*
	(0.08)	(0.05)
Political Theology	0.13**	0.06**
	(0.06)	(0.02)
Party Competition	0.01	−0.00
	(0.02)	(0.01)
Church/State Legacies	−0.01*	−0.01
	(0.00)	(0.00)
Deprivation	−0.26	−0.25**
	(0.18)	(0.12)
Ethnic Heterogeneity	0.02	0.02
	(0.07)	(0.04)
Good Economic Status	0.05***	0.05***
	(0.02)	(0.02)
Bad Economic Status	−0.02	−0.02
	(0.02)	(0.01)
Gender	0.05***	0.05***
	(0.01)	(0.01)
Age	0.01***	0.01***
	(0.00)	(0.00)
Age Squared	−0.00***	−0.00***
	(0.00)	(0.00)
Low Religiosity	0.03*	0.03*
	(0.02)	(0.02)
Moderate Religiosity	0.04**	0.04***
	(0.02)	(0.02)
High Religiosity	0.07***	0.07***
	(0.02)	(0.02)
Year	−0.03*	−0.02***
	(0.02)	(0.01)
Constant	58.28*	39.89***
	(30.68)	(13.07)
Observations	7,098	7,098
Number of Dioceses	85	85

Standard errors in parentheses
***$p < 0.01$, **$p < 0.05$, *$p < 0.1$

Interaction Effects (Discussion)

In Figures 3.5 through 3.7 of the main text, I present figures depicting the predicted probabilities associated with interacting my decentralization, political theology, and religious competition variables against each other. In Figure 3.5, I presented results from a statistical model interacting decentralization with politicized theology. Model 1 in Table A.6 below depicts a table demonstrating results from which Figure 3.5 was derived depicting the decentralization/political theology interaction ("Decentralized X Political Theology"). Furthermore, in Figures 3.6 and 3.7, I presented predicted probabilities from a model interacting decentralization with religious competition, and Model 2 below demonstrates those results in a statistical table ("Decentralized X Religious Competition").

TABLE A.6. INTERACTION EFFECTS

Variables	Model 1 Decent./Theol. Interaction	Model 2 Decent./Comp. Interaction
Decentralized	0.30***	0.27***
	(0.06)	(0.07)
Religious Competition	0.78***	0.60**
	(0.28)	(0.30)
Political Theology	0.25	0.52***
	(0.22)	(0.16)
Decentralized X Political Theology	0.16**	–
	(0.08)	
Decentralized X Competition	–	0.34**
		(0.15)
Party Competition	0.02	0.06
	(0.06)	(0.06)
Church/State Legacies	–0.03	–0.04
	(0.03)	(0.03)
Deprivation	–1.25**	–1.21**
	(0.56)	(0.56)
Ethnic Heterogeneity	0.09	0.12
	(0.17)	(0.17)
Good Economic Status	0.20***	0.21***
	(0.07)	(0.07)
Bad Economic Status	–0.08	–0.08
	(0.06)	(0.06)
Gender	0.20***	0.20***
	(0.05)	(0.05)
Age	0.03***	0.03***
	(0.01)	(0.01)
Age Squared	–0.00***	–0.00***
	(0.00)	(0.00)
Low Religiosity	0.14*	0.14*
	(0.07)	(0.07)
Moderate Religiosity	0.18***	0.19***
	(0.07)	(0.07)
High Religiosity	0.29***	0.29***
	(0.10)	(0.10)
Year	–0.13***	–0.12***
	(0.03)	(0.03)
Observations	7,073	7,073
Number of Dioceses	83	83
Log-Likelihood	–4411.61	–4411.01
AIC	8857.21	8856.01
BIC	8973.9	8972.7

Standard errors in parentheses
***$p < 0.01$, **$p < 0.05$, *$p < 0.1$

Alternative Decentralization Measures (Discussion)

As detailed in the main text of the book, I created my primary deacon measure by taking the natural log of the number of permanent deacons to correct for a nonnormal distribution.[1] Rather than examining the number of permanent deacons this way, I might have alternatively created a categorical variable of the number of deacons in a diocese. Though taking the natural log of the number of permanent deacons helps the normality of the distribution substantially, we are still left with something of a nonnormal distribution in the variable. I created three different dichotomous (yes/no) measures: dioceses with no decentralization, dioceses with moderate decentralization, and dioceses with heavy decentralization. If a diocese has no deacons, the no decentralization variable is coded as 1, and both the moderate and heavy decentralization variables are coded as 0. Alternatively, if a diocese has between 1 and 2 times the standard deviation from the mean of the natural log of the number of permanent deacons, the moderate decentralization variable is given a score of 1. In this case, the no decentralization variable is coded as 0 and the heavy decentralization variable is also coded as 0. Finally, if a diocese has more than two times the standard deviation of the natural log of the number of permanent deacons away from the mean, the heavy decentralization variable is given a score of 1 while both the no and moderate decentralization variables are given a score of 0.

I run this alternative measure of my decentralization variable as a fixed effects logit model (Model 1), a random effects logit model (Model 2), Poisson fixed and random effects models, (Models 3 and 4, respectively), and a negative binomial regression fixed effects model (Model 5). The results of the categorical version of the decentralization variable are substantively very similar to the results of the continuous measure used in the primary models.

TABLE A.7. ALTERNATIVE DECENTRALIZATION MEASURES

Variables	Model 1 Logit Fixed	Model 2 Logit Random	Model 3 Poisson Fixed	Model 4 Poisson Random	Model 5 Negative Binomial
Moderate Decentralization	0.53***	0.27***	0.20***	0.15***	0.18**
	(0.13)	(0.10)	(0.05)	(0.04)	(0.09)
Heavy Decentralization	1.91***	0.65*	1.07***	0.59***	1.08**
	(0.63)	(0.35)	(0.23)	(0.21)	(0.44)
Religious Competition	0.83***	0.41*	0.32***	0.28***	0.36*
	(0.28)	(0.22)	(0.09)	(0.08)	(0.18)
Political Theology	0.56***	0.30***	0.42***	0.31***	0.44***
	(0.16)	(0.11)	(0.07)	(0.05)	(0.12)
Party Competition	0.03	−0.01	0.06***	0.05**	0.04
	(0.06)	(0.06)	(0.02)	(0.02)	(0.04)
Church/State Legacies	−0.04	−0.02	0.00	−0.00	0.00
	(0.03)	(0.02)	(0.01)	(0.01)	(0.02)
Deprivation	−1.29**	−1.16**	−0.31*	−0.23	−0.25
	(0.56)	(0.52)	(0.18)	(0.18)	(0.38)
Ethnic Heterogeneity	0.05	0.07	0.04	0.01	−0.01
	(0.17)	(0.16)	(0.06)	(0.06)	(0.12)
Good Economic Status	0.21***	0.21***	0.12***	0.12***	0.12***
	(0.07)	(0.07)	(0.02)	(0.02)	(0.05)
Bad Economic Status	−0.08	−0.08	−0.11***	−0.11***	−0.10**
	(0.06)	(0.06)	(0.02)	(0.02)	(0.04)
Gender	0.20***	0.20***	0.17***	0.17***	0.17***
	(0.05)	(0.05)	(0.02)	(0.02)	(0.04)
Age	0.03***	0.03***	0.03***	0.03***	0.03***
	(0.01)	(0.01)	(0.00)	(0.00)	(0.01)
Age Squared	−0.00***	−0.00***	−0.00***	−0.00***	−0.00***
	(0.00)	(0.00)	(0.00)	(0.00)	(0.00)
Low Religiosity	0.14*	0.14*	0.10***	0.10***	0.10*
	(0.07)	(0.07)	(0.03)	(0.03)	(0.05)
Moderate Religiosity	0.19***	0.19***	0.09***	0.09***	0.09*
	(0.07)	(0.07)	(0.03)	(0.03)	(0.05)
High Religiosity	0.29***	0.31***	0.22***	0.22***	0.19***
	(0.10)	(0.10)	(0.03)	(0.03)	(0.07)
Year	−0.10***	−0.08***	0.01	0.01	0.01
	(0.03)	(0.03)	(0.01)	(0.01)	(0.02)
Constant		166.63***		−29.35	0.41***
		(56.55)		(20.07)	(0.03)
Observations	7,073	7,098	7,083	7,098	7,098
Number of Dioceses	83	85	84	85	85

Standard errors in parentheses
***$p < 0.01$, **$p < 0.05$, *$p < 0.1$

Clerical/Population Controls
(Discussion)

Furthermore, it may be the case that the size of the clerical population and the size of the Catholic population in each diocese may be relevant control variables to my analysis. To examine whether this is the case, I include both measures in the statistical models presented in this Appendix Table A.8.

I include these control variables in a fixed effects logit model (Model 1), a random effects logit model (Model 2), Poisson fixed and random effects models, (Models 3 and 4, respectively), and a negative binomial regression fixed effects model (Model 5). The results including these control variables are substantively similar to the results of my primary statistical models.

TABLE A.8. CLERICAL/POPULATION CONTROLS

Variables	Model 1 Logit Fixed	Model 2 Logit Random	Model 3 Poisson Fixed	Model 4 Poisson Random	Model 5 Negative Binomial
Decentralized	0.31***	0.10**	0.13***	0.08***	0.12***
	(0.11)	(0.04)	(0.02)	(0.02)	(0.04)
Religious Competition	0.81**	0.40*	0.31***	0.27***	0.33*
	(0.39)	(0.23)	(0.09)	(0.08)	(0.18)
Political Theology	0.60*	0.29***	0.46***	0.34***	0.47***
	(0.35)	(0.11)	(0.07)	(0.06)	(0.12)
Party Competition	0.06	−0.01	0.07***	0.05**	0.05
	(0.10)	(0.06)	(0.02)	(0.02)	(0.04)
Church/State Legacies	−0.03*	−0.02	0.00	0.00	0.00
	(0.02)	(0.02)	(0.01)	(0.01)	(0.02)
Deprivation	−1.20	−1.13**	−0.29	−0.24	−0.24
	(0.77)	(0.52)	(0.18)	(0.18)	(0.38)
Ethnic Heterogeneity	0.12	0.08	0.07	0.03	0.02
	(0.30)	(0.16)	(0.06)	(0.06)	(0.12)
Good Economic Status	0.21***	0.21***	0.12***	0.12***	0.12***
	(0.07)	(0.07)	(0.02)	(0.02)	(0.05)
Bad Economic Status	−0.08	−0.08	−0.11***	−0.11***	−0.11***
	(0.06)	(0.06)	(0.02)	(0.02)	(0.04)
Gender	0.20***	0.20***	0.17***	0.17***	0.16***
	(0.06)	(0.05)	(0.02)	(0.02)	(0.04)
Age	0.03***	0.03***	0.03***	0.03***	0.03***
	(0.01)	(0.01)	(0.00)	(0.00)	(0.01)
Age Squared	−0.00***	−0.00***	−0.00***	−0.00***	−0.00***
	(0.00)	(0.00)	(0.00)	(0.00)	(0.00)
Low Religiosity	0.12	0.13**	0.09***	0.09***	0.08*
	(0.08)	(0.07)	(0.03)	(0.03)	(0.05)
Moderate Religiosity	0.18**	0.19***	0.09***	0.09***	0.08
	(0.08)	(0.07)	(0.03)	(0.03)	(0.05)
High Religiosity	0.29***	0.31***	0.22***	0.23***	0.18***
	(0.11)	(0.10)	(0.03)	(0.03)	(0.07)
Year	−0.14**	−0.09***	−0.00	0.01	−0.01
	(0.06)	(0.03)	(0.01)	(0.01)	(0.02)
Priest Population	−0.01	−0.00	−0.00***	−0.00***	−0.00*
	(0.00)	(0.00)	(0.00)	(0.00)	(0.00)
Catholic Population	0.00	0.00	0.00***	0.00***	0.00***
	(0.00)	(0.00)	(0.00)	(0.00)	(0.00)
Constant		179.71***		−14.29	0.41***
		(57.17)		(20.39)	(0.03)
Observations	7,073	7,098	7,083	7,098	7,098
Number of Dioceses	83	85	84	85	85

Standard errors in parentheses
***$p < 0.01$, **$p < 0.05$, *$p < 0.1$

APPENDIX TABLE A.9

Including 2001 (Discussion)

In addition to the 2003 and 2005 surveys, I can match my diocese-level data from the Catholic Church with an ENCUP survey taken in the year 2001. In this Appendix Table A.9, I also incorporate the 2001 data as a further robustness test of my results, and primarily on my religious decentralization variable.

I do not incorporate the 2001 data into my primary models for several reasons. First, the ENCUP 2001 data does not ask any questions concerning a respondent's religious affiliation or religiosity, two individual-level variables of obvious importance to this study. Furthermore, and at least as importantly, the wording on the political activity questions changed between the 2001 and 2003 versions of the ENCUP, potentially introducing bias. The 2001 survey asks individuals if they have engaged in participatory actions within the last month, whereas the 2003 and 2005 data ask individuals if they have done so within the last year. Nevertheless, keeping this important caveat in mind, the inclusion of the 2001 data does provide an opportunity to assess the robustness of my results to the inclusion of additional observations.

As Appendix Table A.9 demonstrates, the substantive results are generally the same, but there are a few important differences. While religious decentralization and politicized theology both maintain statistically significant and positive associations with activism, the religious competition variable is not statistically significant in two of the models. The biggest difference is associated with the influence of the political competition variable, which is now statistically significant and positive across all the models in this Appendix Table. However, given the caveats noted above, greater weight should be given to the results stemming from the models incorporating only the 2003 and 2005 models. This Appendix Table A.9, again, serves as a useful robustness check on the decentralization result.

TABLE A.9. INCLUDING 2001

Variables	Model 1 Logit Fixed	Model 2 Logit Random	Model 3 Poisson Fixed	Model 4 Poisson Random	Model 5 Negative Binomial
Decentralized	0.25***	0.10***	0.15***	0.11***	0.15***
	(0.04)	(0.03)	(0.02)	(0.02)	(0.03)
Religious Competition	0.30*	0.13	0.25***	0.21***	0.20
	(0.18)	(0.15)	(0.07)	(0.06)	(0.14)
Political Theology	0.29***	0.29***	0.38***	0.36***	0.37***
	(0.09)	(0.08)	(0.03)	(0.03)	(0.07)
Party Competition	0.37***	0.35***	0.28***	0.28***	0.31***
	(0.04)	(0.04)	(0.02)	(0.02)	(0.03)
Church/State Legacies	−0.06***	−0.03**	−0.01*	−0.01**	−0.02
	(0.02)	(0.01)	(0.01)	(0.01)	(0.02)
Deprivation	−1.11***	−1.13***	−0.73***	−0.72***	−0.83***
	(0.40)	(0.38)	(0.15)	(0.15)	(0.31)
Ethnic Heterogeneity	0.16	0.15	0.06	0.04	−0.01
	(0.12)	(0.12)	(0.05)	(0.05)	(0.10)
Good Economic Status	0.21***	0.22***	0.14***	0.14***	0.14***
	(0.05)	(0.05)	(0.02)	(0.02)	(0.04)
Bad Economic Status	−0.08**	−0.08**	−0.11***	−0.11***	−0.11***
	(0.04)	(0.04)	(0.02)	(0.02)	(0.03)
Gender	0.19***	0.19***	0.20***	0.20***	0.19***
	(0.04)	(0.04)	(0.01)	(0.01)	(0.03)
Age	0.03***	0.03***	0.03***	0.03***	0.03***
	(0.01)	(0.01)	(0.00)	(0.00)	(0.00)
Age Squared	−0.00***	−0.00***	−0.00***	−0.00***	−0.00***
	(0.00)	(0.00)	(0.00)	(0.00)	(0.00)
Constant		−1.21***		−0.70***	0.64***
		(0.41)		(0.16)	(0.02)
Observations	12,501	12,511	12,511	12,511	12,511
Number of Dioceses	85	86	86	86	86

Standard errors in parentheses
***$p < 0.01$, **$p < 0.05$, *$p < 0.1$

Broader Mexican Population
(Discussion)

My primary models focus specifically on Catholics in order to assess the impact of the Catholic Church on its own adherents. Given the importance of the Mexican Catholic Church on Mexican life, I also examine the impacts of my variables of interest on the broader population. Accordingly, in Appendix Table A.10, I examine my primary models on all individuals surveyed.

I run this alternative model as a fixed effects logit model (Model 1), a random effects logit model (Model 2), Poisson fixed and random effects models, (Models 3 and 4, respectively), and a negative binomial regression fixed effects model (Model 5). The results are substantively similar to the results of the continuous measure used in the primary models. The most notable difference is that religious competition is now somewhat less robust. As theories of Protestant competition are concerned with the internal dynamics of religious institutions, the models restricted to Catholics may be fairer tests of that particular theory. This is because individuals who are not Catholics are unlikely to be affected by efforts of Catholic clergy to counter Protestant competition.

TABLE A.10. BROADER MEXICAN POPULATION

Variables	Model 1 Logit Fixed	Model 2 Logit Random	Model 3 Poisson Fixed	Model 4 Poisson Random	Model 5 Negative Binomial
Decentralized	0.33***	0.10**	0.13***	0.08***	0.13***
	(0.11)	(0.04)	(0.02)	(0.02)	(0.04)
Religious Competition	0.55*	0.29	0.18**	0.15**	0.16
	(0.32)	(0.19)	(0.07)	(0.07)	(0.15)
Political Theology	0.43*	0.28***	0.39***	0.31***	0.43***
	(0.25)	(0.11)	(0.06)	(0.05)	(0.11)
Party Competition	0.05	0.01	0.07***	0.07***	0.05
	(0.09)	(0.05)	(0.02)	(0.02)	(0.04)
Church/State Legacies	−0.04*	−0.03	0.01	0.00	0.01
	(0.02)	(0.02)	(0.01)	(0.01)	(0.02)
Deprivation	−1.28	−1.29***	−0.38**	−0.35**	−0.30
	(0.81)	(0.48)	(0.17)	(0.16)	(0.35)
Ethnic Heterogeneity	0.07	0.05	0.07	0.04	0.02
	(0.26)	(0.14)	(0.05)	(0.05)	(0.11)
Good Economic Status	0.16***	0.17***	0.11***	0.11***	0.11***
	(0.06)	(0.06)	(0.02)	(0.02)	(0.04)
Bad Economic Status	−0.10	−0.10*	−0.12***	−0.12***	−0.11***
	(0.06)	(0.05)	(0.02)	(0.02)	(0.04)
Gender	0.21***	0.21***	0.18***	0.18***	0.18***
	(0.05)	(0.05)	(0.02)	(0.02)	(0.03)
Age	0.03***	0.03***	0.03***	0.03***	0.03***
	(0.01)	(0.01)	(0.00)	(0.00)	(0.01)
Age Squared	−0.00***	−0.00***	−0.00***	−0.00***	−0.00***
	(0.00)	(0.00)	(0.00)	(0.00)	(0.00)
Low Religiosity	0.13*	0.14**	0.11***	0.11***	0.10**
	(0.07)	(0.07)	(0.02)	(0.02)	(0.05)
Moderate Religiosity	0.17**	0.18***	0.10***	0.11***	0.09**
	(0.07)	(0.06)	(0.02)	(0.02)	(0.04)
High Religiosity	0.21**	0.23***	0.19***	0.20***	0.15***
	(0.10)	(0.08)	(0.03)	(0.03)	(0.06)
Year	−0.10	−0.07***	0.02*	0.02**	0.01
	(0.06)	(0.03)	(0.01)	(0.01)	(0.02)
Practicing Catholic	−0.04	−0.05	−0.11***	−0.12***	−0.12***
	(0.09)	(0.07)	(0.02)	(0.02)	(0.05)
Constant		148.54***		−47.20**	−22.48
		(52.11)		(18.37)	(38.16)
Observations	8,437	8,462	8,447	8,462	8,462
Number of Dioceses	83	85	84	85	85

Standard errors in parentheses
***$p < 0.01$, **$p < 0.05$, *$p < 0.1$

Municipality Selection

Choosing the local municipalities in which I conducted the majority of my interviews was assisted by Guillermo Trejo's *Mexican Indigenous Insurgency Dataset* (MII).[1] Trejo's dataset tracks all indigenous protests from 1976 to 2000 (Trejo 2010), and the unit of analysis is a city-year. As my interest was identifying cities rather than city-years to conduct my qualitative interviews, I summed the total protest events in each municipality of Chiapas and Yucatán from 1976 to 2000 and developed averages of Trejo's provided measures of religious competition, corporatism, electoral competition, repression, poverty, and the proportion of indigenous population for each municipality over the same time period (Trejo 2009, 330–31). I added three additional variables. The first measured the population of each city in the year 2000 (CDI 2000). I also added a binary variable indicating whether the city was in the Catholic Diocese of San Cristóbal de las Casas. This was done to differentiate the Diocese of San Cristóbal de las Casas from the other two dioceses of Chiapas and from the Archdiocese of Yucatán. I developed a final binary variable to assess whether a city belonged in the state of Chiapas or Yucatán. I then regressed the total number of protests in each municipality as a function of religious competition, corporatism, electoral competition, repression, poverty, proportion indigenous population, and the two binary variables for state and diocese.

Following the regression, I computed standardized residuals to exclude deviant cities (Seawright and Gerring 2008). The cities also needed maximum variation in protest events to facilitate the controlled comparison. At the same time, the cities needed to be as near as possible across a range of theoretically relevant independent variables. I identified San Cristóbal de las Casas[2] in Chiapas and Valladolid and Tizimín in Yucatán as the locations to conduct my qualitative interviews. They display wide variation in the number of protest events.

As review of Appendix Table A.11 illustrates, the cities display simi-

TABLE A.11. SAN CRISTÓBAL DE LAS CASAS, TIZIMÍN, AND VALLADOLID

City	State	Protest Events	Population	Poverty	Standardized Residual
San Cristóbal	Chiapas	101	132,421	0.34	1.29
Tizimín	Yucatán	0	64,104	0.39	−0.40
Valladolid	Yucatán	6	56,776	0.33	−0.17

City	ReligiousComp.	Corp.	ElectoralComp.	Repression	Percent Indigenous
San Cristóbal	1.32	0.24	1.65	0.81	0.31
Tizimín	1.58	0.41	1.66	0.00	0.66
Valladolid	1.23	0.49	1.60	0.00	0.64

lar characteristics across a wide range of factors including population size, religious competition, poverty, corporatism, electoral competition, repression, and proportion indigenous, but maximum variance on protest. This makes these cities as representative as possible of communities in Chiapas and Yucatán while maintaining a viable method of contrast across a range of variation in protest (Seawright and Gerring 2008).

The municipality of San Cristóbal de las Casas at the turn of the twenty-first century had a population of around 132,000, and it is located in the central highlands of Chiapas. While San Cristóbal tends to be moderately less indigenous, more affluent, and more Catholic than the rest of the diocese, many of the organizations that developed throughout the Chiapan countryside maintain an organizational presence in San Cristóbal. This made an ideal central location to conduct interviews with organizations spread out all across the state. It is also the headquarters of the Catholic Diocese of San Cristóbal de las Casas. Located in the northeast corner of Yucatán, Tizimín is among the largest geographical municipalities in the state and has a population of around 64,000. Protestant competition here is slightly larger than Yucatán generally. Approximately 52 percent of the population speaks an indigenous language (Yucatec Maya). Thirty-nine percent of the population lives in poverty. About half of the population is made up by the small *comisarías* (small towns) surrounding Tizimín, most of which are at least forty kilometers outside of the city. The comisarías experience little growth and are made up primarily of campesinos. The north of Tizimín is marked by ranches and cowhands, and few in the northern regions attend school. Much of the city is poor and largely populated by Mayan individuals. Finally, Valladolid is located in the southeastern portion of Yucatán with a population of approximately 57,000 individuals, about 63 percent of whom speak an indigenous language. Thirty-three percent of the population lives in poverty. Approximately 86 percent of the population practices Roman Catholicism. Like Tizimín, the parishes in the city center also service comisarías near the city. Also like Tizimín, the people are generally very religious (CDI 2000; Trejo 2010).

Notes

ACKNOWLEDGMENTS

1. Any opinions, findings, and conclusions or recommendations expressed in this material are those of the author and do not necessarily reflect the views of the National Science Foundation.

2. © Religion and Politics Section of the American Political Science Association 2017

CHAPTER I

1. While the term "peasant" may seem antiquated, it is commonly used by experts, including in recent scholarship, to refer to Mexico's poor rural farming class for whom access to land is a dominant preoccupation (Mattiace 2003, 30).

2. As I elaborate in chapter 2, religious institutions emphasize the supernatural, develop comprehensive accounts of human existence, and are collective enterprises that structure local interactions in important ways.

3. Some readers may think of decentralization in a geographic sense, such as the United Kingdom's devolution of governance authority to regional assemblies in Wales, Ireland, and Scotland. However, my understanding of decentralization is borrowed from economic and game-theoretic approaches where local actors share responsibility for monitoring, sanctioning, and decision-making. I am subsequently interested in whether Catholic adherents, rather than clergy, share governance responsibility in the Church more so than whether the Church has devolved authority to geographic regions.

4. More precisely, I utilize a framework of "bounded rationality" as explained more fully at the end of chapter 2.

5. Indigenous and African religious traditions certainly existed, and the Catholic Church often incorporated them (Prokopy and Smith 1999, 4).

6. There is little systematic difference between archdioceses and dioceses. Archdioceses have no governing authority over dioceses, archbishops and bishops enjoy the same rank, and both have a great deal of autonomous decision-making authority over their territory (Camp 1997, 261).

7. These countries include Bolivia, Guatemala, and Peru.

8. When I refer to indigenous activism, I refer to activism around any issue area organized primarily by indigenous populations. Such activism does not need to advance specifically indigenous ethnic interests or be coordinated around indigenous identity politics.

9. Trejo codes protest events as demonstrations, road blockades, hunger strikes, and additional similar actions by indigenous populations across "883 Mexican indigenous municipalities between 1975 and 2000" (Trejo 2009, 329–30). "A protest event is assigned to a municipality every time indigenous villagers or groups from that municipality participate in a protest event, regardless of where the event takes place" (Trejo 2009, 330).

10. These three dioceses are the Archdiocese of Tuxtla Gutiérrez to the northwest, the Diocese of Tapachula to the south, and the Diocese of San Cristóbal de las Casas.

11. Of the 2,382 protest events referenced earlier that have occurred in Chiapas, a full 2,132 (90 percent) of those events have taken place in the Diocese of San Cristóbal de las Casas (Trejo 2010).

12. Chiapas was characterized by a high degree of political activism beginning in the 1970s, long before the Zapatista uprising in 1994. It experienced 937 protest events before the Zapatista uprising in 1994 (spanning a period from 1975 to 1993). Yucatán, on the other hand, had 54 such events during the same time (Trejo 2010).

13. Shannan Mattiace has suggestively pointed to Chiapas and Yucatán as cases where the Catholic Church has differed greatly in prompting indigenous collective action (Mattiace 2009). Utilizing this "diverse cases" method of case selection, the representativeness of my small-N comparison is increased because the full range of variation in the dependent variable is captured (Seawright and Gerring 2008).

14. The characteristics of religious orders in the two regions are also similar in terms of priests per capita (Cheney 2015). Furthermore, individual missions typically serve a specific local area, and their influence cannot account for diocese-wide trends.

15. As of the year 2000, Protestants accounted for 21.9 percent of the population of Chiapas (ranking first among Mexico's thirty-two states), while in Yucatán Protestants accounted for 11.4 percent of the population (ranking fifth among Mexico's thirty-two states). Nationally, Protestants accounted for 7.3 percent of the population (J. Dow 2005, 830). According to the most recent (2010) Mexican census, Protestants accounted for slightly more than 19 percent of the population, suggesting the rapid growth of Protestantism may have crested during the early part of the twenty-first century. Similarly, Protestants accounted for slightly more than 10 percent of the population in Yucatán in 2010, while nationally Protestants were 7.5 percent of the population (INEGI 2011).

16. These numbers are even lower in the city of Cuernavaca where I conducted my qualitative interviews. Only 2.8 percent of the population identifies as indig-

enous and 1.5 percent of the population speaks an indigenous language. According to the most recent census (2010), 1.8 percent of the population of Morelos is indigenous (INEGI 2010).

17. Historians may bring their own theoretical biases into their analyses, and it is subsequently problematic to treat these as pure histories for testing social scientific theories. However, such dangers can be mitigated to the extent that the researcher uses a variety of historical works, each expressing different explanations for the occurrence of the historical phenomenon of interest (Lustick 1996).

18. All interviews were transcribed in Yucatán by Spanish-speaking undergraduate students at the Universidad Autónoma de Yucatán.

19. This project, and my procedure for interviewing respondents, was reviewed by Arizona State University's Institutional Review Board on June 24, 2011.

20. There is also a popular perception of a strong link between the PAN party and the Church, and this might have encouraged Catholic political participation in regions demonstrating higher levels of PAN political strength. However, most scholars generally downplay a Church/PAN link (Camp 1997; Loaeza 2003; Camp 2007, 2008; Blancarte 2006; Mizrahi 2003; Magaloni and Moreno 2003).

CHAPTER 2

1. Though I make it clear here I understand political activism is a specific form of collective action, I default to convention and use the two terms interchangeably throughout the book. See Tilly 1978; Morris 1981, 746; Zald 1996.

2. The very nature of activism involves contentious political issues. The wealthy may not view generous welfare provision as a public good when they pay disproportionate costs to provide it. Nearly everyone can likely point to political activism in certain issue domains that they feel does not produce desirable benefits. However, for the subset of those who do benefit from changes to political policies, political activism results in a public good that cannot be excluded from individuals who did not take on costly activism.

3. Political science has long analyzed political participation from a public goods perspective. A great deal of work has struggled with the application of the public goods approach to voting, for example. However, as we have already seen, voting is a relatively low-cost activity (Pacheco and Owen 2015, 224–25; Aldrich 1993; Lichbach 1998, 6). For this reason, collective action theory, with its emphasis on costs relative to benefits, may be less helpful in explaining voting than other higher cost forms of political participation such as protest (Leighley 1995, 182).

4. My understanding of religious institutions draws heavily from the work of Stark and Bainbridge and from Grzymala-Busse's definition (Stark and Bainbridge 1985; Grzymala-Busse 2012).

5. Christian Smith's influential (1991) examination of liberation theology also examines religiously related activism from the perspective of framing, opportunity, and resource mobilization. The current study builds on that approach by integrating recent theoretical innovations in the religious economy school into that framework, and it also seeks to integrate my own new theory accounting for internal resource mobilization.

6. However, more recent studies have reoriented our focus toward the importance of grievance in explaining collective action. My study takes potential grievances seriously as a potential cause of collective action.

7. Solutions to the collective action problem are vast and a full review is impossible here. Classic solutions tend to focus on the size of the group, selective incentives, club goods, repetitive interactions, the state, political process preferences, ratios of benefits to costs, and community norms (Olson 1965; Buchanan 1965; Hardin 1982; Margolis 1982; Taylor 1987; Hechter 1987; Taylor 1990; North 1990, 13–14).

8. See Berman (2011) for an excellent and accessible further introduction to the club goods approach.

9. An argument could be made that the sacrifice and stigma approach applies to mainstream religious organizations as well, but at a lessened level. In other words, mainstream religious organizations enact some limited sacrifice and stigma requirements and could accordingly prompt some degree of collective action. However, mainstream religious organizations often prompt a wide degree of collective action, often with little recourse to sacrifice or stigma requirements (Warner et al. 2018). Sacrifice and stigma constitutes a powerful means for religious organizations to prompt club goods production, but it is not the only means, and it is likely not extensively employed enough within mainstream religious institutions to prompt large movements of political activism.

10. While I assume individuals generally are boundedly rational, I do not assume individuals are exclusively motivated by rational decision-making, as elaborated in the concluding section of this chapter.

11. A large literature has analyzed decentralization by national states to regional substate units (Hayek 1945; Tiebout 1956; Qian and Weingast 1997; Bardhan 2002, 187–88; Nylen 2002; Goldfrank 2007; Vráblíková 2014). While much of the literature extols the virtues of decentralization by the state, scholarship is mixed and some scholars warn of unintended consequences such as local corruption and increased income inequality (Warner 2007; Prud'homme 1995; Davoodi and Zou 1998; Treisman 2000; Fisman and Gatti 2002; Dasgupta and Beard 2007). Furthermore, this literature has tended to be preoccupied with state outputs such as tax collection and policy, economic performance, and democratic accountability (Wibbels 2006). Less emphasis has been given in this literature to decentralization's impact on grassroots collective action.

12. To be clear, this does not mean there is no distinction between clergy and adherents, and my conceptualization of decentralization does not require complete devolution of ecclesial control from clergy to laity. In most religious settings, there is typically some differentiation between those who are members of the religion and those who are empowered to make doctrinal decisions (Gill 2001, 120). Decision-making is important, but so is lay responsibility for monitoring and sanctioning the production of religious club goods, and this dimension of religious decentralization has largely been ignored by previous literature. As we will see, it has important implications for collective action.

13. Or similarly rational sacrifice and stigma requirements that weed out free riders.

CHAPTER 3

1. The Catholic Church, particularly when it has been anecdotally noted as progressive and decentralized, has been noted to have been a key mobilizer of independent civil society (Olvera 2004, 415).

2. The measure includes organizing, sending letters to a newspaper, complaining to authorities, soliciting support from a civic association, attending marches, petitioning a political party for help, petitioning the federal legislature for help, calling a radio or TV program, writing the president or other authorities, signing petitions, posting letters/fliers, circulating manifestos, carrying signs, or participating in any other form of activism.

3. The results for the Count Activism measure are presented in Appendix Table A.4.

4. To create my "Decentralized" variable, I took the natural log of the number of permanent deacons in each diocese to correct for a nonnormal distribution. To account for dioceses with no deacons, I added 0.5 to the raw value of all deacon values before making the transformation. For a separate analysis, I also created a categorical measure by breaking the number of permanent deacons into three discrete categories. The first category measures only those dioceses with no deacons, and the subsequent **"No Decentralization"** variable accounts for slightly less than half (47 percent) of Mexico's dioceses. The next measure, **"Moderate Decentralization,"** consists of those dioceses possessing between one and forty-seven deacons (one standard deviation from the mean). This measure captures roughly 46 percent of the dioceses in Mexico. Finally, **"Heavy Decentralization"** represents those dioceses ranking in the top 6 percent (beyond one standard deviation from the mean) in numbers of permanent deacons (more than forty-seven deacons). Within these models, "No Decentralization" is the omitted category, and the remaining decentralization variables in the model are interpreted in relation to the "No Decentralization" variable. The results for the alternative categorical measurement of decentralization are presented in Appendix Table A.7. I furthermore present models controlling for the Catholic population and the number of priests in each diocese in Appendix Table A.8.

5. The census provides information on the number of individuals who self-identify as Catholics, historical Protestants, Pentecostals, members of the Church of the Living God, members of other evangelical groups, members of nonevangelical biblical groups, Seventh-Day Adventists, Mormons, Jehovah's Witnesses, Jewish individuals, other, or nonreligious in a reasonably comprehensive accounting of Mexico's various religious groups.

6. Where 1 is divided by the sum of the proportion of individuals adhering to all religious groups: $ENR = 1/\Sigma r_i^2$ where r_i is the proportion of individuals in a municipality adhering to religion i.

7. Alternatively, I might have used the popular seats in the Chamber of Deputies. However, the proportional and popular seats have a correlation of 0.999.

8. Age often has a curvilinear relationship with outcomes of interest. We might reasonably expect individuals are more likely to engage in activism as they get older. However, once they reach a certain age, they become less likely to participate. Because of this, I model the impact of age quadratically as **"Age"** and **"Age Squared."**

9. For my primary models presented in the book, I do not include the 2001 survey data. As I further describe in the description accompanying Appendix Table A.9, the wording of the dependent variable changed between 2001 and 2003, and the 2001 survey did not ask respondents about their religiosity or religious affiliation, two subjects of obvious interest to this study. However, I do run the models including the 2001 data in the appendix to further assess the robustness of my results, and the results are similar to those presented here. Finally, descriptive statistics for all variables used in the models are presented in Appendix Tables A.1a and A.1b.

10. I present the regression results from which Figures 3.1, 3.2, 3.3, 3.4, were derived in Appendix Table A.2. I assess the robustness of these results to random effects logistic regression (Appendix Table A.3), by analyzing my primary dependent variable of political activism as a count of types of activist activities (Appendix Table A.4), and through ordinary least squares regression (Appendix Table A.5). I present interaction effects in Figures 3.5 through 3.7 in the main text, and these figures were derived from the interaction models run in Appendix Table A.6. I also deploy a variety of additional models including alternative decentralization measures, (Appendix Table A.7), controls of the clerical and Catholic populations (Appendix Table A.8), and utilizing the 2001 survey data (Appendix Table A.9). Because my analyses are concerned with factors within the Catholic Church that affect its adherents' activism, my primary models are restricted to self-identified Catholics. However, I also examine models including all Mexicans (Appendix Table A.10). Each of these Appendix Tables is accompanied by a brief description detailing notable results. I have noted in the main text of this chapter those relatively few instances where the results of my appendix models depart from the results presented in the figures in this chapter. The primary difference of note is that the performance of the relative deprivation and Church/state legacy variables is inconsistent across the various models, and overall this analysis provides only limited support for either contention.

11. While my primary models were estimated on conditional fixed effects logistic regression models (Appendix Table A.2, Model 1 and Figure 3.1), I utilized unconditional fixed effects logistic regression models to generate the figures presented in the text as this was more amenable for use with my statistical software. The estimates of both the conditional and unconditional logit fixed effects models are nearly identical.

12. The relationship remains statistically significant with random effects logistic regression as opposed to fixed effects (Appendix Table A.3), with counts of the number of activist events engaged in as opposed to whether an individual engaged in any activist activity (Appendix Table A.4), and with ordinary least squares models (Appendix Table A.5). We further see that the relationship is robust when using the categorical version of the decentralization variable (Appendix Table A.7), with the inclusion of population control measures for the number of clergy and Catholics in each diocese (Appendix Table A.8), when including the 2001 data (Appendix Table A.9), and when the analysis is opened to all Mexican citizens rather than a restricted sample of self-identified Catholics (Appendix Table A.10).

13. The value of 2.3 is approximately one standard deviation from the mean of the natural log of the number of permanent deacons.

14. The only models in which this pops up as statistically significant are the Pois-

son models and the models including the 2001 data. This analysis as a whole, how-ever, provides little support for the contention that political party competition is associated with political activism.

15. It does not show up as statistically significant in most of the robustness checks presented across the appendix except for a few of the models including the 2001 data (Appendix Table A.9).

16. Economic deprivation emerges in and out of statistical significance across the statistical models presented in the appendix.

17. The relationship is not statistically significant in any of the statistical models presented in the appendix.

CHAPTER 4

1. Religious institutions often reorient themselves to respond to demands from adherents (Djupe and Olson 2013). In this case, however, there is little evidence the indigenous populations of Chiapas made demands for decentralization or political responsiveness from Church authorities in the early part of the 1960s.

2. Pastoral workers are the "priests, nuns, and laity who were either assigned to the Maya areas by their religious congregations or who volunteered their services" (Early 2012, 150–51).

3. As will be discussed in more detail in this chapter, many progressive Catho-lic bishops in Mexico and across Latin America attempted to force through their liberation program in a hierarchical manner (Levine 1988, 243; Chand 2001, 191). The Diocese of San Cristóbal de las Casas was very different. Clergy tried to make the Church responsive to their parishioners' own democratically decided agenda.

4. They must also be married and typically serve with their spouses (Interview 46, 2011; Interview 31, 2011).

5. I pushed him on this point, asking him if he had encountered situations where he disagreed with the way the laity ran their organization. "Now, if we didn't agree with something they were doing, that's a tricky situation. You don't say anything publicly. You go to them as you would a friend and say, look, I might do it this way or that way, but that's the extent of it" (Interview 45, 2012).

6. Only one cooperative I spoke with (Interview 83, 2012) had been formed independently of the Church. It was formed in the 1990s, much later than the first wave of cooperatives in the region that formed during the 1960s and 1970s.

7. Some cooperatives provided education and health benefits to nonmembers within their communities. Preferential access to credit, technical assistance, market information, preferential commodity pricing, profit shares, and price floors were restricted to members (Hudson and Hudson 2004, 130–46; Raynolds, Murray, and Taylor 2004, 1109–21; Interview 17, 2012).

8. The spiritual services provided by the Catholic Church were not dependent on working in a cooperative. Religious organizations provide a "menu" of club goods, some contingent on certain forms of participation even if many services are not. Cooperatives provided indigenous Catholic communities a particularly useful organizational model to easily "[identify] and selectively reward high contributors" (McBride 2007, 395).

9. Despite cooperatives' origins within the Catholic Church, cooperative mem-

bership was not restricted to Catholics (Interview 1, 2012; Interview 30, 2012; Interview 17, 2012). Drawn by material benefits, some Protestants came to labor in these groups and were generally welcomed so long as they worked (Interview 1, 2012; Interview 43, 2012). Still, many Protestants stayed away because they were uncomfortable with the cooperatives' Catholic founding. In reality, these cooperatives were almost entirely constituted by Catholics (Womack 1999, 32; Interview 81, 2011; Interview 17, 2012).

10. At the same time, these cooperative arrangements should not be overly romanticized. Communities had serious divisions over whether or not to join and over what would be produced (Interview 1, 2012). Many cooperative members live in conditions of abject poverty and have low levels of education. Variations in land quality give some producers heightened capacities to produce over other members, and international pressures constantly create the danger for increased centralization and technocratization of production (Raynolds, Murray, and Taylor 2004, 1115–16). A cooperative is not "a harmonious space of collective growth but one where political, gender, and class differences have manifested themselves" (Hernández Castillo 2001, 186).

11. By contrast, if cooperatives struggle to produce or to provide their members with tangible material resources, "the interest of producers is lost" (Interview 83, 2012). This is not a hypothetical point. Cooperatives often fail, particularly in situations when they fail to prompt participation from the community (Milford 2012, 2). Recall our observation from chapter 2 that effective group solidarity requires both dependence and control (Hechter 1987). While the cooperatives had means of assuring control through monitoring and sanctioning, they had to foster dependence by giving producers a better price on coffee than by negotiating through traditional intermediaries. If they were not able to do so, people would leave the organization (Jaffee 2007, 56).

12. Like Chiapas, Oaxaca was also characterized by progressive Catholicism, high levels of Protestant competition, and a commitment to decentralization (Norget 1997).

13. These organizations were run by catechists and deacons and predominantly Catholic. "Only Catholics belonged" (Womack 1999, 32).

14. The priest told me that leadership within the EZLN wanted him to travel to Guadalupe Tepeyac to view the preparations they had in place about a month before the uprising (unbeknownst to him at the time). He refused and asked to be transferred to a new location (Interview 45, 2012).

15. The Zapatista uprising elicited a great deal of national and international attention, and the insurgents were savvy in marshaling positive and supportive media coverage for themselves. Soon after the rebellion, the Mexican government adopted the National Mediation Commission, headed by Bishop Samuel Ruiz, to develop a peaceful resolution to the problem. Bishop Ruiz negotiated a ceace-fire within days to prompt a series of talks. These ultimately unraveled in 1998 when Ruiz resigned claiming that the Mexican government was more devoted to war than peace. Despite a military offensive in February of 1995, the government was not able to dislodge the insurgents from their sanctuary in the remote mountains of Chiapas, and the Zapatistas have seemingly forced some concessions from the state. Such apparent concessions included the 1996 San Andrés accords where the gov-

ernment promised that indigenous communities would have autonomous control over their own governance and natural resources. However, the Mexican government has repeatedly reneged on these agreements. Though media interest and the intensity of the conflict have diminished since the early part of the first decade of the twenty-first century, the Zapatistas still organize various marches in San Cristóbal in pursuit of their cause and in solidarity with other social movements across Mexico (Vanden and Prevost 2015, 100–104).

16. This is despite a previous perception by many that he was ideologically conservative while serving as the Bishop of Tapachula.

CHAPTER 5

1. As will be discussed in this chapter, these grievance-based (economic deprivation) accounts of events in Chiapas are unsatisfactory for several reasons.

2. Yucatán is also bordered to its west by Campeche, which had been part of Yucatán until the middle of the nineteenth century. Before Quintana Roo became its own territory at the beginning of the twentieth century, Yucatán was also bordered by the Caribbean to its east.

3. Though the archdiocese gives its priests freedom to formulate their own solutions for local problems, it is important to note that in neither Chiapas nor Yucatán are laity allowed to choose their local parish priests. Priests serve at the pleasure of the bishop, and the bishop has sole decision-making authority over where priests are assigned. Local decision-making authority by priests is not analogous to local decision-making authority by laity.

4. Archbishop Emilio Carlos Berlie Belaunzarán served as the Archbishop of Yucatán until his retirement in 2015 (I conducted my field research in Yucatán in 2011 and 2012). He has been succeeded by Archbishop Gustavo Rodríguez Vega.

5. This is consistent with Mancur Olson's observation that collective action is possible within small groups (Olson 1965).

6. Those individuals I interviewed who did participate civically generally held positions within political parties, were paid salaries for holding governmental positions (Interview 9, 2011; Interview 20, 2011; Interview 25, 2011), or came from families with a history of involvement in politics and holding public office (Interview 67, 2011; Interview 49, 2011).

7. Pastoral assemblies are small jurisdictions where representative members of the laity meet and select individuals to coordinate various activities of the diocese such as lay-manned charitable operations. They may also provide their opinions to the priest. In Yucatán, they meet under the direct supervision and guidance of a parish priest (Interview 11, 2012).

8. Several of my interview respondents suggested the government had been successful in co-opting many organizations (Interview 29, 2011; Interview 32, 2011). "The only thing that the government has done is inject money to divide, to disperse. It's not creating development projects or growth projects. It's only utilizing economic resources to disperse organizations, in order to weaken us" (Interview 43, 2012).

9. The PRD does not have a strong electoral presence in Yucatán (IFE 2010).

10. Though most of the clergy I spoke with suggested the relationship between

the Church and state was respectful, one priest remarked that the relationship between the Church and state was "bad because there has always been confrontation . . . the Church declares the truth" (Interview 31, 2011).

11. Indeed, there is a popular perception of a strong link between the PAN party and the Church. It is possible this could influence political participation in regions demonstrating higher levels of PAN political strength, though scholars generally downplay a strong contemporary Church/PAN link, despite the PAN's Catholic origins (Camp 1997; Loaeza 1999; Camp 2007, 90; 2008; Blancarte 2006; Mizrahi 2003; Magaloni and Moreno 2003).

CHAPTER 6

1. Quoting Bishop Sergio Méndez Arceo.

2. As a point of comparison, the percentage of the indigenous population across the entirety of Mexico is just over 7 percent, and in Chiapas and Yucatán these percentages are 25 and 40 percent, respectively (CDI 2000).

3. Illich's radical ideas were not viewed favorably by the Vatican. In 1969, it forbade clergy from visiting Illich's center in Cuernavaca, the CIDOC (*Centro Intercultural de Documentación*, or the Intercultural Documentation Center), and Illich was encouraged to continue running it in a secular capacity rather than as a member of the Church. While that prohibition was later rescinded, only 15 percent of the individuals who studied there afterward were members of the clergy. The CIDOC closed four years later (Mackin 1997, 62).

4. This commitment was formally expressed later at the bishops' meeting in Puebla in 1979, although most observers attribute the intent of this phrase to the earlier conference in Medellín (Pope 1993, 242).

5. The communities were also aided by the presence of Méndez Arceo, who remained active in the social life of Cuernavaca. He met each Tuesday with lay CEB leaders and with his supporters within the institutional Church. He maintained an active presence in Cuernavaca until his death in 1992 (Mackin 1997, 97; Interview 7, 2012).

CHAPTER 7

1. The degree to which such antagonism is likely is also dependent on how closed the authoritarian political system is, the level of legitimacy of both the religious institution and the state in broader society, the number of adherents of the religion, the degree to which the religion is dependent on the state for resources, and the degree to which the religion usefully provides social services, among other potential factors (Koesel 2014).

APPENDIX TABLE A.7

1. I also added 0.5 to the value of all deacons to account for the substantial number of dioceses with no deacons. This is because the natural log of 0 is undefined.

APPENDIX TABLE A.11

1. With gratitude to Professor Trejo's willingness to share a portion of his dataset.

2. Another reason I chose San Cristóbal de las Casas was because the city serves as a hub and headquarters for civil society organizations throughout Chiapas. In addition to my interviews in San Cristóbal, leads I developed from my own research and subsequent interviews led me across much of the state, including regions as disparate as Bachajón, Chamula, Tuxtla Gutiérrez, Comitán de Dominguez, and Las Margaritas.

Works Cited

Acosta Chávez, Marcela. 2003. "La Quiptic Ta Lecubtesel: Autonomía y acción colectiva." *Nueva Antropología* 19 (63) October: 115–35.

Agrawal, Arun, and Elinor Ostrom. 2001. "Collective Action, Property Rights, and Decentralization in Resource Use in India and Nepal." *Politics and Society* 29 (4): 485–514.

Alchian, Armen A., and Harold Demsetz. 1972. "Production, Information Costs, and Economic Organization." *American Economic Review* 62 (5): 777–95.

Aldrich, John H. 1993. "Rational Choice and Turnout." *American Journal of Political Science* 37 (1): 246–78.

Alesina, Alberto, Reza Baqir, and William Easterly. 1999. "Public Goods and Ethnic Divisions." *Quarterly Journal of Economics* 114 (4): 1243–84.

Allison, Paul D. 2009. *Fixed Effects Regression Models*. Thousand Oaks, Calif.: Sage Publications.

Almond, Gabriel Abraham, and Sidney Verba, eds. 1989. *The Civic Culture: Political Attitudes and Democracy in Five Nations*. Newbury Park, Calif.: Sage Publications.

Andersson, Krister P., and Elinor Ostrom. 2008. "Analyzing Decentralized Resource Regimes from a Polycentric Perspective." *Policy Sciences* 41 (1): 71–93.

Andreoni, James. 1990. "Impure Altruism and Donations to Public Goods: A Theory of Warm-Glow Giving." *Economic Journal* 100 (401): 464–77.

Atran, Scott, and Joseph Henrich. 2010. "The Evolution of Religion: How Cognitive By-Products, Adaptive Learning Heuristics, Ritual Displays, and Group Competition Generate Deep Commitments to Prosocial Religions." *Biological Theory* 5 (1): 18–30.

Bailey, Carol A. 2007. *A Guide to Qualitative Field Research*. Thousand Oaks, Calif.: Sage Publications.

Baklanoff, Eric N. 2008. "Introduction: Yucatán since the 1982 Mexican Debt

Crisis." In *Yucatán in an Era of Globalization*, edited by Eric N. Baklanoff and Edward H. Moseley. Tuscaloosa: University of Alabama Press.

Baldwin, Kate, and John D. Huber. 2010. "Economic versus Cultural Differences: Forms of Ethnic Diversity and Public Goods Provision." *American Political Science Review* 104 (4): 644–62.

Baños Ramírez, Othón. 1988. "Los nuevos campesinos de México: El caso de Yucatán." *Estudios Sociológicos* 6 (17): 309–35.

Bardhan, Pranab. 2002. "Decentralization of Governance and Development." *Journal of Economic Perspectives* 16 (4): 185–205.

Barmeyer, Niels. 2009. *Developing Zapatista Autonomy: Conflict and NGO Involvement in Rebel Chiapas*. Albuquerque: University of New Mexico Press.

Barnes, Samuel Henry. 1979. *Political Action: Mass Participation in Five Western Democracies*. Beverly Hills, Calif.: Sage Publications.

Becker, Penny Edgell, and Pawan H. Dhingra. 2001. "Religious Involvement and Volunteering: Implications for Civil Society." *Sociology of Religion* 62 (3): 315–35.

Bennett, Andrew. 2010. "Process Tracing and Causal Inference." In *Rethinking Social Inquiry: Diverse Tools, Shared Standards*, edited by Henry E. Brady and David Collier. 2nd ed. Lanham, Md.: Rowman and Littlefield.

Berman, Eli. 2011. *Radical, Religious, and Violent: The New Economics of Terrorism*. Paperback ed. Cambridge, Mass.: MIT Press.

Berman, Eli, and David D. Laitin. 2008. "Religion, Terrorism and Public Goods: Testing the Club Model." *Journal of Public Economics* 92 (10–11): 1942–67.

Besançon, Marie L. 2005. "Relative Resources: Inequality in Ethnic Wars, Revolutions, and Genocides." *Journal of Peace Research* 42 (4): 393–415.

Betances, Emelio. 2007. *The Catholic Church and Power Politics in Latin America: The Dominican Case in Comparative Perspective*. Lanham, Md.: Rowman and Littlefield.

Birch, Sarah. 2010. "Perceptions of Electoral Fairness and Voter Turnout." *Comparative Political Studies* 43 (12): 1601–22.

Bishara, Dina. 2015. "The Politics of Ignoring: Protest Dynamics in Late Mubarak Egypt." *Perspectives on Politics* 13 (4): 958–75.

Blackbourn, David. 1991. "The Catholic Church in Europe since the French Revolution: A Review Article." *Comparative Studies in Society and History* 33 (4): 778–90.

Blake, Charles H. 2008. *Politics in Latin America*. 2nd ed. Boston: Wadsworth Cengage Learning.

Blancarte, Roberto. 2006. "Religion, Church, and State in Contemporary Mexico." In *Changing Structure of Mexico: Political, Social, and Economic Prospects*, edited by Laura Randall. Armonk, N.Y.: M. E. Sharpe.

Booth, John A., and Mitchell A. Seligson. 1978. *Political Participation in Latin America*. New York: Holmes and Meier.

Boulding, Carew. 2014. *NGOs, Political Protest, and Civil Society*. New York: Cambridge University Press.

Bowles, Samuel, and Herbert Gintis. 2004. "The Evolution of Strong Reciprocity: Cooperation in Heterogeneous Populations." *Theoretical Population Biology* 65 (1): 17–28.

Brady, Henry E., David Collier, and Jason Seawright. 2010. "Refocusing the Discussion of Methodology." In *Rethinking Social Inquiry: Diverse Tools, Shared Standards*, edited by Henry E. Brady and David Collier. 2nd ed. Lanham, Md.: Rowman and Littlefield.

Brockett, Charles D. 1991. "The Structure of Political Opportunities and Peasant Mobilization in Central America." *Comparative Politics* 23 (3): 253–74.

Bruneau, Thomas C. 1980. "The Catholic Church and Development in Latin America: The Role of the Basic Christian Communities." *World Development* 8 (7): 535–44.

Buchanan, James M. 1965. "An Economic Theory of Clubs." *Economica* 32 (125): 1–14.

Burns, Nancy, Kay Lehman Schlozman, and Sidney Verba. 2001. *The Private Roots of Public Action: Gender, Equality, and Political Participation.* Cambridge, Mass.: Harvard University Press.

Calhoun-Brown, Allison. 2000. "Upon This Rock: The Black Church, Nonviolence, and the Civil Rights Movement." *PS: Political Science and Politics* 33 (2): 169–74.

Cámara Repetto, Oswaldo, and Baltazar Toloza Pasos. 2000. *Marco legal administrativo contable y fiscal del cooperativismo.* Mérida: Grupo Empresarial Cooperativo Mexicano.

Camp, Roderic Ai. 1997. *Crossing Swords: Politics and Religion in Mexico.* New York: Oxford University Press.

Camp, Roderic Ai. 2007. *Politics in Mexico: The Democratic Consolidation.* 5th ed. New York: Oxford University Press.

Camp, Roderic Ai. 2008. "Exercising Political Influence, Religion, Democracy, and the Mexican 2006 Presidential Race." *Journal of Church and State* 50 (1): 49–72.

Camp, Roderic Ai. 2014. *Politics in Mexico: Democratic Consolidation or Decline?* 6th ed. Oxford: Oxford University Press.

Campos Machado, Maria das Dores. 2016. "Christian Churches, Reproduction, and Sexuality in Latin America." In *The Cambridge History of Religions in Latin America*, edited by Virginia Garrard-Burnett, Paul Freston, and Stephen C. Dove. Cambridge: Cambridge University Press.

Caputo, Richard K. 2009. "Religious Capital and Intergenerational Transmission of Volunteering as Correlates of Civic Engagement." *Nonprofit and Voluntary Sector Quarterly* 38 (6): 983–1002.

Castañeda, Quetzil E. 2004. "'We Are Not Indigenous!': An Introduction to the Maya Identity of Yucatan." *Journal of Latin American Anthropology* 9 (1): 36–63.

Catholic Church. 1993. *Catechism of the Catholic Church.* Vatican City: Libreria Editrice Vaticana. http://www.vatican.va/archive/ccc_css/archive/catechism/p2s2c3a6.htm.

CDI (Comisión Nacional para el Desarrollo de los Pueblos Indígenas). 2000. "INI-CONAPO. Estimaciones de la población indígena, a partir de la base de datos del XII Censo General de Población y Vivienda 2000, INEGI." Comisión Nacional para el Desarrollo de los Pueblos Indígenas.

Cederman, Lars-Erik, Nils B. Weidmann, and Kristian Skrede Gleditsch. 2011. "Horizontal Inequalities and Ethnonationalist Civil War: A Global Comparison." *American Political Science Review* 105 (3): 478–95.

CEM. 2011. "Conferencia del Episcopado Mexicano." 2011. http://www.cem.org.mx/.

Chand, Vikram K. 2001. *Mexico's Political Awakening*. Notre Dame, Ind.: University of Notre Dame Press.

Chandra, Kanchan. 2005. "Ethnic Parties and Democratic Stability." *Perspectives on Politics* 3 (2): 235–52.

Charness, Gary, and Matthew Rabin. 2002. "Understanding Social Preferences with Simple Tests." *Quarterly Journal of Economics* 117 (3): 817–69.

Cheney, David M. 2015. "The Hierarchy of the Catholic Church: Current and Historical Information about Its Bishops and Dioceses." http://www.catholic-hierarchy.org.

Cheng, Tun-jen, and Deborah A. Brown. 2006. *Religious Organizations and Democratization: Case Studies from Contemporary Asia*. Armonk, N.Y.: M. E. Sharpe.

Chesnut, Andrew R. 2003. *Competitive Spirits: Latin America's New Religious Economy*. Oxford: Oxford University Press.

Cifuentes, Bárbara, and José Luis Moctezuma. 2006. "The Mexican Indigenous Languages and the National Censuses: 1970–2000." In *Mexican Indigenous Languages at the Dawn of the Twenty-First Century*, edited by Margarita Hidalgo. Berlin: Mouton de Gruyter.

Clark, William Roberts, Matt Golder, and Sona N. Golder. 2012. *Principles of Comparative Politics*. 2nd ed. Washington, D.C: CQ Press.

Cocom, Juan Castillo. 2005. "'It Was Simply Their Word': Yucatec Maya PRInces in YucaPAN and the Politics of Respect." *Critique of Anthropology* 25 (2): 131–55.

Cohen, Nissim, and Tamar Arieli. 2011. "Field Research in Conflict Environments: Methodological Challenges and Snowball Sampling." *Journal of Peace Research* 48 (4): 423–35.

Coleman, James S. 1990. "Norm-Generating Structures." In *The Limits of Rationality*, edited by Karen Schweers Cook and Margaret Levi. Chicago: University of Chicago Press.

Collier, David, Henry E. Brady, and Jason Seawright. 2010. "Causal Inference: Old Dilemmas, New Tools." In *Rethinking Social Inquiry: Diverse Tools, Shared Standards*, edited by Henry E. Brady and David Collier. 2nd ed. Lanham, Md.: Rowman and Littlefield.

Collier, David, Jason Seawright, and Gerardo L. Munck. 2010. "The Quest for Standards: King, Keohane, and Verba's Designing Social Inquiry." In *Rethinking Social Inquiry: Diverse Tools, Shared Standards*, edited by Henry E. Brady and David Collier. 2nd ed. Lanham, Md.: Rowman and Littlefield.

Collier, George Allen, and Elizabeth Lowery Quaratiello. 1994. *Basta!: Land and the Zapatista Rebellion in Chiapas*. Oakland, Calif.: Food First Book, Institute for Food and Development Policy.

Collier, George Allen, and Elizabeth Lowery Quaratiello. 1999. *Basta!: Land and the Zapatista Rebellion in Chiapas*. rev. ed. Oakland, Calif.: Food First Books.

Collier, George Allen, and Elizabeth Lowery Quaratiello. 2005. *Basta!: Land and the Zapatista Rebellion in Chiapas*. 3rd ed. Oakland, Calif.: Food First Books.

Concha Malo, Miguel, Óscar González Gari, Lino F. Salas, and Jean-Pierre Bastian. 1986. *La participación de los cristianos en el proceso popular de liberación en México (1968–1983)*. Mexico City: Siglo Veintiuno Editores.

Conge, Patrick J. 1988. "The Concept of Political Participation: Toward a Definition." *Comparative Politics* 20 (2): 241–49.

Cornes, Richard, and Todd Sandler. 1996. *The Theory of Externalities, Public Goods, and Club Goods*. Cambridge: Cambridge University Press.

Cruz, Alicia Re. 2008. "Cham Kom Tourism and Migration in the Making of the New Maya Milpas." In *Yucatán in an Era of Globalization*, edited by Eric N. Baklanoff and Edward H. Moseley. Tuscaloosa: University of Alabama Press.

Dasgupta, Aniruddha, and Victoria A. Beard. 2007. "Community Driven Development, Collective Action and Elite Capture in Indonesia." *Development and Change* 38 (2): 229–49.

Daviron, Benoit, and Stefano Ponte. 2005. *The Coffee Paradox*. London: Zed Books.

Davoodi, Hamid, and Heng-Fu Zou. 1998. "Fiscal Decentralization and Economic Growth: A Cross-Country Study." *Journal of Urban Economics* 43 (2): 244–57.

Diani, Mario. 1992. "The Concept of Social Movement." *Sociological Review* 40 (1): 1–25.

Diggles, Michelle Eileen. 2008. "Popular Response to Neoliberal Reform: The Political Configuration of Property Rights in Two Ejidos in Yucatán." PhD diss., University of Oregon.

Djupe, Paul A., and Christopher P. Gilbert. 2006. "The Resourceful Believer: Generating Civic Skills in Church." *Journal of Politics* 68 (1): 116–27.

Djupe, Paul A., and Laura R. Olson. 2013. "Public Deliberation about Gay Rights in Religious Contexts: Commitment to Deliberative Norms and Practice in ELCA Congregations." *Journal of Public Deliberation* 9 (1). http://www.publicdeliberation.net/jpd/vol9/iss1/art1.

Domínguez, Jorge I. 2004. "The Scholarly Study of Mexican Politics." *Mexican Studies/Estudios Mexicanos* 20 (2): 377–410.

Dow, James W. 2005. "The Expansion of Protestantism in Mexico: An Anthropological View." *Anthropological Quarterly* 78 (4): 827–50.

Dow, Thomas E., Jr. 1978. "An Analysis of Weber's Work on Charisma." *British Journal of Sociology* 29 (1) March: 83–93.

Durkheim, Émile. 1915. *The Elementary Forms of the Religious Life*. 5th impression 1964. New York: Free Press.

Eakin, Marshall C. 2007. *The History of Latin America: Collision of Cultures*. New York: Palgrave Macmillan.

Early, John D. 2012. *Maya and Catholic Cultures in Crisis.* Gainesville: University Press of Florida.

Eisenstadt, Todd A. 2011. *Politics, Identity, and Mexico's Indigenous Rights Movements.* Cambridge: Cambridge University Press.

ENCUP. 2010. "Encuesta Nacional sobre Cultura Política y Prácticas Ciudadanas." 2010. http://www.encup.gob.mx/en/Encup/Acerca_de_la_ENCUP.

Fallaw, Ben W. 1997. "Cárdenas and the Caste War That Wasn't: State Power and Indigenismo in Post-Revolutionary Yucatán." *The Americas* 53 (4): 551–77.

Fehr, Ernst, and Herbert Gintis. 2007. "Human Motivation and Social Cooperation: Experimental and Analytical Foundations." *Annual Review of Sociology* 33: 43–64.

Fetzer, Joel S., and J. Christopher Soper. 2005. *Muslims and the State in Britain, France, and Germany.* Cambridge: Cambridge University Press.

Fisman, Raymond, and Roberta Gatti. 2002. "Decentralization and Corruption: Evidence from U.S. Federal Transfer Programs." *Public Choice* 113 (1/2): 25–35.

Floyd, J. Charlene. 1996. "A Theology of Insurrection? Religion and Politics in Mexico." *Journal of International Affairs* 50 (1): 142–65.

Fox, J., and S. Sandler, eds. 2006. *Bringing Religion into International Relations.* Houndmills: Palgrave Macmillan.

Frank, Elisa, Hallie Eakin, and David López-Carr. 2011. "Social Identity, Perception and Motivation in Adaptation to Climate Risk in the Coffee Sector of Chiapas, Mexico." *Global Environmental Change* 21: 66–76.

Franklin, Mark N. 2004. *Voter Turnout and the Dynamics of Electoral Competition in Established Democracies since 1945.* Cambridge: Cambridge University Press.

Fu, Diana. 2017. *Mobilizing with the Masses.* Cambridge: Cambridge University Press.

Gabbert, Wolfgang. 2004. *Becoming Maya: Ethnicity and Social Inequality in Yucatán since 1500.* Tucson: University of Arizona Press.

García, María Elena. 2008. "Introduction: Indigenous Encounters in Contemporary Peru." *Latin American and Caribbean Ethnic Studies* 3 (3): 217–26.

George, Alexander L., and Andrew Bennett. 2005. *Case Studies and Theory Development in the Social Sciences.* Cambridge, Mass.: MIT Press.

Gerring, John, and Lee Cojocaru. 2016. "Selecting Cases for Intensive Analysis: A Diversity of Goals and Methods." *Sociological Methods and Research* 45 (3): 392–423.

Gill, Anthony. 1998. *Rendering unto Caesar: The Catholic Church and the State in Latin America.* Chicago: University of Chicago Press.

Gill, Anthony. 1999. "Catholic Responses to Protestant Growth in Latin America." In *Latin American Religion in Motion,* edited by Christian Smith and Joshua Prokopy. New York: Routledge.

Gill, Anthony. 2001. "Religion and Comparative Politics." *Annual Review of Political Science* 4 (1): 117–38.

Gill, Anthony. 2008. *The Political Origins of Religious Liberty.* Cambridge: Cambridge University Press.

Goldfrank, Benjamin. 2007. "The Politics of Deepening Local Democracy: Decentralization, Party Institutionalization, and Participation." *Comparative Politics* 39 (2): 147–68.

González Vázquez, Tonatiuh. 2001. "De la deslegitimación del gobierno al desborde de la sociedad civil en Morelos." Programa Interdisciplinario de Estudios del Tercer Sector, no. 11.

Graham, Jesse, and Jonathan Haidt. 2010. "Beyond Beliefs: Religions Bind Individuals into Moral Communities." *Personality and Social Psychology Review* 14 (1): 140–50.

Grzymala-Busse, Anna. 2012. "Why Comparative Politics Should Take Religion (More) Seriously." *Annual Review of Political Science* 15 (1): 421–42.

Grzymala-Busse, Anna. 2015. *Nations under God: How Churches use Moral Authority to Influence Policy*. Princeton: Princeton University Press.

Gurr, Ted Robert. 1970. *Why Men Rebel*. Princeton, N.J.: Published for the Center of International Studies, Princeton University [by] Princeton University Press.

Habyarimana, James, Macartan Humphreys, Daniel N. Posner, and Jeremy M. Weinstein. 2007. "Why Does Ethnic Diversity Undermine Public Goods Provision?" *American Political Science Review* 101 (4): 709–25.

Hagopian, Frances. 2009. "Introduction: The New Landscape." In *Religious Pluralism, Democracy, and the Catholic Church in Latin America*, edited by Frances Hagopian. Notre Dame, Ind.: Notre Dame University Press.

Hall, Peter A. 1986. *Governing the Economy: The Politics of State Intervention in Britain and France*. Cambridge, U.K.: Polity Press.

Hall, Peter A., and Rosemary C. R. Taylor. 1996. "Political Science and the Three New Institutionalisms." *Political Studies* 44 (5): 936–57.

Hansen, John Mark. 2016. "Mobilization, Participation, and Political Change." *Party Politics* 22 (2): 149–57.

Hardin, Russell. 1982. *Collective Action*. Baltimore: Published for Resources for the Future by Johns Hopkins University Press.

Hardin, Russell. 1990. "The Social Evolution of Cooperation." In *The Limits of Rationality*, edited by Karen Schweers Cook and Margaret Levi. Chicago: University of Chicago Press.

Harris, Fredrick C. 1994. "Something Within: Religion as a Mobilizer of African-American Political Activism." *Journal of Politics* 56 (1): 42–68.

Hart, Paul. 2005. *Bitter Harvest: The Social Transformation of Morelos, Mexico, and the Origins of the Zapatista Revolution, 1840—1910*. Albuquerque: University of New Mexico Press.

Hartch, Todd. 2014. *The Rebirth of Latin American Christianity*. New York: Oxford University Press.

Harvey, Neil. 1998. *The Chiapas Rebellion: The Struggle for Land and Democracy*. Durham, N.C.: Duke University Press.

Hayek, F. A. 1945. "The Use of Knowledge in Society." *American Economic Review* 35 (4): 519–30.

Healy, Teresa. 2008. *Gendered Struggles against Globalisation in Mexico*. Aldershot: Ashgate.

Hechter, Michael. 1987. *Principles of Group Solidarity*. Berkeley: University of California Press.

Hechter, Michael. 1990. "On the Inadequacy of Game Theory for the Solution of Real-World Collective Action Problems." In *The Limits of Rationality*, edited by Karen Schweers Cook and Margaret Levi. Chicago: University of Chicago Press.

Hechter, Michael, Steven Pfaff, and Patrick Underwood. 2016. "Grievances and the Genesis of Rebellion: Mutiny in the Royal Navy, 1740 to 1820." *American Sociological Review* 81 (1): 165–89.

Heckathorn, Douglas D. 1989. "Collective Action and the Second-Order Free-Rider Problem." *Rationality and Society* 1 (1): 78–100.

Heilbronner, Oded. 1998. *Catholicism, Political Culture, and the Countryside: A Social History of the Nazi Party in South Germany*. Ann Arbor: University of Michigan Press.

Henrich, Joseph, Robert Boyd, Samuel Bowles, Colin Camerer, Ernst Fehr, Herbert Gintis, and Richard McElreath. 2001. "In Search of Homo Economicus: Behavioral Experiments in 15 Small-Scale Societies." *American Economic Review* 91 (2): 73–78.

Hernández Castillo, Rosalva Aída. 2001. *Histories and Stories from Chiapas: Border Identities in Southern Mexico*. Austin: University of Texas Press.

Hernández Castillo, Rosalva Aída, and Ronald Nigh. 1998. "Global Processes and Local Identity among Mayan Coffee Growers in Chiapas, Mexico." *American Anthropologist* 100 (1): 136–47.

Heusinkveld, Paula R. 2008. "Tinum, Yucatán." In *Yucatán in an Era of Globalization*, edited by Eric N. Baklanoff and Edward H. Moseley. Tuscaloosa: University of Alabama Press.

Hiskey, Jonathan T., and Shaun Bowler. 2005. "Local Context and Democratization in Mexico." *American Journal of Political Science* 49 (1): 57–71.

Horowitz, Donald L. 1985. *Ethnic Groups in Conflict*. Berkeley: University of California Press.

Hsiung, Benjamin O., and Paul A. Djupe. Forthcoming. "Religion and the Extension of Trust." *Political Behavior*.

Htun, Mala. 2003. *Sex and the State: Abortion, Divorce, and the Family under Latin American Dictatorships and Democracies*. Cambridge: Cambridge University Press.

Hudson, Mark, and Ian Hudson. 2004. "Justice, Sustainability, and the Fair Trade Movement: A Case Study of Coffee Production in Chiapas." *Social Justice* 31 (3 [97]): 130–46.

Huntington, Samuel P. 1993. "The Clash of Civilizations?" *Foreign Affairs* 72 (3): 22–49.

Hurd, Elizabeth Shakman. 2008. *The Politics of Secularism in International Relations*. Princeton, N.J.: Princeton University Press.

Iannaccone, Laurence R. 1992. "Sacrifice and Stigma: Reducing Free-Riding in Cults, Communes, and Other Collectives." *Journal of Political Economy* 100 (2): 271–91.

Iannaccone, Laurence R. 1994. "Why Strict Churches Are Strong." *American Journal of Sociology* 99 (5): 1180–1211.

Iannaccone, Laurence R., and Eli Berman. 2006. "Religious Extremism: The Good, the Bad, and the Deadly." *Public Choice* 128 (1/2): 109–29.

IFE (aka Instituto National Electoral). 2010. "Instituto Federal Electoral, 2000–2005." 2010. http://www.ife.org.mx/portal/site/ifev2.

Inclán, María de la Luz. 2008. "From the *¡Ya Basta!* to the *Caracoles*: Zapatista Mobilization under Transitional Conditions." *American Journal of Sociology* 113 (5): 1316–50.

INEGI (Instituto Nacional de Estadística y Geografía). 2009. "Perfil sociodemográfico de la población que habla lengua indígena." Aguascalientes: Instituto Nacional de Estadística y Geografía.

INEGI. 2010. "Instituto Nacional de Estadística y Geografía." 2010. http://www.inegi.org.mx/.

INEGI. 2011. "Panorama de las religiones en México 2010." Aguascalientes: Instituto Nacional de Estadística y Geografía.

Interview 1. 2012. Church official. Chiapas, August 2.

Interview 2. 2012. Cooperative member. Chiapas, August 2.

Interview 3. 2011. Charitable organization. Chiapas, November 9.

Interview 4. 2011. Church volunteer. Chiapas, December 2.

Interview 5. 2011. Government official. Chiapas, November 11.

Interview 6. 2012. Civic association. Morelos, August 27.

Interview 7. 2012. Civic association. Morelos, August 29.

Interview 8. 2011. Government official. Yucatán, October 27.

Interview 9. 2011. Government official. Yucatán, October 28.

Interview 10. 2011. Citizen. Yucatán, October 28.

Interview 11. 2012. Church official. Yucatán, June 14.

Interview 14. 2012. Civic association. Morelos, August 24.

Interview 15. 2012. Civic association. Morelos, August 23.

Interview 17. 2012. Cooperative member. Chiapas, July 25.

Interview 19. 2011. Government official. Chiapas, November 22.

Interview 20. 2011. Party official. Yucatán, October 21.

Interview 22. 2012. Church official. Yucatán, June 28.

Interview 23. 2012. Church official. Yucatán, June 18.

Interview 24. 2012. Protestant minister. Yucatán, July 9.

Interview 25. 2011. Party official. Yucatán, October 24.

Interview 26. 2011. Citizen. Yucatán, October 13.

Interview 28. 2011. Civic association. Chiapas, November 28.

Interview 29. 2011. Civic association. Chiapas, November 17.

Interview 30. 2012. Cooperative member. Chiapas, July 23.

Interview 31. 2011. Church representative. Chiapas, December 1.

Interview 32. 2011. Civic association. Chiapas, November 29.

Interview 34. 2011. Civic association. Morelos, August 20.

Interview 35. 2012. Civic association. Morelos, August 27.

Interview 37. 2011. Civic leader. Yucatán, October 12.

Interview 38. 2011. Civic leader. Yucatán, October 12.

Interview 39. 2012. Church volunteer. Yucatán, June 21.

Interview 41. 2012. Citizen. Yucatán, June 29.

Interview 42. 2011. Government official. Chiapas, November 15.

Interview 43. 2012. Cooperative member. Chiaps, July 31.

Interview 45. 2012. Church official. Chiapas, July 12.

Interview 46. 2011. Church official. Chiapas, December 1.

Interview 47. 2012. Civic association. Morelos, August 27.

Interview 48. 2011. Civic leader. Yucatán, October 11.

Interview 49. 2011. Government official. Yucatán, October 6.

Interview 50. 2012. Citizen. Yucatán, July 9.

Interview 51. 2011. Church official. Yucatán, October 3.

Interview 52. 2011. Party official. Yucatán, October 10.

Interview 56. 2011. Church official. Chiapas, November 24 and November 27.

Interview 58. 2012. Civic association. Morelos, August 27.

Interview 59. 2012. Civic association. Morelos, August 27.

Interview 60. 2012. Civic association. Morelos, August 21.

Interview 61. 2012. Citizen. Morelos, August 16.

Interview 63. 2011. Church official. Yucatán, October 7.

Interview 67. 2011. Church volunteer. Yucatán, October 12.

Interview 69. 2011. Church official. Yucatán, October 26.

Interview 70. 2011. Citizen. Yucatán, October 29.

Interview 71. 2012. Citizen. Yucatán, September 23.

Interview 81. 2011. Church official. Chiapas, November 4.

Interview 83. 2012. Cooperative member. Chiapas, July 25.

Jaffee, Daniel. 2007. *Brewing Justice: Fair Trade Coffee, Sustainability, and Survival.* Berkeley: University of California Press.

Janssen, Marco A. 2008. "Evolution of Cooperation in a One-Shot Prisoner's Dilemma Based on Recognition of Trustworthy and Untrustworthy Agents." *Journal of Economic Behavior and Organization* 65 (3): 458–71.

Javeline, Debra. 2003. *Protest and the Politics of Blame: The Russian Response to Unpaid Wages.* Ann Arbor: University of Michigan Press.

Jinnah, Muhammad Ali. 1983. "Address by Quaid-i-Azam Mohammad Ali Jinnah at Lahore Session of Muslim League, March, 1940." Islamabad. http://www.columbia.edu/itc/mealac/pritchett/00islamlinks/txt_jinnah_lahore_1940.html.

Jrade, Ramon. 1985. "Inquiries into the Cristero Insurrection against the Mexican Revolution." *Latin American Research Review* 20 (2): 53–69.

Kalyvas, Stathis N. 1996. *The Rise of Christian Democracy in Europe.* Ithaca, N.Y.: Cornell University Press.

Karp, Jeffrey A., and Susan A. Banducci. 2007. "Party Mobilization and Political Participation in New and Old Democracies." *Party Politics* 13 (2): 217–34.

Kaufman, Stuart J. 1996. "Spiraling to Ethnic War: Elites, Masses, and Moscow in Moldova's Civil War." *International Security* 21 (2): 108–38.

King, Gary, Robert O. Keohane, and Sidney Verba. 1994. *Designing Social Inquiry: Scientific Inference in Qualitative Research*. Princeton, N.J.: Princeton University Press.

Kitschelt, Herbert P. 1986. "Political Opportunity Structures and Political Protest: Anti-Nuclear Movements in Four Democracies." *British Journal of Political Science* 16 (1): 57–85.

Klaiber, Jeffrey L. 1998. *The Church, Dictatorships, and Democracy in Latin America*. Maryknoll, N.Y.: Orbis Books.

Klesner, Joseph L. 2007. "Social Capital and Political Participation in Latin America: Evidence from Argentina, Chile, Mexico, and Peru." *Latin American Research Review* 42 (2): 1–32.

Klesner, Joseph L. 2009. "Who Participates? Determinants of Political Action in Mexico." *Latin American Politics and Society* 51 (2): 59–90.

Koelble, Thomas A. 1995. "The New Institutionalism in Political Science and Sociology." *Comparative Politics* 27 (2): 231–43.

Koesel, Karrie J. 2014. *Religion and Authoritarianism: Cooperation, Conflict, and the Consequences*. New York: Cambridge University Press.

Koesel, Karrie J. 2017. "Religion and Regime: Cooperation and Conflict in Contemporary Russia and China." *World Politics* 69 (4): 676–712.

Kollman, Ken. 2013. *Perils of Centralization: Lessons from Church, State, and Corporation*. New York: Cambridge University Press.

Korovkin, Tanya. 2006. "Indigenous Movements in the Central Andes." *Latin American and Caribbean Ethnic Studies* 1 (2): 143–63.

Kovic, Christine. 2004. "Mayan Catholics in Chiapas, Mexico: Practicing the Faith on Their Own Terms." In *Resurgent Voices in Latin America: Indigenous Peoples, Political Mobilization, and Religious Change*, edited by Edward L. Cleary and Timothy J. Steigenga. New Brunswick, N.J.: Rutgers University Press.

Kovic, Christine. 2005. *Mayan Voices for Human Rights: Displaced Catholics in Highland Chiapas*. https://utpress.utexas.edu/books/kovmay.

Kozak, Piotr. 2017. "'A Triumph of Reason': Chile Approves Landmark Bill to Ease Abortion Ban." *Guardian*, August 22, 2017, Global Development. http://www.theguardian.com/global-development/2017/aug/22/chile-abortion-bill-michelle-bachelet-a-triumph-of-reason-ease-abortion-ban.

Kray, Christine A. 2005. "The Sense of Tranquility: Bodily Practice and Ethnic Classes in Yucatán." *Ethnology* 44 (4): 337–55.

Kriesi, Hanspeter, Ruud Koopmans, Jan Willem Duyvendak, and Marco G. Giugni. 1992. "New Social Movements and Political Opportunities in Western Europe." *European Journal of Political Research* 22 (2): 219–44.

Kuran, Timur. 2011. *The Long Divergence: How Islamic Law Held Back the Middle East*. Princeton, N.J.: Princeton University Press.

Lannon, Frances. 1987. *Privilege, Persecution, and Prophecy: The Catholic Church in Spain, 1875–1975*. Oxford: Clarendon Press.

Leech, Beth L. 2002. "Asking Questions: Techniques for Semistructured Interviews." *PS: Political Science and Politics* 35 (4): 665–68.

Leighley, Jan E. 1995. "Attitudes, Opportunities and Incentives: A Field Essay on Political Participation." *Political Research Quarterly* 48 (1): 181–209.

Levi, Margaret, Karen S. Cook, Jodi A. O'Brien, and Howard Faye. 1990. "Introduction: The Limits of Rationality." In *The Limits of Rationality*, edited by Karen Schweers Cook and Margaret Levi. Chicago: University of Chicago Press.

Levine, Daniel H. 1981. *Religion and Politics in Latin America: The Catholic Church in Venezuela and Colombia*. Princeton, N.J.: Princeton University Press.

Levine, Daniel H. 1988. "Assessing the Impacts of Liberation Theology in Latin America." *Review of Politics* 50 (2): 241–63.

Levine, Daniel H. 1995. "On Premature Reports of the Death of Liberation Theology." *Review of Politics* 57 (1) Winter: 105–31.

Levine, Daniel H. 2012. *Politics, Religion and Society in Latin America*. Boulder, Colo.: Lynne Rienner Publishers.

Lichbach, Mark I. 1998. *The Rebel's Dilemma*. Ann Arbor: University of Michigan Press.

Lijphart, Arend. 1971. "Comparative Politics and the Comparative Method." *American Political Science Review* 65 (3): 682–93.

Lipset, Seymour Martin. 1959. "Some Social Requisites of Democracy: Economic Development and Political Legitimacy." *American Political Science Review* 53 (1): 69–105.

Loaeza, Soledad. 1999. *El Partido Acción Nacional, la larga marcha, 1939–1994: oposición leal y partido de protesta*. Mexico City: Fondo de Cultura Económica.

Loaeza, Soledad. 2003. "The National Action Party (PAN): From the Fringes of the Political System to the Heart of Change." In *Christian Democracy in Latin America: Electoral Competition and Regime Conflicts*, edited by Scott Mainwaring and Timothy R. Scully. Stanford, Calif.: Stanford University Press.

Loveland, Matthew T., David Sikkink, Daniel J. Myers, and Benjamin Radcliff. 2005. "Private Prayer and Civic Involvement." *Journal for the Scientific Study of Religion* 44 (1): 1–14.

Lustick, Ian S. 1996. "History, Historiography, and Political Science: Multiple Historical Records and the Problem of Selection Bias." *American Political Science Review* 90 (3): 605–18.

Mackin, Robert Sean. 1997. "The Limits to Radical Reform in the Catholic Church: The Case of Liberation Theology in Cuernavaca, Mexico, 1952–1992." Master's thesis, University of Wisconsin-Madison.

Mackin, Robert Sean. 2003. "Becoming the Red Bishop of Cuernavaca: Rethinking Gill's Religious Competition Model." *Sociology of Religion* 64 (4): 499–514.

Magaloni, Beatriz. 2006. *Voting for Autocracy: Hegemonic Party Survival and Its Demise in Mexico*. Cambridge: Cambridge University Press.

Magaloni, Beatriz, and Alberto Diaz-Cayeros. 2007. "Clientelism and Portfolio Diversification: A Model of Electoral Investment with Applications to Mexico." In *Patrons, Clients, and Policies: Patterns of Democratic Accountability and Political Competition*, edited by Herbert Kitschelt and Steven I. Wilkinson. Cambridge: Cambridge University Press.

Magaloni, Beatriz, and Alejandro Moreno. 2003. "Catching All Souls: The Partido Acción Nacional and the Politics of Religion in Mexico." In *Christian Democracy in Latin America: Electoral Competition and Regime Conflicts*, edited by Scott Mainwaring and Timothy R. Scully. Stanford, Calif.: Stanford University Press.

Mahoney, James. 2010. "After KKV: The New Methodology of Qualitative Research." *World Politics* 62 (1): 120–47.

Mainwaring, Scott. 1986. *The Catholic Church and Politics in Brazil, 1916–1985.* Stanford, Calif.: Stanford University Press.

Manaut, Raúl Benítez, Andrew Selee, and Cynthia J. Arnson. 2006. "Frozen Negotiations: The Peace Process in Chiapas." *Mexican Studies/Estudios Mexicanos* 22 (1): 131–52.

March, James G., and Johan P. Olsen. 2008. "Elaborating the 'New Institutionalism.'" In *The Oxford Handbook of Political Institutions*, edited by Sarah A. Binder, R. A. W. Rhodes, and Bert A. Rockman, Online Publication. Oxford: Oxford University Press.

Margolis, Howard. 1982. *Selfishness, Altruism, and Rationality: A Theory of Social Choice.* Chicago: University of Chicago Press.

Marshall, Martin N. 1996. "Sampling for Qualitative Research." *Family Practice* 13 (6): 522–25.

Martin, David. 1990. *Tongues of Fire: The Explosion of Protestantism in Latin America.* Oxford: Blackwell.

Martin, Kathleen R., and William A. González. 2008. "Embracing Community: An Alternative Tourism for Yucatán." In *Yucatán in an Era of Globalization*, edited by Eric N. Baklanoff and Edward H. Moseley. Tuscaloosa: University of Alabama Press.

Martínez-Torres, María Elena. 2006. *Organic Coffee: Sustainable Development by Mayan Farmers.* Athens: Ohio University Press.

Martínez-Torres, María Elena. 2008. "The Benefits and Sustainability of Organic Farming by Peasant Coffee Farmers in Chiapas, Mexico." In *Confronting the Coffee Crisis: Fair Trade, Sustainable Livelihoods and Ecosystems in Mexico and Central America*, edited by Christopher M. Bacon, V. Ernesto Méndez, Stephen R. Gliessman, David Goodman, and Jonathan A. Fox. Cambridge, Mass.: MIT Press.

Mattiace, Shannan L. 2003. *To See with Two Eyes: Peasant Activism and Indian Autonomy in Chiapas, Mexico.* Albuquerque: University of New Mexico Press.

Mattiace, Shannan L. 2009. "Ethnic Mobilization among the Maya of Yucatán." *Latin American and Caribbean Ethnic Studies* 4 (2): 137–69.

McAdam, Doug. 1982. *Political Process and the Development of Black Insurgency, 1930–1970.* Chicago: University of Chicago Press.

McAdam, Doug. 1996a. "Conceptual Origins, Current Problems, Future Directions." In *Comparative Perspectives on Social Movements: Political Opportunities, Mobilizing Structures, and Cultural Framings*, edited by Doug McAdam, John D. McCarthy, and Mayer N. Zald. Cambridge: Cambridge University Press.

McAdam, Doug. 1996b. "The Framing Function of Movement Tactics: Strategic Dramaturgy in the American Civil Rights Movement." In *Comparative Perspectives on Social Movements: Political Opportunities, Mobilizing Structures, and Cultural Framings*, edited by Doug McAdam, John D. McCarthy, and Mayer N. Zald. Cambridge: Cambridge University Press.

McAdam, Doug, John D. McCarthy, and Mayer N. Zald. 1996. "Introduction: Opportunities, Mobilizing Structures, and Framing Processes: Toward a Synthetic, Comparative Perspective on Social Movements." In *Comparative Perspectives on Social Movements: Political Opportunities, Mobilizing Structures, and Cultural Framings*, edited by Doug McAdam, John D. McCarthy, and Mayer N. Zald. Cambridge: Cambridge University Press.

McBride, Michael. 2007. "Club Mormon: Free-Riders, Monitoring, and Exclusion in the LDS Church." *Rationality and Society* 19 (4): 395–424.

McCann, James A, and Jorge I. Domínguez. 1998. "Mexicans React to Electoral Fraud and Political Corruption: An Assessment of Public Opinion and Voting Behavior." *Electoral Studies* 17 (4): 483–503.

McCarthy, John D. 1996. "Constraints and Opportunities in Adopting, Adapting, and Inventing." In *Comparative Perspectives on Social Movements: Political Opportunities, Mobilizing Structures, and Cultural Framings*, edited by Doug McAdam, John D. McCarthy, and Mayer N. Zald. Cambridge: Cambridge University Press.

McCauley, John F. 2017. *The Logic of Ethnic and Religious Conflict in Africa*. Cambridge: Cambridge University Press.

McClendon, Gwyneth, and Rachel Beatty Riedl. 2015. "Religion as a Stimulant of Political Participation: Experimental Evidence from Nairobi, Kenya." *Journal of Politics* 77 (4): 1045–57.

Menchik, Jeremy. 2017. "The Constructivist Approach to Religion and World Politics." *Comparative Politics* 49 (4): 561–81.

Meyer, Jean. 1978. *La Cristiada.* Vol. 3, *Los cristeros*. Mexico City: Siglo Veintiuno Editores.

Milford, Anna B. 2012. "The Pro-Competitive Effect of Coffee Cooperatives in Chiapas, Mexico." *Journal of Agricultural and Food Industrial Organization* 10 (1) January.

Mitchell, Joshua. 2007. "Religion Is Not a Preference." *Journal of Politics* 69 (2): 351–62.

Mizrahi, Yemile. 2003. *From Martyrdom to Power: The Partido Acción Nacional in Mexico*. Notre Dame, Ind.: University of Notre Dame Press.

Moe, Terry. 1984. "The New Economics of Organization." *American Journal of Political Science* 28 (4): 739–77.

Molinar, Juan. 1991. "Counting the Number of Parties: An Alternative Index." *American Political Science Review* 85 (4): 1383–91.

Morris, Aldon. 1981. "Black Southern Student Sit-In Movement: An Analysis of Internal Organization." *American Sociological Review* 46 (6): 744–67.

Moseley, Edward H., and Helen Delpar. 2008. "Yucatán's Prelude to Globalization." In *Yucatán in an Era of Globalization*, edited by Eric N. Baklanoff and Edward H. Moseley. Tuscaloosa: University of Alabama Press.

Nash, June C. 2001. *Mayan Visions: The Quest for Autonomy in an Age of Globalization*. New York: Routledge.

Nhat Hanh, Thich. 1993. Interbeing: Fourteen Guidelines for Engaged Buddhism. Rev. ed. Berkeley, Calif.: Parallax Press. https://www.lionsroar.com/the-fourteen-precepts-of-engaged-buddhism/.Nigh, Ronald. 1997. "Organic Agriculture and Globalization: A Maya Associative Corporation in Chiapas, Mexico." *Human Organization* 56 (4): 427–36.

Norenzayan, Ara, and Azim F. Shariff. 2008. "The Origin and Evolution of Religious Prosociality." *Science* 322 (5898): 58–62.

Norget, Kristin. 1997. "Progressive Theology and Popular Religiosity in Oaxaca, Mexico." *Ethnology* 36 (1): 67–83.

Norris, Pippa. 2009. "Political Activism: New Challenges, New Opportunities." In *The Oxford Handbook of Comparative Politics*, edited by Carles Boix and Susan C. Stokes. New York: Oxford University Press.

North, Douglass. 1990. *Institutions, Institutional Change, and Economic Performance*. Cambridge: Cambridge University Press.

Nylen, William R. 2002. "Testing the Empowerment Thesis: The Participatory Budget in Belo Horizonte and Betim, Brazil." *Comparative Politics* 34 (2): 127–45.

Oberschall, Anthony. 1996. "Opportunities and Framing in the Eastern European Revolts of 1989." In *Comparative Perspectives on Social Movements: Political Opportunities, Mobilizing Structures, and Cultural Framings*, edited by Doug McAdam, John D. McCarthy, and Mayer N. Zald. Cambridge: Cambridge University Press.

Oliver, Pamela. 1980. "Rewards and Punishments as Selective Incentives for Collective Action: Theoretical Investigations." *American Journal of Sociology* 85 (6): 1356–75.

Olson, Mancur. 1965. *The Logic of Collective Action: Public Goods and the Theory of Groups*. 2nd printing with new preface and appendix. Cambridge, Mass.: Harvard University Press.

Olvera, Alberto J. 2004. "Civil Society in Mexico at Century's End." In *Dilemmas of Political Change in Mexico*, edited by Kevin J. Middlebrook. London: Institute of Latin American Studies, University of London.

Ostrom, Elinor. 1990. *Governing the Commons: The Evolution of Institutions for Collective Action*. Cambridge: Cambridge University Press.

Ostrom, Elinor. 2009. "Collective Action Theory." In *The Oxford Handbook of Com-*

parative Politics Online, edited by Carles Boix and Susan C. Stokes. New York: Oxford University Press.

Ostrom, Elinor, Roy Gardner, and James Walker. 1994. *Rules, Games, and Common-Pool Resources*. Ann Arbor: University of Michigan Press.

Pacheco, Gail, and Barrett Owen. 2015. "Moving through the Political Participation Hierarchy: A Focus on Personal Values." *Applied Economics* 47 (3): 222–38.

Peña, Guillermo de la. 1981. *A Legacy of Promises: Agriculture, Politics, and Ritual in the Morelos Highlands of Mexico*. Austin: University of Texas Press.

Pessi, Anne Birgitta. 2011. "Religiosity and Altruism: Exploring the Link and Its Relation to Happiness." *Journal of Contemporary Religion* 26 (1): 1–18.

Pfaff, Steven, and Anthony J. Gill. 2006. "Will a Million Muslims March? Muslim Interest Organizations and Political Integration in Europe." *Comparative Political Studies* 39 (7): 803–28.

Philpott, Daniel. 2000. "The Religious Roots of Modern International Relations." *World Politics* 52 (2): 206–45.

Philpott, Daniel. 2007. "Explaining the Political Ambivalence of Religion." *American Political Science Review* 101 (3): 505–25.

Piven, Frances Fox, and Richard Cloward. 1977. *Poor People's Movements: Why They Succeed, How They Fail*. New York: Pantheon Books.

Planas, Ricardo. 1986. *Liberation Theology: The Political Expression of Religion*. Kansas City, Mo.: Sheed and Ward.

PNUD (Programa de las Naciones Unidas para el Desarrollo en México). 2008. "Cálculos de la Oficina Nacional de Desarrollo Humano. Índice de desarrollo humano municipal 2000–2005." Mexico City: Programa de las Naciones Unidas Para el Desarrollo en México.

Pope, Stephen J. 1993. "Proper and Improper Partiality and the Preferential Option for the Poor." *Theological Studies* 54: 242–71.

Popkin, Samuel L. 1988. "Political Entrepreneurs and Peasant Movements in Vietnam." In *Rationality and Revolution*. Cambridge: Cambridge University Press.

Powell, Walter W., and Paul J. DiMaggio. 1991. Introduction to *The New Institutionalism in Organizational Analysis*, edited by Walter W. Powell and Paul J. DiMaggio. Chicago: University of Chicago Press.

Prokopy, Joshua, and Christian Smith. 1999. Introduction to *Latin American Religion in Motion*, edited by Christian Smith and Joshua Prokopy. New York: Routledge.

Prud'homme, Remy. 1995. "The Dangers of Decentralization." *World Bank Research Observer* 10 (2) August 1995: 201–20.

Puertas, Pilar. 2015. "La fuerza de lo religioso en la construcción." *Caminhos, Goiânia* 13 (1): 171–84.

Putnam, Robert D. 1993. *Making Democracy Work: Civic Traditions in Modern Italy*. Princeton, N.J.: Princeton University Press.

Putnam, Robert D. 1994. *Making Democracy Work: Civic Traditions in Modern Italy*. Princeton, N.J.: Princeton University Press.

Putnam, Robert D. 2000. *Bowling Alone: The Collapse and Revival of American Community.* New York: Simon and Schuster.

Putnam, Robert D. 2007. "*E Pluribus Unum*: Diversity and Community in the Twenty-First Century; The 2006 Johan Skytte Prize Lecture." *Scandinavian Political Studies* 30 (2): 137–74.

Putnam, Robert D., and David E. Campbell. 2010. *American Grace: How Religion Divides and Unites Us.* New York: Simon and Schuster.

Qian, Yingyi, and Barry R. Weingast. 1997. "Federalism as a Commitment to Perserving Market Incentives." *Journal of Economic Perspectives* 11 (4): 83–92.

Rabe-Hesketh, Sophia, and Anders Skrondal. 2012. *Multilevel and Longitudinal Modeling Using Stata.* 3rd ed. College Station, Tex.: Stata Press.

Raynolds, Laura T., Douglas Murray, and Peter Leigh Taylor. 2004. "Fair Trade Coffee: Building Producer Capacity via Global Networks." *Journal of International Development* 16 (8): 1109–21.

Rosenstone, Steven J., and John Mark Hansen. 1993. *Mobilization, Participation, and Democracy in America.* New York: Macmillan.

Rubin, Jared. 2017. *Rulers, Religion, and Riches: Why the West Got Rich and the Middle East Did Not.* Cambridge: Cambridge University Press.

Rugeley, Terry. 2009. *Rebellion Now and Forever: Mayas, Hispanics, and Caste War Violence in Yucatan, 1800–1880.* Stanford, Calif.: Stanford University Press.

Rus, Jan, and George A. Collier. 2003. "A Generation of Crisis in the Central Highlands of Chiapas: The Cases of Chamula and Zinacantán, 1974–2000." In *Mayan Lives, Mayan Utopias: The Indigenous Peoples of Chiapas and the Zapatista Rebellion,* edited by Jan Rus, Rosalva Aída Hernández Castillo, and Shannan Mattiace. Lanham, Md.: Rowman and Littlefield.

Rus, Jan, Rosalva Aída Hernández Castillo, Shannan Mattiace, and José Alejos García. 2003. Introduction to *Mayan Lives, Mayan Utopias: The Indigenous Peoples of Chiapas and the Zapatista Rebellion,* edited by Jan Rus, Rosalva Aída Hernández Castillo, and Shannan Mattiace. Lanham, Md.: Rowman and Littlefield.

Rydin, Yvonne, and Mark Pennington. 2000. "Public Participation and Local Environmental Planning: The Collective Action Problem and the Potential of Social Capital." *Local Environment* 5 (2): 153–69.

Sabet, Daniel. 2008. "Thickening Civil Society: Explaining the Development of Associational Life in Mexico." *Democratization* 15 (2): 410–32.

Sabet, Daniel. 2008. *Nonprofits and their Networks: Cleaning the Waters along Mexico's Northern Border.* Tucson: The University of Arizona Press.

Sageman, Marc. 2004. *Understanding Terror Networks.* Philadelphia: University of Pennsylvania Press.

Salinas, Salvador. 2018. *Land, Liberty, and Water: Morelos after Zapata: 1920–1940.* Tucson: University of Arizona Press.

Sarkissian, Ani. 2012. "Religion and Civic Engagement in Muslim Countries." *Journal for the Scientific Study of Religion* 52 (4): 607–22.

214   *Works Cited*

Sarkissian, Ani. 2015. *The Varieties of Religious Repression: Why Governments Restrict Religion*. Oxford: Oxford University Press.

Saroglou, Vassilis, Isabelle Pichon, Laurence Trompette, Marijke Verschueren, and Rebecca Dernelle. 2005. "Prosocial Behavior and Religion: New Evidence Based on Projective Measures and Peer Ratings." *Journal for the Scientific Study of Religion* 44 (3): 323–48.

Seawright, Jason, and John Gerring. 2008. "Case Selection Techniques in Case Study Research: A Menu of Qualitative and Quantitative Options." *Political Research Quarterly* 61 (2): 294–308.

Seligson, Amber L. 1999. "Civic Association and Democratic Participation in Central America: A Test of the Putnam Thesis." *Comparative Political Studies* 32 (3): 342–62.

Simpson, Brent, and Robb Willer. 2008. "Altruism and Indirect Reciprocity: The Interaction of Person and Situation in Prosocial Behavior." *Social Psychology Quarterly* 71 (1): 37–52.

Simpson, Charles R., and Anita Rapone. 2000. "Community Development from the Ground Up: Social-Justice Coffee." *Human Ecology Review* 7 (1): 46–57.

Siroky, David S., and Christopher W. Hale. 2017. "Inside Irredentism: A Global Empirical Analysis." *American Journal of Political Science* 61 (1): 117–28.

Siroky, David S., Sean Mueller, and Michael Hechter. 2017. "Cultural Legacies and Political Preferences: The Failure of Separatism in the Swiss Jura." *European Political Science Review* 9 (2): 303–27.

Skocpol, Theda, and Morris P. Fiorina, eds. 1999. *Civic Engagement in American Democracy*. Washington, D.C.: Brookings Institution Press.

Smith, Amy Erica. 2016. "When Clergy Are Threatened: Catholic and Protestant Leaders and Political Activism in Brazil." *Politics and Religion* 9 (3): 431–55.

Smith, Christian. 1991. *The Emergence of Liberation Theology: Radical Religion and Social Movement Theory*. Chicago: University of Chicago Press.

Smith, Christian, ed. 1996. *Disruptive Religion: The Force of Faith in Social Movement Activism*. New York: Routledge.

Snow, David A., E. Burke Rochford, Steven K. Worden, and Robert D. Benford. 1986. "Frame Alignment Processes, Micromobilization, and Movement Participation." *American Sociological Review* 51 (4): 464–81.

Soifer, Hillel David. 2016. "Regionalism, Ethnic Diversity, and Variation in Public Good Provision by National States." *Comparative Political Studies* 49 (10): 1341–71.

Soper, J. Christopher, and Joel S. Fetzer. 2007. "Religious Institutions, Church-State History and Muslim Mobilisation in Britain, France and Germany." *Journal of Ethnic and Migration Studies* 33 (6): 933–44.

Stark, Rodney, and William Sims Bainbridge. 1985. *The Future of Religion: Secularization, Revival and Cult Formation*. Berkeley, Calif.: University of California Press.

Stark, Rodney, and William Sims Bainbridge. 1996. *A Theory of Religion*. Reprint, Brunswick, N.J.: Rutgers University Press.

Stepan, Alfred, and Juan Linz. 2013. "Democratization Theory and the 'Arab Spring.'" *Journal of Democracy* 24 (2): 15–30.

Stoll, David. 1990. *Is Latin America Turning Protestant? The Politics of Evangelical Growth*. Berkeley: University of California Press.

Suárez Blanch, Claudia. 2005. "Situación sociodemográfica de los pueblos indígenas de México." In *Pueblos indígenas y afrodescendientes de América Latina y el Caribe: Relevancia y pertinencia de la información sociodemográfica para políticas programas*. Santiago de Chile: Comisión Nacional para el Desarrollo de los Pueblos Indígenas.

Suarez, Luis. 1970. *Cuernavaca ante el Vaticano*. Mexico City: Editorial Grijalbo.

Székely Pardo, Miguel, Luis F. López-Calva, Álvaro Meléndez Martínez, Ericka G. Rascón Ramírez, and Lourdes Rodríguez-Chamussy. 2007. "Poniendo a la pobreza de ingresos y a la desigualdad en el mapa de México." *Economía Mexicana Nueva Época* 16 (2): 239–303.

Tansey, Oisín. 2007. "Process Tracing and Elite Interviewing: A Case for Non-Probability Sampling." *PS: Political Science and Politics* 40 (4): 765–72.

Tarrow, Sidney. 1989. *Democracy and Disorder: Protest and Politics in Italy 1965–1975*. Oxford: Clarendon Press.

Tarrow, Sidney. 1998. *Power in Movement: Social Movements and Contentious Politics*. 2nd ed. Cambridge: Cambridge University Press.

Tarrow, Sidney. 2010. "Bridging the Quantitative-Qualitative Divide." In *Rethinking Social Inquiry: Diverse Tools, Shared Standards*, edited by Henry E. Brady and David Collier. 2nd ed. Lanham, Md.: Rowman and Littlefield.

Tarrow, Sidney, and Charles Tilly. 2009. "Contentious Politics and Social Movements." In *The Oxford Handbook of Comparative Politics*, edited by Carles Boix and Susan C. Stokes. New York: Oxford University Press.

Taylor, Michael. 1987. *The Possibility of Cooperation*. Cambridge: Cambridge University Press.

Taylor, Michael. 1990. "Cooperation and Rationality: Notes on the Collective Action Problem and Its Solutions." In *The Limits of Rationality*, edited by Karen Schweers Cook and Margaret Levi. Chicago: University of Chicago Press.

Thomas, Scott. 2005. *The Global Resurgence of Religion and the Transformation of International Relations: The Struggle for the Soul of the Twenty-First Century*. New York: Palgrave Macmillan.

Thompson, Ginger. 2002. "Vatican Curbing Deacons in Mexico." *New York Times*, March 12, 2002. http://www.nytimes.com/2002/03/12/world/vatican-curbing-deacons-in-mexico.html.

Tiebout, Charles M. 1956. "A Pure Theory of Local Expenditures." *Journal of Political Economy* 64 (5): 416–24.

Tilly, Charles. 1978. *From Mobilization to Revolution*. Reading, Mass.: Addison-Wesley.

Tilly, Charles. 1984. "Social Movements and National Politics." In *Statemaking and Social Movements: Essays in History and Theory*, edited by Charles Bright and Susan Harding. Ann Arbor: University of Michigan Press.

Tilly, Charles. 1995. *Popular Contention in Great Britain, 1758–1834.* Cambridge, Mass.: Harvard University Press.

Treisman, Daniel. 2000. "Decentralization and Inflation: Commitment, Collective Action, or Continuity." *American Political Science Review* 94 (4): 837–57.

Treisman, Daniel. 2007. *The Architecture of Government: Rethinking Political Decentralization.* Cambridge: Cambridge University Press.

Trejo, Guillermo. 2004. "Indigenous Insurgency: Protest, Rebellion and the Politicization of Ethnicity in 20th Century Mexico." PhD diss., University of Chicago.

Trejo, Guillermo. 2009. "Religious Competition and Ethnic Mobilization in Latin America: Why the Catholic Church Promotes Indigenous Movements in Mexico." *American Political Science Review* 103 (3): 323–42.

Trejo, Guillermo. 2010. *Mexican Indigenous Insurgency Dataset.* Durham, N.C.: Duke University.

Trejo, Guillermo. 2012. *Popular Movements in Autocracies: Religion, Repression, and Indigenous Collective Action in Mexico.* New York: Cambridge University Press.

Turner, Brian. 2002. "Liberating the *Municipio Libre*: The Normalization of Municipal Finance in Yucatan." *Mexican Studies/Estudios Mexicanos* 18 (1): 101–31.

Turner, Ralph H. 1969. "The Theme of Contemporary Social Movements." *British Journal of Sociology* 20 (4): 390–405.

United Nations. 2014. "Indigenous Peoples in Latin America." United Nations Economic Commission for Latin America and the Caribbean. https://www.cepal.org/en/infografias/los-pueblos-indigenas-en-america-latina.

USCCB (United States Conference of Catholic Bishops). 2017. "Selected Quotes of Pope Francis by Subject." 2017. http://www.usccb.org/beliefs-and-teachings/what-we-believe/catholic-social-teaching/upload/pope-francis-quotes1.pdf.

Vanden, Harry E., and Gary Prevost. 2015. *Politics of Latin America: The Power Game.* 5th ed. Oxford: Oxford University Press.

Van Deth, Jan W. 2014. "A Conceptual Map of Political Participation." *Acta Politica* 49 (3): 349–67.

Varshney, Ashutosh. 2002. *Ethnic Conflict and Civic Life: Hindus and Muslims in India.* New Haven, Conn.: Yale University Press.

Vélez-Ibañez, Carlos G. 1983. *Bonds of Mutual Trust: The Cultural Systems of Rotating Credit Associations among Urban Mexicans and Chicanos.* New Brunswick, N.J.: Rutgers University Press.

Verba, Sidney, and Norman H. Nie. 1972. *Participation in America: Political Democracy and Social Equality.* New York: Harper and Row.

Verba, Sidney, Kay Lehman Schlozman, and Henry Brady. 1995. *Voice and Equality: Civic Voluntarism in American Politics.* Cambridge, Mass.: Harvard University Press.

Videla, Gabriela. 1984. *Sergio Méndez Arceo, un señor obispo.* Mexico City: Ediciones Nuevomar.

Vráblíková, Kateřina. 2014. "How Context Matters? Mobilization, Political Opportunity Structures, and Nonelectoral Political Participation in Old and New Democracies." *Comparative Political Studies* 47 (2): 203–29.

Warman, Arturo. 1980. *"We Come to Object": The Peasants of Morelos and the National State*. Baltimore: Johns Hopkins University Press.

Warner, Carolyn M. 2000. *Confessions of an Interest Group*. Princeton, N.J.: Princeton University Press.

Warner, Carolyn M. 2007. *The Best System Money Can Buy: Corruption in the European Union*. Ithaca, N.Y.: Cornell University Press.

Warner, Carolyn M., Ramazan Kılınç, Christopher W. Hale, and Adam B. Cohen. 2018. *Generating Generosity in Catholicism and Islam: Beliefs, Institutions, and Public Goods Provision*. Cambridge: Cambridge University Press.

Warner, Carolyn M., Ramazan Kılınç, Christopher W. Hale, Adam B. Cohen, and Kathryn A. Johnson. 2015. "Religion and Public Goods Provision: Experimental and Interview Evidence from Catholicism and Islam in Europe." *Comparative Politics* 47 (2): 189–209.

Warner, Carolyn M., and Manfred W. Wenner. 2006. "Religion and the Political Organization of Muslims in Europe." *Perspectives on Politics* 4 (3): 457–79.

Washbrook, Sarah. 2007. "The Chiapas Uprising of 1994: Historical Antecedents and Political Consequences." In *Rural Chiapas Ten Years after the Zapatista Uprising*, edited by Sarah Washbrook. London: Routledge.

Weber, Max. 1930. *The Protestant Ethic and the Spirit of Capitalism*. Edited by Stephen Kalberg. Chicago: Routledge.

Weingast, Barry R. 1995. "The Economic Role of Political Institutions: Market-Preserving Federalism and Economic Development." *Journal of Law, Economics, and Organization* 11 (1): 1–31.

Whiteley, Paul F. 1995. "Rational Choice and Political Participation—Evaluating the Debate." *Political Research Quarterly* 48 (1): 211–33.

Wibbels, Erik. 2006. "Madison in Baghdad? Decentralization and Federalism in Comparative Politics." *Annual Review of Political Science* 9: 165–88.

Wickham, Carrie Rosefsky. 2004. "The Path to Moderation: Strategy and Learning in the Formation of Egypt's Wasat Party." *Comparative Politics* 36 (2): 205–28.

Wiktorowicz, Quintan. 2000. "Civil Society as Social Control: State Power in Jordan." *Comparative Politics* 33 (1): 43–61.

Wiktorowicz, Quintan. 2004. *Islamic Activism: A Social Movement Theory Approach*. Bloomington: Indiana University Press.

Wilkie, James W. 1966. "The Meaning of the Cristero Religious War against the Mexican Revolution." *Journal of Church and State* 8 (2): 214–33.

Womack, John, Jr. 1968. *Zapata and the Mexican Revolution*. New York: Vintage Books.

Womack, John, Jr. 1999. *Rebellion in Chiapas: An Historical Reader*. New York: New Press.

Yardley, Jim, and Paulina Villegas. 2016. "At Mass, Pope Francis Embraces 'Misunderstood' of Mexico." *New York Times*, February 15, 2016. https://www.nytimes.com/2016/02/16/world/americas/at-mass-pope-francis-embraces-misunderstood-of-mexico.html.

Yashar, Deborah J. 2005. *Contesting Citizenship in Latin America: The Rise of Indigenous Movements and the Postliberal Challenge*. Cambridge: Cambridge University Press.

Zald, Mayer N. 1996. "Culture, Ideology, and Strategic Framing." In *Comparative Perspectives on Social Movements: Political Opportunities, Mobilizing Structures, and Cultural Framings*, edited by Doug McAdam, John D. McCarthy, and Mayer N. Zald. Cambridge: Cambridge University Press.

Index

activism. *See* political activism

altruism, 50, 51, 110

archdioceses: as administrative units of Catholic Church, 13–14; similar to dioceses, 186n6

authoritarianism: by progressive priests, 97; liberalization of, 118; Méndez Arceo and, 131, 137; in Mexico, 2, 12, 17, 19, 53, 73, 153, 194n1; worldwide, 5, 143, 152

Berlie Belaunzarán, Emilio Carlos, 106–107, 111, 193n4

Bible: indigenous translations of, 77, 146; study groups in Chiapas, 78–79, 96; study groups in Cuernavaca, 128–129, 132–133, 135, 139

bounded rationality, 29, 51, 185n4, 188n10

Buddhism, 4, 5, 143

Calles, Plutarco, 12, 131

Cárdenas, Lázaro, 124, 131

Caste War of Yucatán, 105

Castro, Manuel, 111

catechists, 23, 24, 72, 102; centralized model, 74–75, 108; consciousness raising of, 96–99; decentralized model, 77; as early cooperators, 83–84; leadership of activist organizations, 89–91; leadership positions in cooperatives,

78–80, 87, 146, 155; organizers of indigenous Congress, 88–89

Catholic Chuch: activism in Mexico, 53–54; administrative organization, 13–14, 17, 56, 73; centralization and, 13, 15, 25, 47, 106–111, 126, 128, 147; conservative advocacy and, 152; conservative retrenchment of, 57, 139–142; deacons in, 56; decentralization and, 45, 54, 63–64, 76–83, 101, 125, 129–130, 146–147, 151, 153, 157, 189n1; discouragement of activism in Yucatán, 3, 17, 24, 104; encouragement of activism in Chiapas, 16, 37, 71–72, 89–92; encouragement of activism in Morelos, 18, 135–137; Indigenous Congress and, 89; indigenous religions and, 185n5; initially conservative in Chiapas, 74–75; initially conservative in Cuernavaca, 131; initiator of cooperatives in Chiapas, 3, 23, 78–83, 191nn8–9, 192n13; as metaphor for God, 2; PAN and, 187n20, 194n11; progressive Catholicism (*see* liberation theology); Protestants and (*see* Protestant competition); as rational organizational actor, 35–36; relationship with Mexican government, 12, 58, 122–123, 149; support of Spanish colonialism, 1, 11; Zapatistas and, 92–95

CEFOSEM (Union Training Center in the State of Morelos), 135–136

CELAM (Latin American Episcopal Conference), 133, 138

centralization, Catholic Church and, 13, 15, 25, 47, 106–111, 126, 128, 131, 147; cooperatives and, 82; institutions and, 43–45

Chiapas, 73, activism in, 2, 12, 16–17, 71, 73, 88–96, 186nn11–12; Catholic Church prior to Samuel Ruiz García, 74–75; church/state relationships in, 122, 149; club goods production in, 10, 86–88, 146, 157; coffee and (*see* coffee); cooperatives in, 23, 78–83, 102, 146, 157; decentralization in, 2, 23, 75–83, 101–102, 144, 146, 151, 157; economic grievance and, 70, 115–118, 148; Indigenous Congress and (*see* Indigenous Congress); indigenous population of, 22, 73–74, 124–125, 149, 154–155, 194n2; interview sites, 19; land redistribution and, 74; liberation theology in, 2, 24, 75, 96–100, 102–103, 146–147, 157; liturgical reform, 76–78, 146; Mexican Revolution and, 74; organizational resources in, 3, 88–92, 102, 146, 157; political party competition in, 69, 119–120, 148; prior lack of activism 2, 73; Protestant competition in, 24, 36, 75, 100–101, 102–103, 147, 157, 186n15; qualitative research strategy and, 15–16; rationale for study, 16–17; reciprocity in, 83–86, 102, 146, 157; resource mobilization in, 37; Samuel Ruiz García and (*see* Ruiz García, Samuel); Zapatistas (*see* Zapatistas)

Christian base communities (CEBs), 132; as signifier of decentralization, 56; conservative retrenchment and, 140–142, 194n5; in Cuernavaca 24, 128–130, 132–134, 138–139, 147–148; in Latin America 80, 134–135

church and state legacies, 21, 24; qualitative results for, 121–123, 127, 148–149, 194n10; statistical measurement of, 58; statistical results for, 55, 61, 69–70, 146

CIDOC (Intercultural Documentation Center), 138, 194n3

civil society, 16, 18, 28, 95, 100, 131, 153, 189n1, 195n2

clergy: Catholic clergy on Protestantism, 113–114, 130; centralized Church and, 24, 74, 106–107, 141, 147; decentralization and, 9, 23, 46, 72, 96–97, 132–133, 151, 185n3, 188n12, 191n3; encouraging activism and, 34, 48, 138; initiators of cooperatives 78–80, 82, 83, 102; as rational organizational leaders 58, 73, 100–101; relation with Mexican state, 12, 13, 122, 193–194n10; statistical control of 190n12; trustworthiness and, 49; Vatican II and, 137–138

club goods, 10, 31–32, 39–40, 188n8, 191n8; ethnicity and, 25, 126–127, 155–156; in Chiapas, 73, 86–88, 102, 157; in Cuernavaca, 133–134; from Protestants, 113; lack of Catholic club goods in Yucatán, 103, 109–111, 147; as mechanism leading toward collective action 15, 45, 47, 70–72, 145; religious decentralization and, 46, 49; sanctoining and, 44

coffee: crash in prices 116; metaphor for club goods in Chiapas 1–3, 10, 157; organizational precursor to activism 90–92; production in Chiapas 71, 73, 79–80, 82, 86–88, 146

collective action, 27, 187n1; alternative explanations for, 19, 58–59, 115–126, 148–149; collective action problem, 29, 38; decentralization and, 3, 9, 43–45, 64; deprivation and, 19–22; indigenous collective action, 16, 186n13; individual leaders and, 138; institutions and, 42; lack of across Yucatán, 110; mechanisms leading to, 10, 71; nonstate institutions and, 152–154; political process model and, 6, 10, 26, 33, 47–48, 57, 95–96, 144–145, 150–151; puzzle of religion and, 1, 7; rational choice and, 6, 8, 26, 38–39, 40, 48, 150–151, 188n7; religious elites and, 49; statistical results, 23, 55, 62, 64, 70

rational choice approach, 8, 10, 26, 38–41, 150; criticisms, 50–51

reciprocity: absence in Yucatán, 24; 46–47, 71–72, 144–145; in Chiapas, 80–81, 83–88, 101–102, 146, 157; human behavior and, 50; institutions and, 43–44; as mechanism leading toward collective action, 10, 15–16; in Morelos, 134–135; result of decentralization, 9, 49; in Yucatán, 106, 109–111, 126, 147

religion, 29–32; decentralization and (*see* religious decentralization); framing and, 6–7, 33–35; Mexico and, 13; opportunity and, 7, 35–36; political process approach and, 6, 10–11, 48; prosociality and, 50–51; puzzle of relationship with collective action, 1, 4–5, 144; rational choice approach and, 8, 38–41; rationale for study 49; resource mobilization and, 7, 36–37

religious competition, 7, 11, 36, 48; Catholic Church and, 13; in Chiapas, 100–101; statistical measurement, 57, 189nn5–6; statistical results, 54, 61–70; 146. *See also* Protestant competition

religious economy school, 75, 187n5

religious groups, 31

religious institutions, 31–32, 185n2, 187n4; activism globally and, 4–6; authoritarian regimes and, 152; church/state conflict and, 121–123; club goods and, 39–41; decentralization and, 3–4, 9–10, 26, 45–47, 144, 145, 157; ethnicity and, 154–157; framing and, 34–35; as local community group, 3, 44, 151; mechanisms leading to activism, 10; nonstate institutions and, 152; opportunity and, 35–36; organizational capacities and, 8; political competition and, 21; political process approach and, 47–49, 144, 150, 151, 157; puzzle of relationship with collective action, 1, 157; rationale for study, 50–51; religious competition and, 7, 35–36; resource mobilization and, 36–37

religious orders, 54, 88, 186n14

religious organizations, 31, 35, 49, 150

repression, 35, 94, 119, 120, 127, 148, 155

resource mobilization, 7–8, 36–38; decentralization and, 48, 64, 150, 157; as part of political process approach, 6, 10, 126, 145–146, 150, 157, 187n5; statistical results of, 23, 55, 64, 70

Rodríguez Vega, Gustavo, 193n4

Ruiz García, Samuel, 2, 16, 37, 75–76, 87–88, 93–96, 99–100, 111, 132, 138, 192n15

sacrifice and stigma, 8, 40, 41, 188n9

Salinas, Carlos 13, 119

San Andrés accords, 192n15

San Cristóbal de las Casas, City of, 19, 155, 195n2

San Cristóbal de las Casas, Diocese of: catechists and deacons within, 78; cooperatives and, 78–79, 102; decentralization and, 72, 86, 96, 102, 146; interview information, 19; prior to arrival of Samuel Ruiz García, 73–75; redistricting of, 76, 186n10; relations with Mexican state and, 122–123; as subject of qualitative study, 15, 23; as synonym for Chiapas, 17; Zapatistas and, 93–95. *See also* Chiapas

sanctioning, 9; decentralized, 9–10, 43–46, 144, 185n3; in Chiapas, 23, 72, 81–83, 102, 146; ethnicity and, 124; exclusion and, 10, 44–46, 102, 146; in Morelos, 24, 129, 134, 141; transaction costs and, 42–43; in Yucatán, 24, 109–111, 126

Second Latin American Episcopal Conference, 133

second order collective action problem, 42, 44

See- Judge- Act, 135, 138

semistructured interviews, 18

snowball sampling, 18

social capital, 85, 86, 152

social movements, 27–28, 140, 154, 193n15

Tierra y Libertad, 71, 90, 91